Commuting Stress
Causes, Effects, and Methods of Coping

The Plenum Series on Stress and Coping

Series Editor:
Donald Meichenbaum, *University of Waterloo, Waterloo, Ontario, Canada*

Editorial Board: Bruce P. Dohrenwend, *Columbia University* • Marianne Frankenhauser, *University of Stockholm* • Norman Garmezy, *University of Minnesota* • Mardi J. Horowitz, *University of California Medical School, San Francisco* • Richard S. Lazarus, *University of California, Berkeley* • Michael Rutter, *University of London* • Dennis C. Turk, *University of Pittsburgh* • John P. Wilson, *Cleveland State University* • Camille Wortman, *University of Michigan*

Current Volumes in the Series:

BEYOND TRAUMA
Cultural and Societal Dynamics
Edited by Rolf J. Kleber, Charles R. Figley, and Berthold P. R. Gersons

COMBAT STRESS REACTION
The Enduring Toll of War
Zahava Solomon

COMMUTING STRESS
Causes, Effects, and Methods of Coping
Meni Koslowsky, Avraham N. Kluger, and Mordechai Reich

COPING WITH WAR-INDUCED STRESS
The Gulf War and the Israeli Response
Zahava Solomon

INTERNATIONAL HANDBOOK OF TRAUMATIC STRESS SYNDROMES
Edited by John P. Wilson and Beverley Raphael

PSYCHOTRAUMATOLOGY
Key Papers and Core Concepts in Post-Traumatic Stress
Edited by George S. Everly, Jr. and Jeffrey M. Lating

STRESS AND MENTAL HEALTH
Contemporary Issues and Prospects for the Future
Edited by William R. Avison and Ian H. Gotlib

TRAUMATIC STRESS
From Theory to Practice
Edited by John R. Freedy and Stevan E. Hobfoll

THE UNNOTICED MAJORITY IN PSYCHIATRIC INPATIENT CARE
Charles A. Kiesler and Celeste G. Simpkins

A Continuation Order Plan is available for this series. A continuation order will bring delivery of each new volume immediately upon publication. Volumes are billed only upon actual shipment. For further information please contact the publisher.

Commuting Stress
Causes, Effects, and Methods of Coping

Meni Koslowsky
Bar-Ilan University
Ramat Gan, Israel

Avraham N. Kluger
The Hebrew University of Jerusalem
Jerusalem, Israel

and

Mordechai Reich
Private Practice
Efrat, Israel

PLENUM PRESS • NEW YORK AND LONDON

Library of Congress Cataloging-in-Publication Data

On file

ISBN 0-306-45037-2

©1995 Plenum Press, New York
A Division of Plenum Publishing Corporation
233 Spring Street, New York, N.Y. 10013

10 9 8 7 6 5 4 3 2 1

All rights reserved

No part of this book may be reproduced, stored in a retrieval system, or transmitted in any form or by any means, electronic, mechanical, photocopying, microfilming, recording, or otherwise, without written permission from the Publisher

Printed in the United States of America

To my wife Sandy, a woman of valor in deed and in time of need

—MK

To my late aunt Anna Forster

—ANK

To my wife Sema, navigator par excellence, and our beloved backseat drivers Betzalel, Nechama, Shalom, and Meira

—MR

Preface

Several people have asked what motivated us to write a book about commuting, something that we all do but over which we have very little control. As a matter of fact, the general reaction from professional colleagues and friends alike was first a sort of knowing smile followed by some story. Everyone has a story about a personal commuting experience. Whether it was a problem with a delayed bus, a late arrival, broken-down automobiles, hot trains or subways, during the past year we have heard it all. Many of these stories must be apocryphal because, if they were all true, it is amazing that anyone ever arrived at work on time, at home, or at some other destination.

The interest for us likely stems from many factors that over the years have probably influenced our thinking. All of the authors studied and/or grew up in the New York City metropolitan area. For illustration, let's devote a few paragraphs to describing some of the senior author's (Koslowsky's) life experiences. As a young man in New York City, he was a constant user of the New York City subway system. The whole network was and still is quite impressive. For a relatively small sum, one can spend the whole day and night in an underground world (growing up in New York often makes one think that the whole world is contained in its five boroughs). It is not unusual to wonder who are those passengers who get on only after 2:00 in the morning, or appear to be constantly rushing hither and yon on the subway platform. However, when the subway stopped being a diversion and was needed to get to class on time or to work by 9:00 in the morning, the stressor stimuli and strain responses were suddenly there. The rider's romance with the subways waned, disappeared, and finally turned to frustration; a move away from the city to the suburbs was a relief. The change in living areas was, at least, partially motivated by the desire to say "good riddance" to the subways.

At first, the new mode of transportation, the Long Island Rail Road (LIRR), seemed a welcome change. The LIRR was cleaner, less crowded, and certainly provided a smoother ride; it appeared that a solution to the hassled commuter's traveling requirements was now available. However, frequency of service and, most important of all, punctuality left much to be desired. As a matter of fact, the governor of the state once made an announcement that things would improve and the trains would begin arriving on time. To tell the truth, they *did* change, and the image of the railroad, although never wonderful, did become much better over the years. Although the blizzards in the Northeast during the winter of 1994 were somewhat of a setback contributing to a new set of stories, there is little doubt that the LIRR affords a more pleasant commute than the subways. By the time the stormy weather of 1994 was at its peak, of course, all three authors were living in Israel.

For comparison purposes, it is interesting to examine the situation in Israel over the past two decades. When the senior author moved to Jerusalem in the early 1980s, everything was, at first, much calmer and slower paced than in New York. Less honking, more smoothly flowing traffic, even parking not far from the center of the city was possible. But slowly, the situation began to change in Jerusalem too. By the early 1990s, it looked and sounded very much like New York. Even the pride and joy of the country, the bus system, was starting to deteriorate on several objective measures.

For all three authors, the message from somewhat overlapping life experiences was pretty much the same. Commuting in urban areas is one of life's daily hassles and is likely to have some type of negative consequence—immediate, intermediate, or long-term. Combining life experiences, formal education, and professional practices as lecturers, consultants, and clinicians, we conceived the idea of writing this book as an outgrowth of discussions between the senior author and each of his coauthors over several years. The two junior authors worked hard on different parts of the book, particularly the chapters describing demographics, individual coping, and the physical consequences of commuting. The senior author integrated much of the material from the various sources and used this material for developing the model describing the links between stressor and strain.

The varied industrial and clinical backgrounds of the authors give the book a unique perspective. We have tried to adequately cover the rather limited research, especially as compared to other topics in the stress literature. In addition, a model using structural equation techniques to represent the various stages that lead from the antecedent variables to consequences was presented. Finally, a substantial part of the book is devoted to a discussion of coping techniques that may help to make the commute a more tolerable experience.

Contents

Chapter 1. The Commuting Experience 1

Professionals in the Field 2
The Commuting Experience 4
Defining the Main Variables 6
Mediator and Moderator Variables 8
Stressors, Strain, and Organizational Behavior 11
   Selye's Theory of Stress 11
   Psychosocial Factors and Stress 12
   Coping with Stress 13
   Back to Commuting and Stress 14
   Commuting and Organizational Consequences 14
Summary 16

Chapter 2. Travel and Mobility 17

The GAO Report 18
The Roads That Take Us Home 19
The JCPS Report: The Journey to Work 20
   Workers in the Central City 21
   How Long Does It Take to Get to Work? 21
   Commuter Flows and Transportation Modes 23
   Household Demographics and Mode of Transportation 24
   The Transportation Disadvantaged 26
   Age and the Work Trip 29
   Gender and the Work Trip 29

The Pisarski Update 31
A Case Study: Seattle Commuting Behavior 33
European Travel Behavior 35

Chapter 3. Environmental Factors and Commuting Stress 37

Commuting as an Environmental Stressor 38
Responsivity to Chronic Environmental Stress 39
    Noise 40
    Crowding 45
    Other Environmental Variables 49
Stress, Commuting, and Burnout 53
Combining the Effects of Stressors 56
A Stressor Is Not Always a Stressor 57
Summary 58

Chapter 4. Commuting and Physical Symptoms 61

Research on the Effects of Commuting on Physical Well-Being 62
    Commuting and General Physiological Indicators 62
    Car Driving and Back Problems 63
    Commuting and Cardiovascular Risks 66
    Commuting and Cancer 69
Health Implications of Commuting 71
Special Problems of People Working in Transportation 71
    Long-Distance Truckers 73
    Railroad Engineers 73
Solutions for Various Physical Problems 74
A Methodological Note 76

**Chapter 5. Behavioral, Emotional, and Attitudinal Effects
of Commuting** 79

Commuting and Organizational Behavior 81
    Absenteeism 81
    Lateness 82
    Turnover 83
    Performance 84
Attitudinal and Emotional Behavior 84
Moderators and Intervening Variables 88

CONTENTS

Commuting Measures 88
Mode of Transportation 89
Gender 91
Commuting Couples 93
Driving Stress as a Dependent Variable 95
Lifestyle 96
Information Costs 96
Some Recent Studies 97
Control of the Environment 98
Actual and Perceived Control 99
Operationalization of Commute Predictability 103

Chapter 6. Theory and Model Development **107**

Relevant Stress Theories 109
Person–Environment Fit 109
Expectancies 110
Mediators 111
Moderators 112
Time Urgency 113
Time and the Commuting Experience 114
Other Personality Measures 117
The Commuting Model 118
Some Comments on the Model 124
Links in the Model and Coping Reactions 128

Chapter 7. Individual Coping Strategies **129**

Conceptualizing General Stress-Coping Strategies 129
Commitment as a Buffer 133
Methods for Coping with Commuter Stress and Strain 134
Organization and Self-Discipline 134
General Exercise 136
Morning Exercise 137
Exercise in the Workplace and during the Workday 138
Evening Exercise 138
Integrating Exercise into the Commuting Experience 138
Mediation 139
Cognitive Restructuring 139
Taking Advantage of the Commute 142
Environmental Coping 147

Coping with Crowding 147
Coping with Noise 150
Coping with Heat-Related Stressors 152
Dealing with Commuting Fears 155
Inferences about Individual Coping 156

Chapter 8. Government and Organization Coping Methods 157

The Basis of Governmental Coping Strategies 159
Focusing on Individual Compliance 161
Government Subsidies 163
Car-Pooling 164
  Recommendations for Overcoming the Difficulties of Car-Pooling 166
  Economic and Logic Incentives 167
  Applying Psychological Principles 168
Some New Ideas 171
  Making the Best of Car Driving 176
  Government and Technology 177
Company Coping Strategies 180
  Avoidance or Fleeing 181
  Assessment and Intervention 181
  Flexible Work Arrangements 183
  Telecommuting 185
Summary Remarks 187

Chapter 9. Methodological Issues in Commuting Research 189

Issues Relevant to Field Studies 190
The Structural Equation Model 191
Detecting Moderators and Mediators 192
Common Method Variance 194
Negative Affectivity 194
Cause–Effect Relationships 196

References 199

Index 215

1

The Commuting Experience

Each day tens of millions of men and women from every social stratum commute between home and work in the United States and most other industrialized countries. This morning and evening ritual involves billions of person hours every year, has wide-ranging implications for the way business is conducted, and impacts on the physical and psychological health of workers and their families.

United States government reports indicate that changes in the work force, greater availability of automobiles, and the shift of jobs to suburban locations have significantly increased commuting by private automobile (Pisarski, 1987). In an article on some creative approaches for improving mass transportation, *The New York Times* (Passell, 1992) graphically describes the magnitude of the problem. Between the years 1970 and 1989, the number of cars on the road increased by 90%, whereas urban road capacity increased less than 4%. For the year 1984, traffic delays averaged 5 hours per employed person, and the 10-mile commute in Los Angeles which took 20 minutes to complete in 1990 had become 30 to 35 minutes in 1992—an increase of about 50% in just 2 years.

Besides the loss in productivity experienced by profit-making as well as nonprofit organizations, the direct and indirect costs to the individual and society cannot be measured solely in monetary terms. According to Cervero (1986), a well-respected Professor of City Planning, the American life style is being threatened by the transportation situation. Middle-class Americans left the inner city several decades ago looking for uncluttered environments where traffic congestion, pollution, and lack of space would be problems of the past. Instead, the building boom in the 1980s and lack of intelligent regional planning often produced traffic problems in the suburbs equal to those found in congested downtown areas.

Cervero feels that planners and decision makers must adopt an entirely new approach if the future is to be made livable, if not enjoyable. Employer initiatives that reduce trip length or frequency of trips such as flex-time and telecommuting (both of which are defined and analyzed later in the book) provide only part of the solution. These tactical remedies do not remove the underlying problem. Radical approaches that view the problem of mass transportation as a strategic issue are required. Altering the future makeup and relationship among the cities, suburbs, and rural areas would ultimately provide the only long-lasting solution. Planning on a much grander scale, which takes into account the present and future regional traffic patterns, is essential. Outside the city, community decision makers must redesign suburban work places into denser clusters and plan for phasing in new jobs, housing, and services gradually into a specific area.

An analysis of the entire process beginning with an examination of individual and organizational variables and proceeding with the local, regional, and national concerns is necessary for providing a comprehensive solution to the commuting predicament. As most researchers and practitioners tend to tackle only one aspect of the entire commuting process (e.g., the relationship between commuting stress and organizational behavior or the causes of suburban gridlock), an interdisciplinary approach is needed for tackling all aspects of the problem. Although it is our intention to emphasize individual and organizational variables in explaining some of the antecedents and consequences involved in the commuting process, the macro perspective, including the community planner's input into the decision process, will be incorporated when discussing recommendations for ameliorating the present situation. As the primary goal of the book is to be as objective and exhaustive as possible, an attempt will be made to identify critical variables from various disciplines and perspectives.

PROFESSIONALS IN THE FIELD

It would appear appropriate at this point to describe how several disciplines have studied or tried to deal with commuting. Just in the past few years, the number and variety of professionals examining these issues from an organizational, individual, and societal perspective have increased substantially. Within the organization, psychologists and personnel managers are wrestling with many of the more blatant negative consequences of the commuting experience. Outside the organization, community or environmental psychologists, clinicians (psychologists, psychiatrists, etc.), and government experts of all types have also become involved in various aspects of the problem.

In practical terms, this means that the industrial psychologist is frequently interested in identifying causes or correlates of relevant behaviors such as lateness or absences. If a systematic relationship between variables is found, then methods for modifying the link may be tried. Although traffic-associated problems are one of the many logical causes for the behavioral outcomes measured in an organizational context, they are among the least understood variables. Researchers are not sure what aspect of the drive between home and work is the primary cause in the process, and, therefore, it is often relegated to minor status in organizational behavior studies (Muchinsky, 1977). An appreciation of the many links between independent and dependent variables is necessary before the problem can be managed intelligently.

The environmental psychologist also plays a crucial role in researching various aspects of the problem. By identifying relevant variables from different social domains, a clearer picture of the numerous linkages is obtained. This is most striking in the work of Novaco and colleagues (e.g., Novaco, Stokols, & Milanesi, 1990; Novaco, Kliewer, & Broquet, 1991). Several of their articles have appeared in the *American Journal of Community Psychology* in a section devoted to environmental ecological psychology. The authors present their results in an ecological framework implying a network of reciprocal links among the residential, commuting, and occupational spheres. The data collected from the series of studies conducted by Novaco and colleagues have been the basis for much of the modern thinking in the field.

On the other hand, the clinical psychologist, psychiatrist, and social worker are the professionals primarily responsible for treating symptoms associated with commuting stress both on the job and at home. Although the ailment, as presented to the clinician, is rarely, if ever, labeled as a commuting stress disorder, it may be viewed as yet another life stressor that initiates or aggravates psychological, physiological, or behavioral changes in the individual. We can apply some of the theory and practice available in the stress literature for understanding and treating the consequences of the commuting experience.

A clinician's perspective and appreciation of individual differences often yield an awareness of the existence of underlying causes and provide guidelines for a suitable course of action. Individual differences, according to Payne (1988), play a crucial role in the perception of the stressor. For example, personality (Type As have been suggested by some investigators), self-image, and locus of control are only some of the constructs that have been studied in the field. Other stress investigators (e.g., Gellalty & Meyer,

1992) have focused on cognitive processes and styles, including ability to attend to relevant information as a predictor of arousal or the effects of stress. As the literature in the field begins to accumulate and as more studies take on a comparative approach, it will be easier to pinpoint those variables that contribute most to stress reactions.

Finally, in its attempts to intervene for the common good, the government, as always, has some advice to offer. Employers in the United States are being told by the federal government to reduce the number of cars driven to work, to increase car occupancy and utilization of public transportation, and to adopt other measures for reducing both traffic congestion and emission of car pollutants (Cervero, 1986).

It is clear that the commuting experience as it exists today in the United States may have wide-ranging ramifications. In addition to the individual commuter, deleterious effects on the environment, the employer, and the family (this last area, in particular, was the focus of a recent study by Novaco et al., (1991) have been reported. Identifying intervening variables and outcomes related to the drive between home and work can serve two purposes: (1) provide an understanding of the variables and links that comprise the commuting experience and (2) suggest methods of intervention for reducing or, at least, controlling some of its negative effects at either the individual, company, or societal level.

THE COMMUTING EXPERIENCE

Everyone who drives a car is familiar with the experience of being cut off by another driver. There you are sputtering in rage as the driver of the other car speeds off with nary a glance behind him. Do you remember the effect of the incident on your mood? Did it affect your work performance during the first segment of your workday? If the incident occurred on your way home did it affect the way you greeted your spouse or children? Many transit commuters experience other stressors such as standing-room-only conditions on a crowded bus or subway car on a hot summer day, or being drenched in a rainstorm during the three-block walk from the subway station to work.

Although various consequences of commuting have been studied, the findings are generally inconsistent. Direct effects are obvious and include hours lost from work or leisure activities, vehicle wear and tear, excessive gasoline consumption, and the like. Air pollution, the noise of honking horns, drivers screaming, and traffic accidents are also quite common in areas with high traffic volume and congestion. The above consequences are all worthy of study and are usually part of the research domain of transportation experts and regional planners. However, clinicians, personnel managers, and organizational psychologists generally deal with more indirect effects that appear to emanate from commuting but are harder to trace. One such particular effect is strain (the difference between strain and stress is discussed below), which is posited as having organizational consequences such as withdrawal, attitude change, and lowered performance levels and appears to be one of the logical consequences of commuting.

A particularly troublesome issue for many investigators is the inconsistency of findings from the field. Some individuals react negatively to a specific stressor, whereas others do not. A later chapter in the book describing in detail the linkages among the variables including relevant mediator and moderator variables (see Chapter 9) may help to explain some of these inconsistencies.

Individual and organizational effects have economic implications too. What first appears as only psychological or physiological is often followed by various behavioral changes reducing efficiency or productivity. Thus, a long, difficult commute may raise certain body fluids or chemicals resulting in fatigue, difficulty in concentration, or other undesirable effects. Family, friends, and fellow employees may become affected when employees become irritable or uncooperative. Although psychological states are somewhat difficult to quantify, other organizational effects including absence, lateness, and performance are more objective and have clear monetary costs associated with them. An understanding of the entire process necessitates an analysis of a host of variables at one time. Unfortunately, the literature largely consists of analyses of the relationship between commuting and specific intermediate or ultimate outcomes. A thorough review of the findings and the development of a model that provides an explanation of the following process is needed: how does the individual's commute translate, at later stages, to the various individual, family, and organizational effects hypothesized and/or observed by researchers?

There is no simple answer to this question. As studies in the applied psychological literature are often based on very little theoretical background, the results were often inconsistent, ambiguous, or, at best, inconclusive. For example, if sex is an important moderator in the link between stress and certain negative outcomes, and several studies seem to indicate that it is, an investigator who examined only male or only female subjects could not draw a meaningful inference about the effects of stress. Also, if a study with car drivers rather than users of mass transportation finds a significant correlation between distance traveled and lateness, a lack of theoretical understanding prevents us from drawing any generalizations to other situations.

Independently of the commuting experience, interventions have been proposed both in the work place and at home for dealing with various types of stress at the individual level (e.g., Corey & Wolf, 1992; Guest, 1981). At the same time, stress researchers have examined questions associated with prediction, developed models of relevant determinants and consequences, and initiated training and desensitization programs to reduce the level of stress at many companies (e.g., Fletcher, 1988; Ilgen, 1990; Netermeyer, Johnston, & Burton, 1990; Motowidlo, Packard, & Manning, 1986; Bruning & Frew, 1985). An attempt will be made to integrate these approaches and apply them to the commuting experience. The comprehensive approach is essential before meaningful intervention can be proposed for the suffering commuter. According to Corey and Wolf (1992), when referring to the need to blend clinical and organizational efforts in stress research and management, there is as yet "no evidence in the literature that these efforts have been integrated in any coherent and systematic way" (p. 65). Only by examining and understanding the process from a broad perspective, do Corey and Wolf feel the deleterious effects associated with various individual and organizational outcomes can be improved.

The remainder of the book, after a brief discussion of several important issues related to commuting, specifically, and stress, generally, covers the following topics: (1) a description of commuting patterns in the United States (based on census data and national transportation surveys); (2) commuting as a stressor, i.e., the description of the independent variable; (3) direct effects of commuting including certain physiological changes; (4) mediators and moderators in the commuting process; (5) organizational consequences; (6) formulation of a commuting model that integrates the above data and permits methods of testing; and (7) intervention and recommendations.

Before delving into some of the aspects of the stress literature that can be applied to the commuting experience, it is necessary to define several terms that will be important throughout the book.

DEFINING THE MAIN VARIABLES

There is great difficulty in trying to specify what the independent variable or causal agent is in the commuting process and how it should be measured. Initially, commuting was defined in terms of distance or time traveled (or average speed). Martin (1971) cites data to support the practical equivalence of the two terms (time and distance), particularly, in studies of public transportation near the worker's home. Novaco, Stokols,

Campbell, and Stokols (1979) have reported a correlation of .93 between the two measures.

These were the independent variables used in most of the early reports on the effects of commuting. Novaco et al. (1979) formulated a new concept of *commute impedance*. Impedance was defined as a behavioral restraint on movement or goal attainment (Novaco et al., 1991). Essentially, impedance consists of anything that frustrates the goal to arrive at a particular destination—for example, distance, slow speed, or traffic congestion. Novaco et al. (1979) observed that commuting can be a significant stressor when measured in terms of the degree of commute impedance. Extending this definition to public transportation, commuting stress may be a function of the number of stages in the commute (Taylor & Pocock, 1972), the crowded conditions of the commute (Aiello, DeRisi, Epstein, & Karlin, 1977), or the complexity of the journey to work (Knox, 1961). Steers and Rhodes (1978) simply used the phrase transportation problems for the independent variable. Finally, Ivancevich (1986) considers commuting one of life's hassles and, as with other obstacles in life, feels that it often leads to stress and behavioral changes (see Dohrenwend and Shrout, 1985, for a general discussion of various "hassles" as examples of life-stress variables).

At first glance, it would appear that average speed is an ideal measure of impedance. If it takes longer to get to work (or to return home), more impedance is implied. However, this simple measure is confounded with so many other extraneous factors so as to nearly completely obscure its meaning. For example, a commuter driving at 35 mph is not necessarily experiencing more impedance than another driver driving at an average speed of 50 mph. The former may be using only local streets and going at the maximum permissible speed and actually experiencing no "obstacles" along the way, whereas the latter may be driving on a superhighway (on a German autobahn, this driver would probably be only crawling) and experiencing many "obstacles" along the way. Interestingly, Novaco et al. (1990) found that "average speed increases as an artifact of commuting distance" (p. 234), a further indication that speed is not a function of impedance but of other extraneous variables.

Another ambiguity, artificially imposed by researchers' disregard of proper terminology, relates to the general issue of job stress in an input–output (I/O) context (Beehr & Franz, 1987). In particular, the terms *stress* and *strain* have not been adequately distinguished, and the lack of clarity here has often caused confusion in distinguishing between the independent and dependent variables across studies. Using a manual search of journals in organizational behavior, Jex, Beehr, and Roberts (1992) found that in nearly 40% of the articles stress was used either incorrectly or ambiguously. The authors feel that a stress questionnaire that does not define its terms adequately may yield erroneous results especially if vague usage allowed each respondent to interpret the word stress as either stress or strain.

According to the correct usage, *stress* refers to the job stressor, the stimulus part of the equation and is usually the cause or outside force. *Strain* is the response part of the equation and is the potential harmful effect of a force on the object. Part of the blame for the confusion in terminology can be placed on Selye (1976), who used the term stress to refer to a syndrome of human responses.

Therefore, it would be advisable to distinguish between the two terms. In the present context, commuting stress refers to environmental or outside variables that cause strain. Both stress and strain can be measured with either psychological or physiological (or objective) measures. For our purposes, both terms are important. The objective (e.g., number of traffic lights on the route from home to work) or subjective (e.g., perception of number of times brakes were applied) stressors may cause objective strain responses (e.g., change in blood pressure), and subjective strain responses (e.g., self-reports of fatigue and lack of concentration).

MEDIATOR AND MODERATOR VARIABLES

Whereas impedance can be objectively measured by a speedometer, odometer, or number of cars on the road, investigators have suggested that another factor, the perception of the commuting experience also needs to be taken into account. Koslowsky and Krausz (1993) noted that it may be *more* important to use the commuter's reaction to the trip between home and work than some objective indicator. For example, while an hour train ride may involve more time and distance than a 35-minute commute by car, for some people, the train ride may be perceived as less stressful because they would not have to buck traffic or fight to find a parking space. For others, time alone in a car might be perceived as less stressful than being a passenger in a train (or, especially, a commuter subway with other people). Thus, the measure that may be required is some type of qualitative indicator rather than a quantitative one. Perception variables are a good example of mediators that explain, often, a substantial part of the variance in the dependent variable.

The idea of subjective impedance as an index of perceived constraints was suggested and operationalized by Novaco et al. (1990). Specifically, four components of subjective impedance were identified: evening commute congestion (e.g., perception of times brakes were deemed necessary, etc.), aversiveness of travel (e.g., ratings of the commute in terms of slow–fast, stop-and-go, etc.), morning commute congestion (e.g., necessity to apply brakes on the way to work, etc.), and surface street constraints (travel speed reduced by stop signs, etc.). It is interesting to note that the evening commute was perceived as significantly different from the morning commute in the Novaco et al. (1990) study; the former also showed considerably higher internal consistency (.89 vs. .75). Kluger (1992) also included this distinction as part of his predictor variables.

Aware of the inconsistent results in the field of commuting, Kluger (1992) has included a different mediator in his study of the commuting process. He proposed a measure that has both objective and subjective components. What needs to be considered, according to Kluger, is the variance (or standard deviation) of the commute measure and not its mean. Average speed, even if it is rather low, does not necessarily yield any specific effect. Considerably more important is the predictability of the commute. Thus, a drive that consistently takes 1 hour, give or take a few minutes, to work every day may not lead to any negative consequences as the individual adjusts to this time period. However, a mean drive of 30 minutes, that is accompanied with a standard deviation of 30 minutes is more likely to yield negative consequences. The driver in the latter case may perceive a lack of control, a situation that has been associated with stress (Perlmuter & Monty, 1977).

The lack of control manifests itself in another aspect of the commute. An individual who has a relatively short commute (as defined by the driver) may take longer to get to work than other commuters who live much further away. This is readily seen in a place like Manhattan, where driving crosstown (i.e., east–west or vice versa) during the rush hour may take many times longer than a mass transit trip or even a bus ride that goes straight along one of the north–south avenues. Again, the lack of control and the cognition or awareness that fellow employees arriving from further away have shorter trips may be stressful. This would imply that the time to get to work is meaningful only in its proper context. A commute is "long" only if the driver perceives it as such.

Concepts similar to those described above can be found in the general stress literature. Specifically, Thompson (1981) indicates that work stress is related to the discretion lattitude that is available to the individual in avoiding some undesirable event. When the course of action available to the employee is not under the individual's control, the environment is likely to become stressful. As applied to commuting, a driver who must arrive at work by a certain hour is liable to experience levels of discomfort and stress if alternative routes are not available and he or she perceives a lack of control. As such, the independent variable may be defined as the difference between perceived (or even, actual) demand and perceived alternatives available.

Whether or not a person feels he or she can exert control in a stressful situation directly influences the mode of reaction to the stress. For example, recent research has indicated that many hospital patients worry that pain medication will not be immediately available when they need it or that they will have to wait until the next prescribed time for administration despite the fact that their pain level is high. Those patients who were offered the opportunity to control their administration of pain medication were found to be less anxious and required less pain medication overall. The "learned helplessness" paradigm of Seligman (1975) posits that people confronted with stressors who feel they cannot exert control in that situation are more likely to give up or become depressed.

Moderators also play a role in explaining the links between the independent variable and outcomes. Let's start our explanation of moderators with an illustration. Two people exposed to the same stressor are not likely to have the same reaction. Personality and context play an important role in determining the effects of stressors. Thus, response is often modulated by the degree to which an event is perceived as threatening, harmful, or challenging (Lazarus, 1966). A performance review may indeed be stressful, but if the employee views his supervisor as warm, supportive, and fair, a good deal of the stress involved in the appraisal experience can be mitigated, if not entirely removed. Interpretation is also directly related to one's personal and cognitive style. Some people tend to see things as problems, whereas others view them as challenges. People who tend to become easily depressed or who have low self-esteem may become overwhelmed by some psychological stressors, whereas others with a more optimistic attitude or positive self-image find they can deal with the stressor more effectively. Variables that can be split into several groupings with greater effects observed for one of the categories than some or all of the others are commonly called moderators.

Researchers in other applied areas make distinctions between objective and subjective stressors (Wells, 1982) and *acute* versus *chronic* stress (Eden, 1982). In the Wells study, modest correlations were observed between objective job conditions and perceived work stressors indicating that the concepts overlap but also contain unique components for prediction. As regards the second distinction, commuting has both acute and chronic characteristics. A commuter who has the same trip each day may experience strain continuously during work and at home (chronic), experience it only after a specific event such as observing the aftermath of a serious car accident (acute) or some combination of the two (at peak levels right after the journey with less striking effects the rest of the day).

The comparisons with other investigations illustrate very clearly that the commuting process involves stressors that are both unique and similar to that reported in the literature.

STRESSORS, STRAIN, AND ORGANIZATIONAL BEHAVIOR

Two particular streams of research are relevant for understanding the effects of the commuting experience on the individual and the organization: (1) stressor stimuli and strain responses, and (2) stressors and organizational behavior. By briefly reviewing some of the work in these areas, it may be possible to apply many of the same principles to the commuting process.

Arriving at work after a harrowing morning drive that has included traffic delays, a few doses of noxious exhaust fumes, and an ominous rattling in the motor that is the harbinger of auto repair bills yet to be paid, many people complain about being exhausted or "stressed out." The same complaint can be heard from those who make their way to work on overcrowded buses or trains. They have been subjected to unforeseen delays, inclement weather, and sometimes multiple transfers from one train or bus to another. How can we understand the demands and strains on the commuter in the light of stress research?

Selye's Theory of Stress

Selye (1976), one of the original investigators of stress and its effects defined it as the "nonspecific response of the body to any demand." A stressor is an agent that produces stress. Stressors are often physiological. For example, running a marathon, sitting in a hot room, or cutting oneself while shaving are all physiological stresses that require the body to make an adjustment. While Selye did not emphasize emotions as stressors, it has become clear that love, hate, fear, and a host of other questions can also be agents of stress.

Selye explained that the body adapts to stress with what he called the *general adaption syndrome*. When first exposed to a stressor, the body responds with an "alarm reaction." In essence this is the response of the body as it mobilizes its coping abilities. The body then enters a stage of "resistance" as it continues to work toward coping and adapting to the stressor. However, when stressors occur too often or when coping mechanisms do not work successfully, the body enters a stage of exhaustion. In this stage, resistance is intermittent or weak, there are signs of physiological breakdown, and the body is particularly vulnerable to illness or disease.

In other words, the body becomes less and less successful at adjusting to the stressors because of their frequency or intensity.

Psychosocial Factors and Stress

The relationship between psychosocial and physiological factors in understanding the effects of stress has become a focal point of research during the last half of the century. Systematic studies of the relationship between life events and bodily reactions can be said to have begun with the investigations by two researchers, Stewart Wolf and Harold Wolff (McLean, 1973). An accident at a young age had resulted in their patient Tom having his esophagus sealed off and his stomach opened and connected to his abdominal wall. This artificial opening, essentially a window into Tom's stomach and digestive system, enabled the investigators to observe Tom's digestive system reacting to emotionally changed situations. Among their findings, Wolf and Wolff observed an inhibition of secretory activity and vascularity when Tom was depressed and a large increase of gastric secretions and acidity when Tom was angry (McLean, 1973). Their research had many interesting implications for Americans who spend hundreds of millions of dollars every year on laxatives and antacids. During World War II and the Korean War that followed, a great deal of research was conducted that studied the relationship between psychological reaction to combat and resulting physiological stress.

Everyone reading this book has, at one time or another, experienced stress resulting from an emotional reaction to some stimulus. The anxiety preceding a first date, a particularly important interview, the joy of being reunited with a loved one, or anger at begin rejected or insulted are all examples of psychological stressors. Each can have an effect on our bodies by increasing blood pressure or heart rate, releasing catecholamines or other hormones, or producing any one of a number of "fight or flight" reactions. Perhaps it should be noted here that not every form of stress is bad. Bringing home a new baby, receiving a promotion, or moving to a new home may be stressful events, but they certainly have many positive connotations. At the same time, our bodies are amazingly resilient, and we are able to cope constantly with a variety of stressors. Stress can actually improve our performance at times. Some veteran actors welcome stage fright because it helps to keep them extra sharp during a performance.

Strain, in many cases, involves some form of physiological response or arousal. Based on the findings from several studies, it appears that the demands of the task situation are related to activity in the sympathetic nervous system (Gellatly & Meyer, 1992; Levenson, 1988; Kahneman, 1973). Many variables influence the level of the arousal including the behavioral and cognitive demands of the task (McGrath, 1976).

Especially important from the cognitive perspective is the task-relevant information that the individual attends to (Gellatly & Meyer, 1992). When task demand is low and the accompanying arousal is low, an individual can concentrate and deal with all sorts of activity, and strain is not a factor. This is illustrated by a commuter who drives while holding a conversation on a cellular phone and is as productive as when he or she is sitting at the office desk. During rush hour when traffic problems exist, the demands and arousal level are higher, and the driver's concentration must focus only on task-relevant information. This in turn may increase arousal and, at some point, cause performance decrement and behavioral changes. How long this pattern lasts is not clear, but if arousal is chronic, the individual's defenses may become ineffective or wear down (e.g., listening to music in the car may not produce a calming effect anymore). This approach holds much promise in understanding the relationship between the cognitive and behavioral domains in any potentially stressful situation.

Coping with Stress

The cognitive aspect of "perceived control" in a stressful situation is directly related to coping with stress. In fact, many practitioners in the health, industrial, and clinical fields of psychology teach their clients how to cope more effectively with stress when it cannot be avoided. Today, several cognitive–behavioral-type approaches including stress inoculation training have become very popular (Meichenbaum & Cameron, 1983). One of the more innovative clinicians in the cognitive area, Albert Ellis (1962) and his rational emotive theory teach clients to evaluate psychological stressors as well as their own abilities more realistically. The theory has many applications to coping in an organizational environment (Ellis, 1978). Ellis suggests that many people have unrealistic expectations of themselves. They feel that "I must get everyone to like me" or "I should succeed at everything I do." Changing a self-centered attitude to a more realistic response will help the client reduce internal conflict and experience stressors as less threatening. Various other cognitive therapy approaches (Beck, Rush, Shaw, & Emery, 1979) enable the client to interpret stressful situations more realistically and optimistically and thereby increase their capacity for coping.

Lazarus (1966) speaks of two different coping strategies. When faced with a stressful situation a person can take *direct action*. He or she may proceed to gather more information about the nature of the stressor, remove the stressor, or leave the scene. An example of direct action would be buying your teenager a Walkman to take the place of the stereo blasting in his room or buying yourself earplugs if that doesn't work. The other alternative is *palliative coping* where the person reacts to the stressor by adjusting his or her internal environment. This approach can include utilizing some of the cognitive approaches referred to previously: being more realistic in appraising the stressors, self-coaching in assertiveness or optimism, or taking time for relaxation or meditation. Negative examples of palliative coping would include dealing with a stressful situation by ingesting drugs or alcohol or resorting to other self-destructive behaviors.

Back to Commuting and Stress

It might seem as though we got detoured in our discussion of commuting and stress, but in fact we can now better understand their relationship. A typical commuter is exposed to a multitude of stressors on the way to and from work. Physiological stressors include environmental factors such as noise, crowding, heat, and noxious fumes. Time pressures and aggressive or reckless behavior on the part of other commuters are just a few examples of the psychological stressors that affect commuters. As with stress in general, the effects of commuting stress are influenced by moderators and mediators. It is apparent that the linkages here are complex, involve a multivariate perspective, and clearly defined hypotheses must be generated and tested before meaningful conclusions can be reached.

One can also see how the concepts of perception and coping are intertwined in the commuter's reactions to the negative stimuli. Does the commuter have the possibility of choosing an alternative route? Can the radio be tuned to a station that offers constant traffic reports and enables the commuter to be armed with all the information vital to a decision? Can a Walkman be used to filter out the noise and discomfort caused by a crowded subway ride to work? Can a portable phone help maintain communication with home or office and provide some relief from time pressure? Many of these coping styles will be discussed in greater detail later in the book.

Commuting and Organizational Consequences

Organizational psychologists use many types of outcome measures as the dependent variable. A good starting point would be to look at some of the common withdrawal measures such as lateness, absence, and turnover with the purpose of determining if generalizations from the effects of other types of stress (e.g., role conflict, role ambiguity, etc.) can be applied to commuting. In other words, is commuting one of the variables that have an influence on whether we show up to work and when we show up at work?

On a typical work day in America about 2% to 4% of the work force is absent (Rosse, 1991). The direct and indirect cost of these absences cost the United States about $30 billion in 1984 (Rosse, 1991). Nominally, the costs are much higher today. Accurate data on the antecedents and consequences of absences are hard to come by (Rosse, 1991). Many of the researchers of absence behavior complain about a lack of compatibility in the measures used. Some even insist that measuring absence is misleading and prefer measuring attendance behavior. Meaningful statistics on the cost of lateness to the organization are nonexistent, so it's hard to draw many conclusions from the phenomenon of tardiness. Using some of the recent procedures in the field of utility analysis, we will present some estimates of the monetary effects of various outcomes on the organization.

Unlike absences and lateness, turnover has been studied quite extensively, and there is a general consensus on how to measure the variable (Koslowsky & Krauss, 1993). From one perspective, the various withdrawal measures can be considered as ways to cope with stress. It is as if the individual is trying to "escape" or avoid contact with the stressor (Edwards, 1988). When stress is present within an organization, the worker may choose several courses of action. A progression model from lateness to turnover is advocated by Mitra, Jenkins, and Gupta (1992). This does not imply that the same set of antecedent variables are associated with each behavioral outcome; specific causal variables, as well as the moderators and mediators, must be considered (Mitra et al., 1992; Rosse, 1991). Thus, turnover may be more a function of outside economic variables such as job alternatives, whereas absences may be more a function of personal and situational variables such as commuting stress. Nevertheless, the authors who posit a progression (Gupta & Jenkins, 1983; Rhodes & Steers, 1990; Rosse, 1991), argue that withdrawal tends to follow a sequence, from mild withdrawal (e.g., lateness) to more severe forms of withdrawal (e.g., turnover). Findings from other researchers did not support a progression hypothesis (Mckee, Markham, & Scott, 1992; Mobley, 1982).

One other type of measure that is often used as an outcome indicator is attitude. This includes job satisfaction, organizational commitment, and job involvement. Rosse and Hulin (1985) argue that job attitudes may underlie a spectrum of behavior and stimulate a desire to withdraw from the situation. Other attitudes may serve as moderators as well as dependent variables. For example, although stressors are generally found to correlate moderately with job satisfaction (Kasl, 1978; Murphy, 1988), some investigators argue that the association is moderated by locus of control (Abdel-Halim, 1980). In any event, if attitudes are intervening variables between stress and future behavior, it would appear that a comprehensive model of the entire process needs to include an attitude link.

Initially, it seems to make sense that there should be a relationship between some aspects of the commuting experience and absenteeism or tardiness. Almost everyone can attest to the experience of arriving late at work because of heavy traffic or delays in public transportation. Some of us awakening to a snowstorm or heavy rain and thinking about the long commute to work have pulled the blankets back over our heads. At times the length of a commute or the idea of facing bumper-to-bumper traffic can help convince us to stay home one more day to nurse a cold or backache.

In fact, very few researchers have included "distance from work" or commuting as one of the variables that needs to be studied when predicting organizational withdrawal. They have generally chosen to look at motivational factors such as work attitude and job satisfaction, or past absentee behavior and organizational factors (tenure, shiftwork) as precursors of future behavior.

By surveying the studies that have been conducted with commuting as the independent variable and one of the behavioral measures as the dependent variable, it may be possible to draw some inferences that can be of aid in building a model that includes the commuting experience as an independent variable. Intuition would seem to indicate that commuting could be a significant factor influencing these variables, and a comprehensive model should include these measures.

SUMMARY

As we have seen, in the first stage, the commuting process involves some type of objective or subjective experience. Variables acting as mediators or moderators then come into play yielding the various individual, organizational, and family effects reported in the literature. After a review of the relevant independent and dependent variables in the process, an integrative multidisciplinary model will be suggested. Methods for testing and verification that avoid some of the methodological pitfalls will then be proposed.

2

Travel and Mobility

An understanding of commuting patterns and behaviors is necessary for identifying the antecedents and consequences of stress. In addition, coping behaviors, both individual and organizational, are to a large extent a function of the quantitative and qualitative features of the trip to work and back home. Governmental intervention for reducing some of the negative effects of commuting also requires an appreciation of the way people get to work, their preferences, and, in cases where warranted by societal needs, persuading individuals to change their behavior.

Where people live and work, the mode of transportation used to get there, and the ramifications of this choice are of major concern to employers, community/urban planners, and employees. For the employer, available commuting patterns help determine the makeup of the labor market. In this sense, commuting can be seen as the lubricant of the labor market (Jansen, 1993, p. 101). The community planner is most interested in the mode of transportation used as well as that preferred by the people living in a specific area as this data will be the major input for budgeting and allocating required resources for managing traffic- and transit-related issues. Road congestion, train and bus crowding, dependable and timely schedules for the journey, and environmental impact are only a few of the concerns that must be dealt with in planning a commuting network from scratch. Finally, relevant commuting variables, such as the quality of housing and schools in an area, time and distance to work, mode of transportation available, and job opportunities all are part of the process involved in deciding where to live. It is recognized that the commute affects the individual and, we contend, that reactions or responses to this experience involve a complete spectrum of other major targets including the family, the organization, and the society. The usual government reports and scholarly texts on commuting patterns hardly ever mention the issue of stress. It is not a topic commonly discussed by economists, demographers, or most transportation experts. Nevertheless, as we will try to show, stress often has a major impact on all of these disciplines because of the physical, emotional, and behavioral consequences of the commuting experience.

In order to understand the interaction among the various factors in the process, it is necessary to appreciate some of the demographics that make up the commuting experience. Although most of our discussion will focus on the situation in the United States, some data from Europe will be presented for comparison purposes. The information in this chapter was culled from several sources. American road conditions and individual commuting patterns were derived from two of the major government sponsored technical summaries over the last decade: The General Accounting Office (GAO, 1989) report on traffic congestion and the Joint Center for Political Studies (JCPS, 1985) report, much of which is derived from the United States Census data.

In order to update these findings, two other sources were also consulted. The first is a report prepared by Pisarski (1992) for the United States Department of Transportation. The second uses survey results generally not available from governmental data banks and focuses on the commuting situation in a fairly large and typical Standardized Metropolitan Statistical Area (SMSA). The presentation of the responses by motorists in Seattle, Washington, will help us illustrate some of the general, as well as unique, commuting characteristics of an urban area in the United States faced with some of the issues described in the book.

THE GAO REPORT

In 1988, the U.S. General Accounting Office was asked to report on federal efforts to improve mobility and recommend ways for dealing with the issue of traffic congestion. The report, addressed to the U.S. Senate Subcommittee on Transportation and Related Agencies found that federal efforts focused on three methods to reduce traffic congestion: road construction and reconstruction, transportation systems management, and advanced technology.

The GAO report noted that in a survey of 20,000 respondents, 80% said that traffic congestion was a major problem in their communities. Highway statistics reported by the Federal Highway Administration in 1989 indicated that by 1987, 46.4% of all urban interstate roads were congested. During commuting hours in the same year, 65% of urban interstate travel was congested. The GAO report recognized that labor force changes, a decline in new highway miles, suburban expansion, and more trucks on the road were significant contributors to traffic congestion.

THE ROADS THAT TAKE US HOME

The Federal Aid Highway Program distributes funds to the 50 states to construct and reconstruct urban and rural highway systems. Although the federal government supervises disbursement of the funds and approves the work to be done, each state is responsible for administering the program. Roads are classified as being part of: (1) the interstate system, which includes highways that comprise the nation's transportation network; (2) the primary system, which consists of interconnecting roads important to interstate, statewide, and regional travel; (3) the urban system, which consists of urban highways and arteries; (4) the secondary system, which includes rural collector routes. The GAO reports that nearly 75% of travel occurs on the interstate, primary, and urban systems despite the fact that the total mileage of these systems is only 12% of the total for the United States.

In an effort to increase the capacity of roads to carry traffic, the Federal Highway Administration provides funds for new construction. At the same time, with the ageing of the national highway system, the government has also emphasized reconstruction. The *4r program* involves the resurfacing, restoring, rehabilitating, and reconstructing of the interstate system. The GAO report points out that the fourth "r," reconstructing, means that the government can support not only preservation of existing highway miles but also subsidizes functional improvements that will result in highways being able to bear additional traffic. Adding lanes or widening highways is an example of highway reconstruction. Thus federal funds help to reduce traffic congestion by adding new routes and highway miles as well as by providing additional lanes on existing highways.

The federal government invests a great deal of money subsidizing the construction and reconstruction of highways. However, building roads and adding lanes is expensive, and it is not the only way to handle traffic congestion. Some of these other techniques will be discussed later in the chapters devoted to coping with commuting problems (Chapters 7 and 8). Although the GAO report describes the general problem of traffic congestion, some of the more specific characteristics of the commuting experience are not mentioned. What happens during the commuting hours? What types of transportation do people use? What is rush hour really like? To answer some of these questions, we need to look at the journey to and from work. Another report does exactly that. Written by the Joint Center for Political Studies and prepared for the U.S. Department of Transportation Urban Mass Transportation Administration, the report examined and compared the trends in commuting between 1970 and 1980 using the U.S. census data for those years.

THE JCPS REPORT: THE JOURNEY TO WORK

According to the JCPS report, approximately one third of all local trips are work-related ones, and there have been significant changes in the way people get to work. The years between 1960 and 1980 brought many changes for work travel. Gasoline prices rose and even tripled between 1970 and 1980. The cost of operating an automobile increased by about 250% during the 1970s. Despite the fact that transit fares rose only 44% from an average of 27.6 cents in 1970 to 39.7 cents in 1980, there was a decline in the use of public transportation for the commute to work (JCPS, 1985). Between 1960 and 1980, 30 million people were added to the work force, but the number of people using public transportation was reduced by more than 1½ million. The JCPS suggests a number of demographic changes that may account for this trend: (1) During the 1960s and 1970s, many people were moving out of large cities where there were well-developed public transit systems into smaller cities, particularly in the Sunbelt where well-developed transit systems were not extant. (2) The Baby Boom generation started buying automobiles. There were 20 million more cars being driven in 1980 than in 1970. The number of people getting to work by private automobile rose from 61.7 million in 1970 to 82.8 million in 1980. During that time, the number of occupied housing units increased by 17 million people, whereas the average household size dropped from 3.14 persons in 1970 to 2.76 persons in 1980. That meant that there were more "smaller households" than during the 1970s, and this fact made ride-sharing less likely. (3) In urbanized areas, the trends were similar. The number of workers living in urban areas and using public transportation for this work commute fell from 6.4 million in 1970 to 5.9 million in 1980. About 16 million more urban workers used private vehicles to get to work in 1980 than in 1970. However, there was an increase in the number of urban workers who walked to work or conducted their work at home during the 1970s.

 The JCPS report revealed a strong relationship between the use of public transportation and the number or cars available in a household. About 56% of workers who had no car used public transportation to get to work in 1970, and 49% did in 1980. People with no car available need to walk, bike, boat, or share a ride to work with someone else; these are popular alternatives in addition to public transportation.

At the other end of the spectrum, only about 3% of workers living in a household with three or more automobiles made the trip to work by public transportation. About 75% of those who used public transportation in 1980 came from households that had no car or one car available.

The report indicated that the highest rate of public transportation use was found among people living in a central city, working in the central business district (CBD), and having no car available to them—about 71.6% in 1980. Those least likely to use public transportation worked outside a central city, lived in the suburbs, and came from a household with 3 or more cars available—only 0.7% in 1980.

Workers in the Central City

Workers who commute into a CBD use public transportation about four times as frequently as other workers. Two factors that contribute to this phenomenon are: (1) more well-developed public transportation systems in central cities; and (2) limited space, expensive parking, and extreme traffic congestion as one comes closer to the CBD. The most urbanized areas in the United States, such as New York, New Jersey, and Pennsylvania, have well-developed transportation systems and also have a substantially higher percentage of workers arriving at work with public transportation. In 1980, about 33% of all U.S. workers who used public transportation to get to work lived in the New York City–northeastern New Jersey area.

How Long Does It Take to Get to Work?

The JCPS analyzed U.S. Census Bureau data and arrived at the following average times for a one-way trip to work. The national average travel time for workers in urbanized areas was 22.5 minutes. Teenage workers, 16 to 19 years old, had an average 16.5-minute work trip. The JCPS posited that many teenagers take part-time jobs closer to home.

Workers who live in group quarters had an average of a 10.6-minute travel time. This group included soldiers, college students, and workers in sheltered workshops. Many of these people walked to work. Workers with no automobile available averaged 29.2 minutes on their work trip. Overall, workers who used public transportation spent about twice as long on their trip to work as workers using private vehicles—21.1 minutes for autos compared to 42.2 minutes for public transportation. To round out the picture, average travel time in 1980 for bus or streetcar travelers was 37.8

minutes, subway or elevated train riders averaged 47.4 minutes, and railroad commuters had an average 63.8-minute one-way ride. Taxi riders had an average ride of 18.6 minutes.

The JCPS also analyzed average travel time according to commuter flow statistics. Among their findings they noted that workers living in the urban fringe and working *outside* a central city averaged an 18.8-minute work trip. The percentage of these people using public transportation was very low, about 2.1%. People living on the urban fringe and traveling into the CBD averaged a 35.1-minute ride. About 32.1% of these people used public transportation.

Average work trip time is a result of many factors including mode and availability of transportation, as well as the point of origin of the work trip and the traveler's destination. Getting across town in a central city during rush hour can take the same amount of time as traveling from one suburb to another. As we noted, traveling with public transportation takes, on the average, twice as long as commuting by automobile. Let's take a closer look at who uses public transportation, and what type of public transportation they choose.

The JCPS (1985) reported that streetcars and buses were the most frequently used form of transit for the work trip. About 62% of people who used public transportation to get to work arrived in a bus or streetcar. About 27% took subways or elevated trains. About 7% of those using public transportation used the railroad and about 3% arrived at work with a taxi. The number of workers living in cities and urbanized areas increased in the years between 1970 and 1980, but public transport use generally declined. In 1970, 8.6% of urbanized workers used buses or streetcars, but only 6% utilized them in 1980. Subway and elevated train riders comprised 3.8% of urbanized workers in 1980 but only 2.45% in 1980. Approximately 0.4% of all workers used taxis in 1970, and that number declined to 0.21% in 1980. Railroad commuters comprised 0.99% of all workers in 1970 and 0.85 in 1980 (JCPS, 1985).

Although the use of public transportation declined among urbanized area workers as a group, railroad usage among those who did utilize public transportation increased. In 1970, about 7.1% of public transportation work trips took place by railroad. That number represented about 453,000 workers. In 1980, about 8.9% of public transportation users arrived at work by railroad, about 524,000 workers in all (JCPS, 1985).

The increase in railroad use took place mainly in two geographical regions—the Middle Atlantic region, which includes New York City and Philadelphia, and the East North Central region, which includes Chicago. The JCPS reports that 93% of the national increase in railroad use for the work commute took place in these two areas. The choice of public transportation mode for the work trip was also related to place of domicile and place of work. The JCPS found that workers who lived in the central city, as well as those who resided in the urban fringe, used buses and streetcars to get to work more than any other mode of transportation, as noted previously around 62%. For workers living in central cities, subways and elevated trains were the next most commonly used mode of public transportation, whereas workers who lived in the urban fringe utilized the railroad. About 33% of central city dwellers used subways as opposed to about 10% in the urban fringe. About 25% of public transportation commuters living in the urban fringe used the railroads as opposed to about 2% of central city residents.

The JCPS divided job location into three categories: (1) the central business district (CBD) or downtown core of commercial activity, (2) the central city (CS), which represents the portion of the central city outside the CBD, and (3) work places located outside the CS (OCS), which can include locations outside of urbanized area boundaries.

In 1980, among workers living in an urbanized area and working in a CBD, approximately 58.5% arrived at work by bus or streetcar, and 26.6% arrived by train. Railroad commuters represented 13.7% of workers and taxicab riders, 1.2%. Among workers who traveled to the CS but outside of the CBD, about 59.9% used buses and streetcars, about 29.9% used subways or els, about 8.1% used the railroad, and 2.1% hailed taxis. Workers in these two areas were basically similar in their choice of public transportation with the most significant difference occurring in railroad and taxi usage (JCPS, 1985).

Among people who resided in an urbanized area and worked in the urban fringe, there was a large jump in bus or streetcar use to 84.2% and a drop in subway or el use to 6.3%. Railroad use dropped to 5.1% , and taxi use increased to 4.3%. Thus, as one moves away from the CBD, the number of commuters relying on buses or streetcars increases. The opposite is true for subway or "el" riders. As one moves further away from the central core of the city, subway and el use decreases. Concerning use of railroads in the commute to work, whereas the percentage of commuters who used the railroads to get to work in the CBD (10.5% in 1970 and 13.7% in 1980) and CS (4.6% in 1970 and 8.1% in 1980) increased between the 1970 and 1980 census, the percentage of public transportation commuters working in the urban fringe and utilizing the railroad actually decreased from 11.7% in 1970 to 5.1% in 1980. A decline in railroad service to urban fringe areas may account for the decreased use of railroads to get to work in those locations (JCPS, 1985).

Commuter Flows and Transportation Modes

The JCPS organized its findings concerning mode of public transportation for the work trip around six commuter flows that took into account residence and job location. In 1980, among workers living in a CS and working in a CBD, 60.3% rode to work on buses or streetcars, and 34.7% used subways or els; however, 84.8% of workers living in the CS and working outside of a CS used buses to get to work, with only 9.1% traveling by subway or el. Work trip commuters traveling entirely within CSs used subways and els at a higher rate than those traveling to the urban fringe or coming into the CS from the suburbs. The JCPS saw this as reflective of the fact that subways and els are more available within the CSs. About 30% of work trip commuters from the suburbs to the CS (outside the CBD) job locations used railroads, whereas only about 2% of workers who moved exclusively within the central city utilized the railroad.

Household Demographics and Mode of Transportation

The JCPS examined a number of factors relating household patterns in the United States to the use of public transportation. Households vary in terms of the number of people living in a particular house, how many workers there are in the household, and what demands there are in terms of transportation needs. The JCPS assumed that the more people there are in a particular household with demands for an automobile, the more likely it is that some members of the family may need to depend on public transportation to get to work. That is, there just won't be enough automobiles to go around.

Although earning a living is obviously a high priority in any household, workers are not the only members of the family who require the use of an automobile with regularity. Young children may need to be taken to school. Older children may require a car to get to college classes. Household tasks such as shopping, bringing children to the doctor or dentist may also require the use of a car, particularly in suburban areas. As the demand increases for use of family vehicles, workers seek other forms of transportation for their work trips including public transportation (Kasoff, 1970).

The JCPS (1985) reports on the basis of the U.S. Statistical Abstract of 1984, Table 60, that during the 1970s the numbers of small households increased while the number of large households fell. The average household size fell from 3.14 persons in 1970 to 2.76 persons in 1980 and to 2.71 persons in 1984. Among households in urbanized areas with at least one person traveling to work, the number of one-person households increased from 3.6 million in 1970 to 6.7 million in 1980. At the other end of the spectrum, the number of "large" households with 10 or more members fell from 166,200 in 1970 to 97,000 in 1980.

The expected direct linear relationship between size of household and use of public transportation was not found after an analysis of the

1980 Census Bureau data. Instead of showing minimal public transportation use among single and small households and greater utilization among large households, a curvilinear relationship was found. Very small households as well as very large households used public transportation more than average-sized households.

The JCPS interpreted this finding along the following lines. Large households tended to use public transportation more than average households because there was more of a demand on the family automobile(s). The great demand for private transportation among other family members encouraged working family members to seek alternative forms of transportation, including public transportation. Small households, and particularly single-person households, were not as well off financially as larger households, and, therefore, less likely to own an automobile. Single-person households also tend to be located in CSs where public transportation is more likely to be available.

Until this point, we have addressed households in terms of the number of members. The JCPS also looked at households in terms of the number of workers in a home in relationship to public transportation use for the work trip. United States Bureau of Census data from 1983 (Table 37) identified two significant trends during the 1970s: (1) The number of women aged 16 and over in the work force increased from 35.7% in 1960, to 41.4% in 1970, to and 49.9% in 1980, almost half of the labor force, and (2) the number of multiple-wage-earner households increased. The Bureau of Labor Statistics reported that 21.9 million families had two or more wage earners (JCPS, 1985). That number represented about 54% of all wage-earning families.

More multiple wage earners and more female participation in the work force made it more likely that travel to work *at different locations* would be necessary. If there are not enough automobiles for all the workers in a particular family, then public transportation could be a likely alternative. The confounding factor in this equation is that as the number of wage earners in a household increases, the household income also tends to increase making it more feasible to purchase additional automobiles. In fact, the JCPS analysis of 1980 Census Bureau data indicated that most households with one earner had one car, most households with two earners had two cars, and most households with four or more earners had three or more cars. On the other hand, there were still a significant number of households with fewer cars than workers. About 37% of households with two workers had one or no cars available, and about 58% of households with three or more workers had fewer than three cars available. In 1980, the JCPS reports, about 19.1 million workers in urbanized areas resided in households where there were fewer cars than workers. That made it likely that public transportation had become a work trip alternative for many members of those households who could not have use of the family car(s).

The JCPS found that the most important factor in terms of household patterns and public transportation use was the ratio of cars in the family to the number of workers (JCPS, 1985). A worker from a household with less than one car per worker was 4.5 times more likely to choose public transportation as a means to get to work than a worker coming from a household with at least one car per worker. Over half of the households with *no car available* in 1980 were households with only one worker, and these single-worker families, as noted before, used public transportation more than any other type of household. The JCPS reported that overall the number of workers living in a household with less than one car per worker increased by almost 2 million during the 1970s, but the number of workers using public transportation for the work trip during that period fell by about 900,000.

The Transportation Disadvantaged

The JCPS (1985) looked at work trip commuting trends of demographic groups identified as the "transportation disadvantaged." Among these groups, blacks, women, the poor, teenagers, and older workers were looked at as particularly representative of the transportation disadvantaged. Each of these groups used public transportation at a higher rate than the national average.

The JCPS analysis of Census Bureau data indicated that in 1970 about 30.9% of black workers residing in urbanized areas used public transportation to get to work. That percentage diminished to 21.8 percent in 1980. However, in both cases the percentage of black workers using public transportation was almost three times as high as white workers. In 1980 the JCPS reported, blacks consisted of 11.7% of the work force but represented 26.7% of the workers who used public transportation for the work trip.

As we already pointed out, the lack of available private transportation often leads an individual to choose public transportation alternatives. The JCPS analysis of Census Bureau data for 1980 indicated that about 32.6% of all black households in the United States had no car compared with only 10.2% of white households. Overall, 30% of all workers living in a household without a car in 1980 were black. Only 5.6% of workers coming from households with three or more cars were black.

In general, blacks demonstrated a greater tendency to use public transportation than Caucasians overall. Among households with no car available 61.6% of black workers in urbanized areas used public transportation to get to work compared to 42% of Caucasians. In households with at least one car, Caucasians used public transportation for the work trip at only half the rate as blacks.

Residential distribution of blacks is an additional factor in their greater use of public transportation. Most blacks living in urbanized areas tend to reside in CSs where public transportation is more readily available. In both 1970 and 1980, the majority of white workers resided outside of CSs. In 1980, about 41.6% of white workers lived in CSs as compared to 71.8% of black workers.

Even within the CS, blacks in the work force used public transportation for the work trip at about twice the rate as Caucasians. About 11% of white, CS dwellers used public transit as compared to 25.6% of blacks residing in the CS. Even in the suburbs, blacks tended to utilize public transportation at about twice the rate as Caucasians, 10.8% of black suburban dwellers in 1980 as compared to 21.9% of white suburbanites.

The JCPS (1985) reported that in every commuter flow pattern blacks tended to use public transportation at a higher rate than the Caucasian population. For whites, the heaviest commuter flow remained outside the CSs in 1970 and 1980 with over 38% of white urbanized area workers traveling from the urban fringe to a job outside of a CS in 1980. The corresponding figure for blacks was 17.4%. In 1980 about 71.8% of blacks lived in the CS, with 28.2% living in the urban fringe. The heaviest commuter flow for blacks took place between a residence in the CS to a job in the CS (JCPS, 1985).

The JCPS quoting Kain (1967) points out that at the same time that the heavy concentration of blacks live in the CSs, the majority of new jobs for which they are qualified are emerging in the suburbs. This creates a major obstacle for blacks' economic progress and for their future employment in particular. Lack of adequate public transportation from the CS to suburban job locations is a contributing factor to this situation.

Despite the facts that most black workers in 1980 resided in CSs and commuting time to work from CS residences is generally faster than other commuter flows, the average work trip time for blacks in 1980 was 27.1 minutes compared to 21.5 minutes for whites. The JCPS reports that a gap between average work trip commute time between blacks and whites was evident for all six major commuter flows that the study examined. The exception to this phenomenon was average time travel for blacks and whites residing in the urban fringes and working in the CBD. In this commuter flow, blacks and whites utilized public transportation at almost the same rate (32.3% and 32.2%, respectively), and blacks traveled to work an average of 35.1 minutes as compared to whites with an average of 34.9 minutes per work trip (JCPS, 1985).

Data on work trip commutes were collected for other minorities, including Asian Americans, Pacific Islanders, Eskimos, Aleuts, and Native Americans, but interpretation of the data was difficult because the sources were from such diverse groups. Hispanics were considered an ethnic group and not a racial group. Hispanics were also identified differently in 1980 than they were in the 1970 census. The JCPS interpreted the 1980 data concerning Hispanics with the caveat that the analysis might not be accurate.

The JCPS described Hispanic use of public transportation for the commute to work occurring at a rate higher than whites but lower than blacks, about 14.6% of the Hispanic work force in 1980. In 1980, about 13.4% of Hispanic workers resided in a home with no car available as compared to 4.9% of whites and 17.8% of blacks. Average work trip time for Hispanics dwelling in an urbanized area was 23.8 minutes, once again higher than the average time for whites but lower than the average trip time for blacks. The pattern repeats itself in five out of six of the commuter flows that were studied (JCPS, 1985).

Poverty, of course, denotes decreased income. In practical terms, an inability to purchase and maintain an automobile can result in a lack of overall mobility and a reliance on public transportation. (While we are addressing the issue of a work trip, imagine for a moment a different scenario—taking a sick child to the doctor on a rainy, cold day by public transportation versus by car. That's one of the advantages of mobility in terms of private transportation.) As mentioned previously, households without a car use public transportation for the work trip at a higher rate.

The JCPS analysis revealed that in both 1970 and 1980, workers in families with lower incomes used public transportation for the work trip at higher rates than workers from families with greater incomes. Public transit use dropped significantly as family income increased to about $20,000 a year (in 1970 and 1980), and then the usage values leveled off. According to the data, workers from families that earned less than $10,000 used public transportation for the work trip at a rate almost twice as high as workers from families with an income at or above the median (JCPS, 1985).

In 1970, 21.8% of workers who lived at or below the poverty level used public transportation for the work trip compared with 13.6% of other workers. In 1980, 16.7% of workers from poverty households used public transit as compared to 9.2% of others. Workers from low-income or poverty households were also more likely to reside in CSs where public transportation is more accessible and better developed. In 1983, 36.5% of people at or below the poverty level resided in CSs compared to 28% of the total population. The fact that the poor are concentrated in CSs is associated with their higher use of public transportation on their journey to work (JCPS, 1985).

Age and the Work Trip

Both in 1970 and 1980, the group of workers who used public transportation at the highest rate was workers in the 55+ category. In 1980, about 10% of workers in the 55- to 59-year age group used public transportation for the work trip, 11.5% in the 60- to 64-year age group, 13.5% in the 65- to 69-year age group, and 14.5% in the 70+ age group. In the 30- to 54-year age group about 8.5% of the workers used public transportation to get to work. About 10% of the 20- to 29-year age group used public transport, and about 9.3% of the 16- to 19-year age group commuted to work with public transport (JCPS, 1985).

The trend in these numbers is clear. The older the worker, the higher the rate of public transit usage. The JCPS sees this as the outcome of a number of factors:

1. Some of today's elderly workers grew up at a time when automobile use was not as common as it is today and may never have learned how to drive a car.
2. Physical disabilities, illness, reduced reaction time, and other physical and psychological factors may work to discourage the older worker from getting behind the wheel and encourage him or her to utilize public transportation, particularly when it is readily available.
3. Older workers who may be semiretired may choose jobs for different reasons than they did when they were younger. Often their choice of a job is, at least, partially, based on convenient location and easy access to public transportation.

The fact that teenage workers used public transportation at a lower rate than any group except the 30- to 54-year age range is hard to explain in light of the fact that many teenagers do not have a car, are part-time employees, and tend to live in the highly populated urban core. It may be that teenagers who are working part-time work closer to home within walking, jogging, or biking distance and do not need to rely on public transportation to get to work as much as other groups.

Gender and the Work Trip

When we discussed multiple-wage-earner households, this question could have arisen: When there is a car in the family, who gets to use it and who must travel with public transportation? In general, women use public transportation at a higher rate than men (Fox, 1983). The JCPS analysis demonstrated that in 1970 19.9% of female workers used public transit for the work trip compared to 10.2% of male workers. Although women comprised only 38% of the work force, they represented almost 55% of public transit work trippers. In 1980, the numbers were different, but the trend was similar. About 12% of female workers used public transit as compared to 7.5% of male workers (JCPS, 1985).

The JCPS (1985) offered a number of reasons for the higher rate of public transportation use for the work trip by women:

1. A group of women workers are heads of households. Households headed by women often have much lower incomes than those headed by men. The median income for households headed by women in 1983 was $11,789 compared to married-couple households with a median of $27,286. Lower income often implies no private vehicle and a heavier reliance on public transportation.
2. Women are more likely than men to work in temporary or part-time jobs, which are often located closer to home. The average work trip in 1980 was 9.2 miles for men (23.6 minutes) and 6.7 miles for women (20.4 minutes). Data from the 1982 Census Bureau Population Survey analyzed by the JCPS indicated that, in most cases, men were the primary earners in their families. Their jobs and work trips were likely to be viewed differently than those of women. If there was a choice between public and private transportation for the work trip it is possible that men were more likely to get the use of the car (JCPS, 1985).

A summary of the JCPS analyses of the 1970 and 1980 Census Bureau data (JCPS, 1985) yields the following facts:

1. As compared to 1970, fewer people used public transportation in 1980 for the work trip. About 15 million workers joined the work force in urban areas during that time, but by 1980 the overall number of workers using public transit had decreased by almost half a million from 1970. In terms of percentages, 13.9% of the urban work force used public transportation in 1970 compared to 9.5% in 1980. This decline occurred in all regions of the country except the West. Even in the West, it must be noted, transit use for the urban work trip in 1980 occurred at a rate of 6.2% as compared to 18.9% in the Northeast.
2. The 25 urbanized areas in the country that had a population of a million or more in 1970 and 1980 comprised 82.5% of work trip transit users in 1980.
3. In 1980, the average work trip by car was 21 minutes compared to 42 minutes by public transportation.
4. Suburbanization was a significant factor in the 1970s and continued into the 1980s. Census Bureau statistics indicated that between

1981 and 1982 there was a net migration from the CSs of 2.2 million and a net immigration to the suburbs of 2.0 million. The numbers again increased the next year. Between 1981 and 1982 the CSs lost 2.5 million people, and the suburbs had a net immigration of 2.4 million people. Public transportation facilities in the suburbs did not expand as rapidly as the rate of population growth (JCPS, 1985).
5. Four groups used public transportation to get to work at a consistently higher rate than other demographic groups: (a) workers who lived in a household without a car available to them (Overall there was a decrease in the number of households with no car available from 10.5% in 1970 to 6.9% in 1980. This was a contributory factor to decreased use of public transit.), (b) workers whose employment was located in the CBD (In 1980 almost a third of these workers used public transportation for the work trip, and they accounted for 31% percent of all work trip transit users.), (c) workers who lived in densely populated areas (About 25% percent of workers living in domiciles with 50 or more apartment units used public transportation for the work trip in 1980. They accounted for about 14% of all work trip transit users. These buildings are generally located in higher density, CS neighborhoods.), and (d) minorities, women, older workers, and the poor, who used public transportation for the work trip at higher than average rates (JCPS, 1985).

In the conclusion to its report, the JCPS (1985) quoted a 1980 U.S. Department of Transportation study that indicated that nearly 59% of the urban work force lives within 2 miles of employee's place of work, and 33% of workers reside within a quarter of a mile of public transportation. When asked by the researchers why the workers chose not to use public transportation when it was relatively close to home, several different responses were offered. Somewhat more than 16% of the workers replied that they prefer private transportation, 13.3% replied that public transportation does not reach their job location, and 11.1% spoke of the inconvenience of the time schedule (JCPS, 1985).

THE PISARSKI UPDATE

Pisarski (1992), using the 1990 Nationwide Personal Transportation Survey (NPTS), provided some new insights and emphases in understanding commuting patterns in the late 1980s and the beginning of the 1990s. As the wealth of data available to him and the possible analyses could fill many books, examples of some of the chapter titles provide an overview of some of the issues that the author felt were most important in describing current travel behavior: "What Has Happened with Transit," "Vehicle Alternatives to Work," and "Women's Travel Behavior."

Although there had been many attempts and campaigns over the years to get people out of their cars and into other modes of transportation, the beginning of the 1990s saw a slight increase, over 1980, in work travel times to somewhat more than 20 minutes (Pisarski, 1992). The 1990 preliminary census data put the value at about 22.4 minutes for the nation, nearly 2 minutes more than the NPTS data of the previous decade. Nearly 70% of the population spend less than one-half hour getting to work. The average distance from home to work is close to 11 miles. These figures yield a speed in miles per hour for NPTS data of 32 to 33 miles per hour (Pisarski, 1992). A breakdown by mode of transportation is provided in Table 2.1. An analysis by mode of transportation shows that personal vehicle travel time was around 19 minutes, but for transit users it was nearly 50 minutes in 1990.

Many of the speed figures in 1990 show an increase over 1980. Several explanations for this fact were offered by Pisarski. First, it "reflects the improvement in individual speeds obtained by shifts to the single occupant vehicle from car pooling, mass transit, and walking" (1992, p. 71). In the latter modes, times were traditionally longer. Another reason suggested by the author was the slight shift away from peak hour usage of the various modes of transportation. Although more workers (29%) still depart from their homes for work between the hours of 7 A.M. and 8 A.M. than any other hour, a large number (nearly 50%) of the new employees added to the work force during the 1980s reported beginning work before 7 A.M. This last pattern seems to have several explanations including the fact that more people are joining the service industries where starting times are more flexible and also require working hours outside the usual 9 A.M. to 5 P.M. routine.

Table 2.1. Some National Demographics of Commuting Speeds in America: 1983 versus 1990 NPTS Data[a]

	1983	1990
1. Mean commuting speed (all modes of conveyance)	29.1	32.3
2. Mean commuting speed (automobile)	31.7	34.7
3. Mean commuting speed (transit)	19.7	15.2
4. Mean commuting speed (walking)	2.7	3.1

[a]From Pisarski (1992).

In trying to understand the increase observed in the use of personal vehicles and the decrease in the use of all other means of getting to work, Pisarski indicates that the move away from the city has allowed or perhaps has necessitated greater automobile reliance. Only about 2% of all trips nationally use some form of transit vehicle, with residents of CSs being the largest users. Nearly 11% of the latter go to work by some form of transit compared to 5% in the overall population. What is remarkable in these data is that a breakdown by various demographics (age, sex, income, and region) all show this trend. Pisarski (1992) finds most interesting that the gap in favor of men versus women among commuters is decreasing, and it appears that for the latter group greater access to the automobile has meant less reliance on the transit system.

A CASE STUDY: SEATTLE COMMUTING BEHAVIOR

Besides the overall measures mentioned above, another way to understand commuting in America is to examine the behaviors and commuting patterns of a specific urban area. An intensive survey was recently done on the habits of the Seattle commuter, based around a typical urban center, whose findings may provide some insight into the situation in America at the beginning of the 1990s. Besides presenting the data for the commuter in the Seattle area, comments that are relevant for the stress–strain relationship and for the coping process, will be inserted.

Spyridakis, Barfield, Conquest, Haselkorn, and Isakson (1991) analyzed the responses from approximately 4,000 motorists in the Seattle area as they were leaving one of the local highways. Approximately, two-thirds of the commuters interviewed here work 5 days a week. In this group, 75% of the motorists commute alone. Although not particularly surprising, this last statistic is particularly relevant as it indicates that authorities have a long way to go before they can achieve even reasonable numbers of car-poolers or mass transportation users.

The data showed that the average morning commute was 31 minutes as compared to 35 minutes for the evening commute. These numbers are somewhat higher than the values cited in the government reports mentioned above. The previous numbers are an average across large, medium, and small communities. Although Seattle does not include the population and traffic densities characteristic of the Northeast or Southern California, it is, nevertheless, larger than most of the metropolitan areas in the United States and would be expected to have people traveling over greater distances, experiencing greater traffic congestion than would be found in many of the smaller communities around the United States.

Confirming the findings from other studies mentioned in Chapter 1, distance and time of the commute calculated separately for the morning and evening rush hours had relatively high correlations: .81 for the former and .76 for the latter. The authors also reported that the correlation between the time to work and the time to get home from work correlated .86. Although these indicate high associations, there may be some qualitative differences between the two time periods of the day. Spyridakis et al. (1991) felt that the time spent coming home from work is more likely to include other chores and activities, whereas in the morning, the commuter is inclined to go to work without any detours, personal or otherwise.

This may explain different stress phenomena including the differences in measured strain levels between the morning and evening and between men and women (Novaco et al., 1991). If we assume that during the evening rush hour, women are more likely to perform family chores (such as shopping, picking up the children from school, etc.), the difficulties and time pressures involved in performing them may have some impact on stress reactions. The more complicated an activity or the more functions it contains, the greater the expected stress. Perrewe and Ganster (1989) used the term quantitative overload as a potential stressor that can have negative attitudinal or behavioral consequences. Although a majority of the commuters (58%) reported stress as part of their commuting experience, the women reacted more negatively to both components of the commute, the trip to work and the trip home.

The mean kilometers traveled by women (23) to work was less than that for men (25). This difference in the commuting distance is apparently in contradiction to the self-report measure of stress obtained in the study, namely, the women perceived their commutes to be more stressful than men. However, it is supportive of the major premise of the book that calculating distance or time alone is not sufficient for predicting commuting stress; other considerations such as the quality of the trip and the personal variables of the commuter must be determined as well.

Commuters reported greater variability in the hour that they leave work as compared with the time that they arrive at work. This implies that when going to work the commuter is much more likely to follow habitual behavior. During the evening trip, other demands (including family obligations) may require the commuter to be more flexible in determining when to return home. Approximately two-thirds would like to reduce their commuting time, and one-third would like their commute to be more enjoyable. A little more than 60% of the sample are familiar with alternative routes, and about 58% said that the routes on the way home are more easily modified than those on the way to work (37%). All these responses are clues to the type of stress intervention techniques that might reduce stress. In our discussion of individual and organizational coping methods, some of the recommendations that will be made are in response to the time involved in the actual commute, the control experienced over the trip to and from work, and what could be done during this interval. Interestingly, and consistent with the notion that less control may increase perceptions of stress, female commuters, who experienced greater stress, reported using alternative routes less frequently than male commuters.

The authors also looked at the variables that influence route choice. Approximately 76% of commuters stated that traffic reports impacted their behavior, 61% were influenced by time of day, 50% by time pressures, and 37% by weather conditions. About 50% stated that getting traffic information before starting the commute (i.e., at home or in the office or factory) was preferred. Not surprisingly, nearly 98% of the people get their traffic updates from the commercial radio, 53% from electronic messages over the highway, and 29% from television. It would appear from the data here that the optimal procedure for reducing uncertainty, a prime correlate of stress, would be to prepare psychologically and factually for what is in store. This will be the basis for some of the individual methods discussed later for mitigating the effects of the noxious stimuli associated with commuting.

As part of this information "gathering," the commuters were asked what would help them or would be useful in preparing for the commute. The responses included a radio station dedicated to traffic information only (92%), a phone hotline (34%), TV/video (25%), and a computer (15%). It is likely that incorporating the computer into the automobile and teaching the motorist how to use it (especially its ability to relay real time data to meet driver demands) will become more popular over time. Again, some of these facts are the bases for several of the recommendations for individual and organizational coping methods that will be proposed later on.

EUROPEAN TRAVEL BEHAVIOR

The European commuting situation is different from that of the United States and, according to Orfeuil and Bovy (1993), the unique nature there can be attributed to several features of the society including the "long tradition of planning, economic welfare, concern for the environment, and the transition to a single Europe" (p. 13). According to data collected from many sources, the authors found that American car ownership, as measured by cars owned per 1,000 inhabitants, is much greater than it is in Europe, or even in Japan. In the United States, the value for this measure is 560, whereas for the European Economic Community (EEC) it is 360 and for Japan, 240. Overall, the price for transport is higher in the EEC and, in particular, the relative cost (amount of hours needed to work for purchasing a car) is much higher in the EEC than in the United States. Car and truck usage is much greater in the United States, and accompanying these statistics are the larger number of road casualties and noxious pollutants (both values are about 30% to 80% higher in America). Interestingly, noise exposure is about twice as high in Europe than it is in the States. With a few notable exceptions such as are found in the northeastern part of the United States, density is higher and proximities to noise stimuli much greater in Europe.

With these distinctions in mind, it is interesting to examine some of the parameters of commuting in the EEC. First, as compared to the United States data or the Seattle survey, the average distance traveled in Europe is considerably less than in the United States. In the EEC as a whole, 71% of all trips to work are less than 10 kilometers with an average of approximately 10 (as extrapolated from the chart reported by Jansen, 1993, p. 115). It should be noted, however, that these numbers are changing rapidly (e.g., in France, the distance has doubled in the 20 years between 1967 and 1986), and the emerging single-Europe concept will cause the trend to move more in the direction of the United States, where values are double or more than in the EEC.

A few words about public transport are also necessary. In their article on public transport in Europe subtitled "Requiem or Revival," Stern and Tretvik (1993) find an ambivalent attitude across the continent. In some ares, such as interurban travel, there has been a remarkable improvement, whereas in regional areas, service has, if anything, declined over the last decade. A survey of average public transport usage showed that values range from 11% (in France and Belgium) to 30% (in Greece and Turkey) of daily commuting trips. These values compare favorably with the United States (the numbers are not exactly comparable so that it is hard to say whether one of the regions is using public transport more than the other). However, high-speed trains and their use in commuting travel constitute a noticeable trend; they may be the savior for Europe and prevent the type of high automobile usage and long commuting trips found in the States.

3

Environmental Factors and Commuting Stress

The effects of environmental stimuli on the individual have been the focus of many investigations over the years. Indeed, social psychologists and health practitioners long ago recognized this area as a legitimate subspecialty within their fields. Periodicals such as the *Journal of Environmental Psychology, Work and Stress,* and the *Journal of Human Stress* as well as numerous books have analyzed and discussed the relationship between potential environmental stressors and well-being (Evans, 1982; Proshansky, Ittelson, & Rivlin, 1970; Keating, 1979; Sauter, Hurrell, & Cooper, 1989).

The commuting experience has been seen by several researchers as another reaction of the individual to the environment. In such an ecological model, the influences on the individual during the day are too numerous to mention. Nevertheless, among the most conspicuous noxious stimuli particularly relevant for commuting are air pollution, lack of comfort, noise, and crowding (see Table 3.1). This approach considers reactions to the commute as caused by a combination, not necessarily linear, of various factors in the environment.

Another approach somewhat unique in the literature considers the commuting experience as a response rather than a causal phenomenon. In developing a driving behavior inventory (DBI), Gulian, Matthews, Glendon, Davies, and Delaney (1989) utilized the transactional view of psychological stress (Lazarus & Launier, 1978) to explain their view of driver stress. Applying this perspective in a commuting context, an individual who perceives and evaluates the journey between home and work as being demanding or requiring more resources than can be readily provided is liable to experience stress from the mere fact that he or she is

Table 3.1. Examples of Environmental Stressors

Stressor	Manifestation during commuting
1. Noise	Subway entering platform; horn honking; road construction
2. Crowding	Subway cars during rush hour; pushing and shoving in any mass transit mode
3. Weather	Heat; cold; humidity
4. Environmental features	Aesthetics; lighting; pollution

involved in the commuting process. An important feature in this conceptualization is the necessity to posit interactions between situation/environmental variables and extraneous (personal, demographics, etc.) variables.

COMMUTING AS AN ENVIRONMENTAL STRESSOR

Most of the theories in commuting are derived from the stress literature. Brehm and Kassin (1990) divided stressful events into two main categories: macrostressors and microstressors. The former refers to (relatively) major life events including marriage, divorce, bereavement, leaving home for the first time, and so forth. The latter events, according to the authors, refer to strained relationships, deadlines, running the rat race, and fighting traffic. Such routine and daily hassles tend to build up and produce stress. Using the perspective of environmental and social psychology, this chapter analyzes what aspects of the commute are potentially stressful and may lead to a strain response.

Although the commute itself has rarely been listed explicitly as an environmental stressor or even a daily hassle in organizational psychology, it easily fits into one of the many formulations that have been suggested for linking the stages between stressors and reactions in theoretical models of stress.

A good illustration of this appears in the model presented by Kahn and Boysiere (1991). Their approach, similar to others discussed in the literature (e.g., Cooper & Payne, 1992; Singer, Neale, & Schwartz, 1987), includes a category called organizational antecedents of stress. The variables listed in this all-inclusive category (size, work schedule, etc.) confront the worker when he or she arrives at the job. Commuting can easily be conceived as another variable whose potential influence exists before the beginning of the work day. It can be viewed in such models as potential baggage accompanying the worker to the organization.

Similarly, the commuting variable also takes on personal characteristics labeled "properties of the person" by Kahn and Byosiere. However, the latter variables appear to be more permanent parts of the individual and are not as readily subject to daily change as is commonly found with commuting. As a matter of fact, it is the *variability* of the commute that may play a critical role in some of the negative consequences associated with commuting. This concept is an important feature of the conceptual model of the commuting process that will be presented in detail in Chapter 6.

One of the few investigators bothered by this absence of relevant environmental studies in the area of commuting was Novaco and his colleagues (Novaco et al., 1979; Novaco et al., 1991). They noted that a basic text in the field by Altman and Werner (1985) neglected to mention the influence of the commuting experience on the home. The Novaco group proceeded to conduct a series of studies examining the impact of commuting on the home that represented a potentially major new focus not only for environmental psychologists but also for personnel managers.

As was already suggested by many researchers and supported by some of the findings of Novaco et al. (1990), the possibility of the existence of interdomain transfer effects requires practitioners and investigators from various specialties to be aware of the possible consequences of the ride to and from work. The concept of interdomain transfer emphasizes the fact that the psychological and behavioral "fallout" of one area can influence another domain. For the commuter, the ride to work and its effects there can influence his or her homelife, and the ride home, which frequently disturbs the commuter's relationships with the family, can have far-ranging consequences on performance at work.

RESPONSIVITY TO CHRONIC ENVIRONMENTAL STRESS

Responsivity to environmental stress has focused on three major areas: physical health, mental and attitudinal states, and behavior. Physical health includes most of the common ailments (headaches, stomachaches, etc.) that we are familiar with but also more serious problems such as heart disease, high blood pressure, and ulcers (Steffy & Jones, 1988). The process by which stress acts on an individual to produce strain responses is quite complex, and studies have shown that stress plays a role in the onset as well as the intensification of many health problems. However, as Baron (1986) so aptly writes about the stress variable, it is only one of many possible causes that directly or indirectly affect health, and a researcher in the field must recognize that other factors are also involved. In any study, where only a limited set of variables can be examined, one can expect, at best, moderate relationships.

Similarly, the influence of environmental stress on emotional and attitudinal variables has been reported quite frequently. Anxiety, depression, and fatigue are just a few of the examples in this area (Baron, 1989).

Job satisfaction, commitment, and involvement are some of the typical attitudinal responses that have been investigated in connection with the environment (Weinstein, 1978).

For most commuters, one of the distinctive features of the journey to work and back is that the general environment (not necessarily the commuting time) remains relatively constant from day to day. Although, as we will see later, there are several techniques for mitigating some of the negative effects of the ride, the individual who begins the trip to work at the same time each day is confronted with approximately the same stimuli (noise, crowding, poor lighting, etc.). Responses to such environmental stimuli have been examined from many perspectives, and we will deal with a few of the recent approaches to this issue. Some of the potentially noxious stimuli studied in environmental psychology that are particularly relevant for the commuting experience are presented below.

Noise

A characteristic of many commuting experiences is the noise factor. Although in certain situations, such as some commuter trains, the noise is only a background stimulus and is hardly noticed, in other circumstances, it so dominates the entire experience that "tuning out" the noxious stimulus is nearly impossible. The mass transportation subway systems of major cities like New York fall into this latter category. It should be pointed out that in many urban areas such as Washington, DC, the metro network functions relatively quietly.

The manner in which noise affects people has been investigated in several other settings, including worksites and airports. Theoretical explanations and methods of coping have been offered by several investigators, and several of these can be presented here and applied to commuting. In one approach, discussed by Broadbent (1971), noise stimulates a form of arousal that forces the individual to attend to certain features of the environment and not to others. Performance that requires a wide range of cues may be affected as the noise does not permit the individual to readily focus his or her attention on the necessary inputs required for accurate or speedy work.

Cohen (1978) and Cohen and Weinstein (1982) argue that this narrowed focusing caused by arousal is not only a function of the magnitude of the stimulus but also of the meaning and the degree of control that is present in the noisy situation. Thus, loud radio music may have a positive performance effect as the listener has control and actively chooses the music that is being played (assuming it can readily be turned off by the listener). In situations where the noise is not under the individual's control and has no particular meaning for the individual, as occurs when a subway enters a station, the reaction may be considerably more negative.

One other theory that may have particular relevance for commuting is the contention that only the onset of noise may be disruptive and stimulative (Poulton, 1979). According to Cohen and Weinstein (1982), this may indicate that some form of adaptation takes place over time, and much of the negative characteristics slowly dissipate over time. More interestingly, however, is the case of intermittent noise that is quite common in commuting environments. Here, negative consequences have been attributed to learned helplessness (Cohen & Weinstein, 1982) and cognitive fatigue (Cohen, 1978). Both of these explanations are consistent with one prominent feature of commuting, namely, the limited control that individuals feel about their experience. Although this description is particularly appropriate for mass transportation users, many car drivers in and around urban centers have quite similar experiences. Thus, noise levels as well as other distractions during the trip between home and work (and return) are bothersome *because* the individual does not feel that it will stop or end through his or her actions.

Physical Impact of Noise on the Commuting Experience

As commuters drive to or from work, many of the tasks that are required of them may be affected by the noise level. For example, vigilance or monitoring of the environment is essential for a safe trip. Cohen and Weinstein (1982) concluded that certain intensity and features of noise may interfere with performance. First, at 95 decibels or more, noise begins to affect individuals; below this level, negative effects are less likely. Also, deleterious effects can be expected under conditions of unpredictable, intermittent noise and during the onset or cessation of the stimulus. However, it appears that varied and discontinuous noise under the driver's control such as is commonly found with the car radio or tape deck may actually enhance the driving experience. Also, it appears that noise that has been present for a considerable period of time no longer has much of an effect.

Another set of studies on the aftereffects of noise have particular relevance for the commuter. Under certain conditions, even after the noise itself has stopped and the commuter is no longer in the car or bus, subsequent behavior at work or at home may be affected from the exposure to noise. For example, Glass and Singer (1972) reported that subjects performed poorly after the cessation of unpredictable noise of 108 db or even 58 db. Of particular interest, was the reported drop in tolerance for frustration. Cohen and Weinstein concluded that the major issue here again is the degree of control available to the subject. According to the authors, cognitive variables play a critical role in determining whether the individual will experience negative aftereffects. By providing a means for the subject to modify the stimulus, or just as effectively, providing the perception that the stimulus can be turned on or off at will, the situation may be markedly improved.

These findings have great implications for the driver, some of which will be discussed in the context of the model presented later in the book (Chapter 6). As a commuter on a train, for example, an individual may want to turn out certain noises in the environment by donning a walkman or sitting with windows closed and the air conditioning turned on. Incidentally, the humming effect of an air conditioner or the swaying rhythms often accompanying a train ride may be quite soothing and, as mentioned above, are not necessarily bothersome after the onset. Similarly, a driver who can shut the window and eliminate to a large degree the noises in the environment would be well advised to do so. As this allows actual control over the stimulus, not just perceived control, it should be especially effective.

Also, predictability can be used to the driver's advantage. A trip that takes the driver over areas that are uncommonly noisy, such as construction sites, can either be avoided or, at least, prepared for by using methods that block out or filter the noise in the environment. By not being surprised and by expecting the stimulus to occur at a certain time and place, even if it cannot be controlled, the individual has probably lessened the impact of the noise. Finally, it is interesting to note, that many of the negative effects of noise in the literature are similar to the findings reported with other types of stimuli including electric shock and, even, confrontation with bureaucrats in governmental offices. In making this observation, Cohen and Weinstein (1982) imply that certain types of stimuli act on the individual in a similar pattern. It can be inferred from this line of research that each individual has the ability to accommodate certain groups of stimuli without any negative effect but, when confronted with other additional stimuli, an actual or cognitive attempt must be made to deal with the new input. Failure to do so can only lead to some form of negative consequences.

Emotional Effects of Noise

In Landy's (1992) article on work design and stress in an organization, noise is seen as a potential precursor for psychological problems, as well as many other dependent variables. Much of the seminal research in this area was actually done about 20 years earlier. In summarizing one group of studies, Cohen and Weinstein (1982, p. 54) described insensitivity to the needs of others as a possible effect of noise. For example, Page (1977) and Sherrod and Downs (1974) reported that noise was more likely to reduce compliance to requests for verbal aid or offers of assistance.

In an interesting study on the effects of traffic noise on residents in nearby buildings, Damon (1977) showed that people who were closer to the origins of the noise were generally found to have more asocial behavior (truancy, crimes, etc.) than those who lived further away. However, as the study was carried out in the field, several critical demographic variables were not controlled making it difficult to draw accurate conclusions (Cohen & Weinstein, 1982).

A Model for the Effects of Traffic Noise

Although the effects of traffic noise on the commuter have not been adequately examined, studies of its impact in other settings have been reported. The effects of outside noise such as that caused by traffic flow on a person watching television or in the middle of a conversation have been described as annoying or disturbing (Gunn, 1987; Williams, Stevens, & Klatt, 1969). Also, noise has been found to be particularly disturbing at night (Leboyer & Naturel, 1991). This is probably true for several reasons. During the night hours, when background noises are relatively low, the introduction of any new stimulus is perceived much more acutely, and its potential impact on people so exposed is much greater. The conclusion of Leboyer and Naturel (1991) from the various studies is that the type of sound or even its intensity does not necessarily cause a reaction. What is much more important is the degree of actual or perceived control caused by the stimulus. If the commuter is disturbed because it is undesirable to him or her at this time, then it may become a negative experience. This is actually a cognitive process whereby perceptions play a vital role on whether the victim will suffer. Thus, the same noise in some cases will have a negative effect and in other cases no effect at all.

For the case of a car-pool driver or user of mass transportation, the trip to work will be considerably more uncomfortable if conversations with fellow passengers are interrupted. Of course, this assumes that the conversation is desirable on the part of the commuter. In the case of a passenger in a car pool or user of mass transportation who wants to sleep, commuting stimuli may have unpleasant consequences if the sleep is disturbed. Again, it is obvious that for the same person under different conditions (sometimes sleep is desired, whereas other times conversation may be preferred), noise will have different effects.

There is an additional variable in the commuting situation that may influence the consequences. According to a model of environmental stress presented by Henry and Meehan (1981), the stress experienced is a function of the behavioral alternatives available to an individual. Thus, a potentially noxious stimulus may require of an individual a fight or flight response. However, if neither of these responses is available under the present circumstances, a strain response is likely to occur.

Unlike the commuter, an individual at home or even at work may have a larger repertoire of flight or fight responses available. The commuter who is stuck in traffic, either in a private car or in some form of mass transportation, confronts an external stimulus that cannot be handled with the limited alternatives available. Based on movies as well as news stories, it is easy to conjure up the image of the hapless passenger in New York or Tokyo crammed into a subway car and unable to extricate himself.

In addition, knowledge of the fact that under different circumstances a present stressor would not have much of an effect provides a potentially new source of stress. A good illustration of the type of setting where this occurs is the rush hour commute by automobile. Thus, a driver coming to work at 8 A.M. is all too aware that in another 2 hours, the noxious stimulus being experienced now could be dealt with much more easily either by driving faster or taking an alternative route. However, during the morning rush hour, this may not be possible. What we have is an additional cognitive factor that probably plays a role in the stress–strain linkages observed in the commuting experience.

In a recent analysis of neighborhood noise, Leboyer and Naturel (1991) suggested a new approach to understanding the annoying effects of noise on individuals. Although it had been suggested previously by investigators in the field that degree of control perceived by a victim of noise is a critical element, whereas absolute noise level alone is not meaningful, the authors feel that just as important are the motivations attributed to the person experiencing the noxious stimulus. In summarizing the findings, Leboyer and Naturel (1991) noted that two specific situations stand out as likely to produce negative reaction: (1) those where the sufferer accuses the person making the noise as being inconsiderate and of being unlike himself and others, (2) unusual noise or exceptional noise where the source is unknown (p. 84).

Applying these concepts here, it is possible to make several inferences relevant to the commuter's experiences. Horns honking in a traffic jam or jackhammers working at construction sites, often every day at the same hour, are common occurrences for car drivers. These situations contain many of the characteristics described previously by Leboyer and Naturel

(1991). The perpetrator of the noise does not really care much about the victim, does not have any relationship to the driver, and the latter may very well view the former as inconsiderate. The driver can do very little about his or her predicament (although to some extent, of course, noise can be filtered out by closing windows of the car).

Thus, a constant and uncontrolled noise emanating from a construction site contains the ingredients described above. The annoyance experienced by the driver manifests itself in many ways including feelings of strain or frustration, especially if the situation is not controllable, which is the usual case when we are considering the commuting experience. Other possible reactions that may crop up over time include lack of concentration (as the noise becomes more noxious objectively or subjectively) and less regard or concern for other drivers. These reactions may have much more deleterious effects on the driver as well as on others than mere psychological annoyance.

Crowding

It appears that one of the major negative components of urban life is the large number of people found per unit area. In rural societies, an individual encounters one's neighbors less frequently, and the space available for these encounters is much greater. Nevertheless, as mentioned already in Chapter 1, the trends are for fewer farms and greater movement to urban environments. This change in the environment has introduced the problems associated with crowding to nearly the entire population.

Epstein (1982) suggests a model for understanding the problems identified with crowding or density (number of people per unit space). Although its focus is broad, the conceptualization has many applications to the commuting experience. An individual in a particular work or leisure setting is assumed to be striving for accomplishing a goal or goals. This may be writing a book, talking with friends, answering the phone, or running a company board meeting. In all cases, the environment has specific characteristics that permit the goal to be achieved. When other people enter into proximity, an individual's "resources, activities, level of interpersonal reaction, and spatial location" (Cohen & Weinstein, 1982, p. 133) must be coordinated with the needs of people sharing the same environment.

If there is enough space for all and interference is not a problem, then negative consequences are not expected. However, if the number of people in the environment begins to increase, density increases, competition for the available space becomes more pronounced, and goals originally fixed at the beginning of the task may now become thwarted. This is especially true in a situation where others in the environment are competing for similar goals. The repeated hassles experienced by a commuter using some form of mass transportation illustrates the problem quite well. A crowded train, bus, or subway may make it impossible to read a paper or even just sit and relax. More importantly, if too many people are waiting at a station for a train, the commuter may not even be able to board. This latter issue is salient for the passenger not only because it may lead to a missed train, but the uncertainty that accompanies waiting on a crowded platform is anxiety producing. A crowded platform requires the individual to evaluate his or her chances of getting on the train and, if lucky enough to board, the probability of getting a seat.

An aspect of the commute on a rush-hour train or subway that may be particularly irritating is the repetitive nature of the stimuli that one encounters. Many a commuter waking up in the morning is only too well aware that in a very short time the pushing and shoving will begin again. Epstein (1981) considers the chronic, repeated, and unwanted experiences as stressful. A person who rarely uses a train may not mind the ride and show little, if any, negative response after exposure to crowds pushing and shoving their way in and out of the doors. As a matter of fact, the scene may look quite humorous. But for those who encounter this spectacle daily, it is anything but humorous.

Although several irritants that make the situation difficult can be identified, the breach of accepted rules by others or violation of spatial norms is particularly aggravating. Thus, a person who pushes ahead in line or does not allow another individual his or her turn to board, is creating the basis for negative reactions. This can also be seen when a road narrows and two lanes become one. If cars take their turn, then a somewhat difficult situation is dealt with the best way possible. However, when one car refuses to give up rights to another and pushes through, a "violation of spatial norms [occurs that] may increase arousal and discomfort (Epstein, 1982, p. 134).

A few years ago, *The New York Times* described in vivid detail the experiences of a commuter. In an article by Finder (1991b), the situation on a platform in one of the busy subway stations in New York City was described. The city, which has over 3.5 million daily commuters with thousands of people coming down onto the platform every minute, is particularly crowded at Roosevelt Avenue in Queens, a major switching point for many daily commuters.

Crowding here is so severe that, when the trains are not running because of mechanical problems or other difficulties, the conductors sometimes have to close off the stairways leading to the platform. Otherwise, they say, the area could get so overcrowded that passengers might fall to the tracks. Unlike their more famous counterparts on the Tokyo subway, the platform conductors at Roosevelt Avenue do not actually push passengers into the trains. They rely, instead, on persuasion. The conductors have a mandate to move morning trains in and out within 45 seconds. This goal was met 92% of the time in a typical month at the end of 1991. However, the feeling of being crushed is so pervasive that many people laugh when confronted with the question "What do you think of Roosevelt Avenue station?" Perhaps, a defensive mechanism or a denial process to forget the daily nightmare is being activated.

Evans and Lepore (1992) argue that the negative effects of crowding are often accompanied by lack of control and uncertainty. Both are likely precursors of psychological stress. Cooperation, which, in this case, is the converse of lack of control, is one method of preventing the appearance of the negative consequences of crowding. Many studies in residential settings and laboratories have shown this to be true, and, we quote only a few that are particularly relevant to the commuting experience.

Stress reactions as indicated by various physiological and psychological measures are common findings from studies of residential settings and laboratory experiments (Cox, Paulus, McCain, & Schkade, 1979; Fleming, Baum, & Weiss, 1987; Nicosia, Hyman, Karlin, Epstein, & Aiello, 1979). For example, Fleming et al. (1987) showed that emotional and behavioral measures of residents were associated with the crowding found in their neighborhoods. Also, they reported that the degree of perceived control was found to mediate this relationship. By considering the effects of perceived control, the relationship between density and outcome was reduced.

Of particular relevance to commuting research are the findings from two laboratory studies. In the first study, Karlin, Rosen, Epstein, and Woolfolk (1979) reported that, after just a few exposures, the effects of crowding were found to persist and subjects continued to react negatively. In the second study, effects were observed prior to the actual crowding but following the anticipation of future crowding (Baum & Greenberg, 1975). The ramifications of these studies are very clear. The effects of crowding on a bus or train may linger after the journey is over and continue to influence the person psychologically or physiologically during work hours, especially for the first few hours of the work day. Similarly, these effects can be expected to occur after arrival home following a commute that included crowding.

The Baum and Greenberg study indicates that the commuter may be affected just through anticipation or the knowledge gained from previous trips to work or home. This would imply that the actual reduction of crowding experiences would probably not affect the individual *unless* he or she expected the change to occur. It appears that crowding, similar to noise, involves some form of cognitive process that needs to be altered before the negative consequences can be eliminated or reduced.

In reflecting on some of the differences between crowding and other environmental stressors, Epstein (1982) identifies one distinct feature of the former stimulus that contributes to making the commuting experience particularly problematic. Crowding is a group phenomenon not a spatial one. A lone rider in a small or narrow railroad car may, if the dimensions are small enough, feel uncomfortable but probably not suffer from the negative consequences associated with crowding. The method for removing the effects of crowding is, according to Epstein, quite simple. Cooperation or planning together is required in order to best allocate available resources. However, in many commuting environments this is not really practical. People tend not to know each other on a crowded railroad platform and verbal, as well as nonverbal, interaction is minimal, at best.

In applying some of the findings from crowding research to commuting, Epstein writes (1982, p. 144) that the "chances of reducing the stressful effects of crowding in mass transportation ... [are] smaller, because the problems are attributable to others who are not cooperatively linked to the individual."

What then is to be done about crowding? The unfortunate commuters are caught in a situation that is not of their making and in which they have little chance of controlling the other actors, who, according to Epstein, are critical players in the entire process. In Chapter 8, a discussion of flex-time, which permits the commuter to avoid the most crowded hours, illustrates some of the benefits that this new and growing trend provides, particularly as it affords the individual greater control of the situation.

It should also be noted that the implications of some of the findings challenge the arguments put forth by many urban planners and transportation experts. With the clear emphasis and strong suggestion by all relevant authorities that mass transportation is to be preferred over driving, crowding stress is bound to increase. Although driving a car on a congested road contains some of the features found in crowding stress (e.g., the general inability of getting others in your environmental space to cooperate for achieving the desired goal in the most efficient way), it is the commuter train, subway, and bus that constitute the biggest area of concern for those studying the problems of crowding in work settings. Of course, there are other variables involved that are relevant for making the decision in favor of mass transportation including lower commuting costs, less environmental pollution, and, frequently, a faster journey between work and home. Interestingly, those who do use their car during the rush hours will often cite crowding as one of the chief reasons that the bus or train is not considered an attractive alternative.

In this context, some of the findings reported by Flannely and Mcleod (1989) are particularly relevant. The authors examined the factors influencing commuters' choice of travel mode. First, they found that solo drivers to work and car-pool drivers rated the automobile as a very important means for getting to work. Understandably, bus riders did not rate the automobile as very important for commuting. All types of respondents did recognize the societal benefits that would result if solo drivers to work were eliminated or cut down. The automobile was rated low on saving energy, reducing pollution, and reducing traffic congestion. Nevertheless, all the different commuting modes in the study (driving, car-pooling, and riding a bus) saw the advantage of the car, specifically, in the area of comfort and convenience. The authors concluded that the obvious noneconomic advantages of the automobile over alternative modes of commuting travel makes it quite difficult to convince people to give up their cars for mass transportation as it exists today.

Perhaps we can leave this topic with the advice provided by Evans and Lepore (1992). As the literature seems to indicate that some subgroups may be particularly vulnerable to the effects of crowding, minimizing their exposure could have an impact on the mode of transportation used to work and home. Even the car driver, aware of the crowding problems associated with bus or train travel, who is not readily willing to give up the comfort levels afforded by the automobile, might be swayed if the setting could be made to provide a more positive experience including more personal space.

By approximating the conditions of a solo trip, by offering amenities such as first-class service in commuting trains or cellular phone service, the provider of mass transportation can induce the commuter to change his or her mode of transportation to work. For others, particularly where personality measures or indicators of social interaction show that truly private, solo travel is best for them psychologically, it may not be worth the effort, and, everything considered, these individuals' may indeed be better off taking a car to work, even if the other associated costs, individual and societal, are great.

Other Environmental Variables

Of the variables typically considered as environmental, noise and crowding are the most salient for the commuting experience. Nevertheless, a few other environmental stimuli that have been investigated in other contexts and that may contribute to the quality of the trip between home and work are mentioned and discussed briefly. Thermal stress, heat and cold, has been found to have a wide range of effects on humans, and, in situations where the individual has little control, these effects may be magnified.

Much of the pertinent research in the field was done with high temperatures, rather than low temperatures, and these will be the focus here.

High Temperatures

Generally, the body adapts to changes in the core body temperature of about 37° C through self-regulation procedures. If the thermoregulatory systems fail to restore temperature to normal levels after some perturbations, there is a possibility of physiological damage including heart damage, blood pressure increases, and muscular rigidity (Bell & Greene, 1982). Among the many complicating factors that are relevant for the commuter are high humidity and excess clothing. High humidity, endemic to some of the larger mass transportation systems, nearly guarantees an uncomfortable ride. For example, the temperature equivalent of 30° C (not unusual in a subway platform during the summer) with a humidity of 80% is 44° C (Landsberg, 1969).

The commuter using mass transportation must often wear the right combination of clothing or be subjected to extremes in temperature. Thus, on a cold day, the outside air requires a heavy coat, but in the heated railroad car, a jacket or even a short-sleeved shirt, may be adequate. Too much clothing retards heat loss and may produce a very uncomfortable, and as described below, stressful ride.

The problem with the research in the area of thermal effects on psychological and performance indicators is the inconsistent findings. At the introduction of high temperatures, some studies showed an orientation or positive arousal effect followed by stabilization or adaptation. However, as arousal intensifies, coping may become more difficult, which, in turn, is followed by performance decrement as attention is drawn more and more to the thermal stimulus. This reasoning was used by Bell and Greene (1982) to hypothesize that an increase in aggression or other asocial behavior may result. Combining the heat stimulus with a crowded environment—a nearly perfect description of the conditions inside some subway cars or trains during morning or evening rush hours in the summer—yields a particularly stressful situation.

How this feeling of aggression extends over time, including the period after the cessation of extreme cold or heat stimuli, is not clear from the literature and needs to be explored. Future emphasis of this type of research may have implications for some of the psychological and behavioral responses observed after commuter arrival at work or at home.

Tranquility of Environment

Recently, aesthetic aspects of environments have been the focus of research by some environmental psychologists (Hartig, Mang, & Evans, 1991; Herzog

& Bosley, 1992). The argument made by investigators in the field is that certain types of natural environments are associated with tranquility, serenity, and peace. Even more so, it is possible that an environment may have restorative effects and help to reduce the strains encountered in normal or daily life activities. In particular, the fact that many subway platforms in the United States remain barren, if not bleak, is a criticism of the authorities in these urban areas. Although transportation officials often contend that beautifying or enhancing the quality of empty platforms is difficult as well as costly, the effort made in many areas around the world, particularly some of the larger European capitals, may very well pay off. The implication from research in this area indicates that people often seek out such environments to help them cope and revive fatigued attention capacity (Hartig et al., 1991). As one of the problems commonly cited by users of mass transportation is the strain that the environment precipitates, it may both help to reduce negative consequences, and from a societal viewpoint, bring more people to subways and trains. Scenes of mountains or field-forests, identified by Herzog and Bosley (1992) as tranquil stimuli, can be placed on subway car walls or platforms to produce positive effects.

Lighting Problems

Lighting has several features that may impact on the users of mass transportation. First, the issue of crime, associated with subways, is to some extent a function of the lighting (or lack of lighting) found in the tunnels, platforms, and subway cars themselves. It is not clear whether crime is actually reduced as lighting becomes more attractive or effective, but it appears that individual fears and perceptions of safety are lessened (Tien, O'Donnell, Barnett, & Mirchandani, 1979; Zimring, 1982). Also, light is associated with positive feelings and personal comfort, whereas poor lighting is associated with more negative affect (Wineman, 1982). Such studies would indicate that among the reasons that people avoid some forms of public transportation is the fear element or lack of feelings of security resulting from poor lighting. Constant exposure to such an environment can be expected to lead to psychological strain and other health problems.

Energy Conservation

Over the past two decades, energy conservation has been one of the important economic and social issues in the country. The economic costs are clear because a large percentage of the money spent on energy in the purchase of petroleum and natural gas leaves the country. Socially, the problem is multifaceted, as it includes pollution and resource abuse caused by certain users such as homeowners and industrial plants. Social scientists have been involved in the field of energy use and conservation in an attempt to understand the source of people's attitudes and to alter their behavior.

The transportation industry is a major user of petroleum products. Zerega (1981) points out that the major share of petroleum production goes to the automobile. As far back as the early 1980s, data such as the fact that a 1-mile one-person trip consumes between 2 and 10 times as much energy as a bus, train, or subway ride of equal distance was often discussed. The government treated this problem as an issue of marketing and economics and not a social issue. So federal funds were allocated to entice consumers toward car-pooling, or special bus lanes were built to speed the commute for the driver. What this has meant is that the cost for mass transportation has decreased in relationship to driving an automobile, but automobile usage keeps growing nevertheless. More and more people are on the roads than ever before. Thus, the actual statistics in the field show that commuter car-pooling plans have been ineffective and ride sharing has not caught on (Darley & Gilbert, 1985).

What is needed here is the social scientist's perspective on the environment and how people can be made to comply. In Chapter 7 on coping strategies, some of these methods are discussed and presented for consideration.

Air Pollution

One additional environmental stressor that may be relevant to several topics in this book is air pollution. Novaco et al. (1991) state that air pollution is a possible cause for strain reactions. Similar to other stressors, its linkage to the dependent measure may be direct as well as indirect. However, unlike most of the other stressors, here the commuter is both a victim and perpetrator. For the victim, it has been shown, in both indoor and outdoor settings, that pollutants can cause emotional and physiological changes (Evans & Jacobs, 1982; Hedge, Erickson, & Rubin, 1992). For example, poor air quality may depress mood and, in areas where certain chemicals or oxidants are in the atmosphere, may have some negative effect on psychiatric admissions and measures of social pathology (Strahilevitz, Strahilevitz, & Miller, 1979).

However, in addition to its effects on individual behavior, pollution is related to human behavior as an effect variable. Evans and Jacobs (1982, p. 127) say that it (i.e., the quality of the air) is affected by an individual's decision to use mass transportation rather than another mode of travel. From this perspective, mode of transportation serves as a causal variable having potentially a societal, as well as an organizational, impact. This can readily be seen in the case of a large manufacturing plant newly located in a pristine area outside the city. The quality of air (as well as water and other natural resources) will be affected by commuting behavior.

In their comprehensive article on the social psychological aspects of environmental psychology, Darley and Gilbert (1985) presented the view that for an organization, and perhaps, for the individual, immediate gain may not always be the best course of action. Thus, profits for a company may increase temporarily when a pollutant is introduced by a large company (often in a manufacturing process), but eventually society, if not the organization itself, begins to realize that the sum of all the negative consequences to the natural surroundings, good will, and employee health may not be worth the short-term gain.

A similar process and trade-off can also be applied to the commuting process. In trying to minimize employee discomfort and also make a contribution to the society, the organization and the individual may have different and conflicting objectives. On the one hand, being able to decide by oneself when to leave home or office without recourse to a bus or train schedule is one of the freedoms provided by the automobile. Many commuters are quite reluctant to part with this positive feature of their daily routine. Indeed, the organization may very well recognize this need for many of its workers (as evidenced by the large parking areas of number of company cars and various other amenities available to employees).

However, on the other side of the equation is the organization's responsibility to make sure that the employee arrives on time and is ready to work, something a long car ride may not permit. A lesser concern but nevertheless a legitimate issue in many places, particularly where climactic conditions such as smog or air inversions are common, is to try to minimize automobile usage by encouraging alternative methods. Given these disparate needs, an organization may often act against its best interests by either not taking a clear position or act so as to encourage both behaviors. Such an anomaly occurs when an organization subsidizes car pooling for its workers while it also provides free parking. As we see below, government can play a role through legislation and economic incentives to nudge the organization and the worker in directions that reduce air pollution and maximize as much as is possible the comfort of the individual's trip to work and back home.

STRESS, COMMUTING, AND BURNOUT

Of particular importance for the commuter is the potentially harmful consequence of burnout as a reaction to environmental stress, particularly chronic stressors. The commuter who follows the same route each time is likely to confront the same stimuli daily. The honking horns on the congested streets or hot subway cars in the morning are examples of chronic stressors. Prolonged exposure to such stimuli can result in emotional, physical, and mental exhaustion. According to Baron (1986), these are the major components of burnout.

As many other disorders have similar characteristics, the presence of burnout symptoms is not conclusive proof that an individual is inflicted with the malady. Nevertheless, the symptoms that manifest themselves are quite easy to spot. First of all, the physical aspects of burnout include features such as headaches, nausea, back pain, sleep disturbances, and changes in eating habits. The emotional aspects of the illness, according to Baron, include depression, hopelessness, and entrapment. Mental exhaustion refers more to such variables as negative attitudes toward others, cynicism, and reduced self-esteem.

A frequent consequence of burnout in whatever form it occurs is a reduction in the ability to perform one's job. Individuals who start high may wind up performing at such perfunctory levels that management or the employee him- or herself decides that it would be better to work somewhere else. Baron refers to the common phenomenon of "dropping out" as a consequence associated with burnout that may have negative implications for the organization as well as for the individual.

A commuter is a logical candidate for burnout stress. At least as far as physical symptoms are concerned, many commuters report a tiredness or exhaustion when they arrive at work or return home. In an analysis of chronic demands or repeated exposure to stressors, Schaubroeck and Ganster (1993) write that the accumulation of such negative stimuli begins to have a toxic effect on the individual. Adaptive physiological responses are reduced, and the falloff in individual performance appears in many measures of productivity including a greater likelihood of becoming a victim to a workplace accident (p. 73).

Schaubroeck and Ganster argue that so-called challenge situations are dealt with inefficiently, and critical faculties may not be brought to bear just when they are most needed. The challenges defined by the authors are not the usual ones confronting the individual. In their paper, they cite the air traffic controller who faces chronic stress every day because of the nature of the work. However, when two airplanes are suddenly on a direct collision course, the decisions that must be made are no longer the usual ones, and the controller is confronting a challenge wherein resources must be garnered for coping with the crisis. It is during such predicaments that the individual becomes less able to cope with the new and potentially harmful stimulus. In an environmental psychology context, the formulation of stress effects presented by Schaubroeck and Ganster is consistent with a review of the topic as presented by Poulton (1978). Poulton showed that human subjects exposed to noise stressors were often found as manifesting reduced arousal levels toward various task stimuli.

The commuting situation has many of the so-called challenge characteristics described above, and a crisis may actually have to be dealt with *during* the commute as well as afterwards in the office or at home. The latter two periods are the ones that have generally been the concern of the organizational and environmental psychologists who have looked at the topic. For a driver, the chronic stress caused by traffic congestion or stop and go traffic may hinder or reduce the ability to arrive at optimal decisions. A commuter on a long, slow trip to work may see an overtaking driver as a situation that is not only stressful (Gulian et al., 1989) but as one requiring a reaction. Under such circumstances, the commuter may behave inappropriately and speed up or drive uncomfortably close to the other car. During non-rush hours an automobile driver may not be particularly bothered by an overtaking car; however, during rush hour, the accumulated stress that has consistently been shown to produce reduced arousal (as measured by increased adrenaline secretions and other psychophysiological indicators) may provide for poor recovery for coping with the challenge or minicrisis confronting the driver.

Evidence for poor physiological recovery to a normal state after exposure to traffic-related stimuli was provided by an ingenious experiment set up by Ulrich et al. (1991). After all their subjects were presented with a stressful stimulus, recovery, as measured by several physiological indicators, was compared under several experimental conditions. Using video clips, the conditions consisted of natural and man-made scenes presented to all subjects. For comparison purposes, the authors collapsed the visual stimuli into three main settings: (1) natural (either vegetation, water), (2) traffic flows (heavy—as represented by 24 vehicles per minute and light—as represented by 4 vehicles per minute), and (3) pedestrian malls. Results showed that recovery was best for the natural condition and worst, in general, for the traffic groups. In addition, comparison of the two groups within the traffic condition found no significant differences in stress recovery. From the data, it can be inferred that an individual's perception of light or heavy traffic, as compared to either a bucolic or a crowded environment, does not readily permit restoration of the original physiological state. It may very well be that the mere presence of traffic stimuli, no matter how innocuous, has deleterious effects.

This finding complements the previously cited contention of Schaubroeck and Ganster (1993) that an individual confronting a challenge after a chronic stress may experience difficulties in coping. The implications for the driver of a car are apparent: responsivity in dangerous or challenging situations during or even after a long, tedious commute may be negatively affected.

In a slightly different explanation of the environmental impact of stress on the driver, Gellalty and Meyer (1992, p. 695) see that informational cues may be not be integrated by the individual if the arousal levels have gone beyond certain levels. Using the driving situation as an example, the authors write that as road conditions become more difficult and demanding, attention may shift from task-irrelevant activity (talking to a fellow passenger) to task-relevant activity (watching the road). After a certain amount of arousal builds up, performance (such as braking behavior) may deteriorate as some task-relevant cues are ignored. This is an update of the arousal–performance inverted U curve often presented in textbooks (Landy, 1985) that has been criticized by many investigators as not providing an adequate description of the relationship between performance and stress (Baron, 1986).

COMBINING THE EFFECTS OF STRESSORS

Another issue of particular importance to the commuter is the possible consequences of several environmental stressors. In statistical terminology, we often talk of the sum of the significant main effects and/or significant interaction terms as the explanation for the observed explainable variance in a study. Here, too it is legitimate to ask how does the simultaneous exposure to crowding and heat affect the subway rider or pollution and noise stimuli influence a car driver. Are they acting independently or not?

Although such a study using commuters as subjects has not yet been reported, several environmental investigators in other contexts have studied such phenomena. A model of multiple stressors based on the work of Broadbent (1971) was discussed by Landy (1985). In his presentation, Landy identifies three types of situations: *superadditive, linear,* and *canceling effects.*

In the first, the environmental stressors produce an interaction or superadditive affect. This implies that, when presented together, the performance decrement or strain reaction is greater than the sum of the effects if each were introduced separately. The explanation for such a phenomenon is quite creative. According to Broadbent, human performance contains a "margin of safety" wherein a stressor's effects are not yet felt. This concept refers to the fact that an individual has the ability to absorb or muffle a moderate degrees of stress. Before a negative reaction can be observed, the stressor must be strong enough to go beyond the "margin of safety." Now, if two stressors were to act separately, each would have to pass the "margin of safety" before the individual could be expected to respond; however, when acting together, if one has enough intensity to go beyond this point, the other stressor's total impact on the individual comes into play.

Let's illustrate this with an example from the domain of commuting. Assume that certain levels of noise and heat, when encountered separately, will cause a 10% decrease in commuter performance as measured by a commuter tracking task done immediately after coming to work. Now let us also assume that this decrement includes a "margin of safety" of 5%. That means that even after a stressful commute, the individual, whose normal performance is 95% of true capacity, and can easily absorb and not respond negatively until the stimulus intensity is strong enough to overcome this 5% level. Thus, the observed performance decrement of 10% caused by each stimulus is actually 15% since it also includes the "margin of safety." When acting together, only one stimulus is needed before the "margin of safety" is surpassed. The total effect would then be 25% (10% from the first stimulus and 15% from the second).

One of the classic studies that supported the superadditive model of stressor effects was the study carried out by Colquhoun (1962). The use of alcohol and certain drugs (hyoscine and meclozine), commonly used stressors, were found to produce short-term memory effects greater than expected from the sum of their independent effects. More recently, using a psychosomatic complaints scale as a measure of strain, Greller, Parsons, and Mitchell (1992) also reported an interaction effect among a list of stressors. Interestingly, the authors found that certain social support variables acted *additively* as moderators (or buffers, using their term) in mitigating the relationship between stressors and strain.

Landy feels that such findings may be particularly meaningful for two reasons: The aggregate negative consequences from two or more stressors is greater than predicted from data on each one separately. Also, superadditive effects indicate that the same mechanism is at play for both stressors. Individual or organizational methods of coping with both stressors need only focus on one process rather than two separate mechanisms.

Studies that have shown straight additive effects or even cancellation effects are more common. Thus, Ganster, Fusilier, and Mayes (1986) and Russell, Altmaier, and van Velzen (1987) reported more or less linear effects between stressors (as well as other predictors) and dependent variables.

A STRESSOR IS NOT ALWAYS A STRESSOR

Some of the major problems in trying to understand the stressor–strain relationship include the inconsistent findings. This phenomenon is referred to several times throughout the book. One aspect of the relationship that has not been studied adequately is the possibility that, for some, the stressor variable may actually have a positive relationship with certain effect indicators. Many solo drivers will tell you that the time spent in the car on the way to work or back home is the only time when they are able to think and plan their future activities. At the end of the day, many commuters may perceive of such time as a chance for peace and quiet after a hectic day; it is the time for unwinding before facing the family or some other activity that will require the commuter's active participation.

For the senior author, whose office at the University is a 50-minute bus ride from home, the commuting time is spent efficiently by preparing for a class lecture or a meeting that requires some preparation. Many people treasure these moments and are actually reluctant to give them up. Nevertheless, even such descriptions do not preclude a threshold associated with different stimuli that, once breached, is likely to lead to stress. For example, a crowded bus ride, which happens frequently to the senior author, prevents any work from being done. If the ride is also accompanied by some teenagers acting up and creating noise, the threshold for tolerance is quickly reached, and coping mechanisms to reduce strain reactions must be attempted.

SUMMARY

What must be remembered at all times is that stressor stimuli, environmental or otherwise, do not affect all people in the same way. For some, the threshold is never reached; for a few the threshold may be reached only after a very high intensity or duration of the stimulus is experienced; and, finally, for others, the threshold is realized after some reasonable period of exposure. In the model that is introduced in Chapter 5, the scenarios described here are best explained by moderators such as personality that play a key role in most psychological processes.

It appears that the various environmental stimuli discussed here, noise, crowding, aesthetics, and lighting, as well as many others identified by social psychologists, are potential contributors to the quality of the commuting experience and one's reaction to it. However, a major problem with analyses that only consider the objective factors as affecting the individual's reaction are the dubious assumptions that everyone reacts the same way to an external stimulus and that an individual's reaction is simply a function of one or more environmental factors. Instead, research has shown that responses are anything but uniform, and, though expected, negative consequences are often not observed. Thus, noise or crowding may seem to researchers as meeting the minimum requirements for a noxious stimulus. Laboratory studies may even have shown that an effect exists. Yet, the organism in the natural environment does not always react according to theory.

It is, therefore, necessary to postulate intervening variables, especially moderators and mediators, as playing a role in the process. In this chapter, we have dealt with some of the external factors, already identified in other stress contexts, that initiate the chain. It is still incumbent upon us to ferret out variables that enable or permit such trigger stimuli to produce, at the end of some process, behavioral or emotional changes in the individual. Ultimately, then, we may be able to explain more of the variance in the dependent variable. The lesson from social research is that some relationships will never be explained entirely. The goals should be to understand what has been done, what we can learn from it, and how to proceed in the future. Examining and explaining these are the aim of the next few chapters.

4

Commuting and Physical Symptoms

Whereas commuting seems to be related to stress-induced emotional strain and will be the focus of the next chapter (Chapter 5), there is also evidence that commuting, particularly by car, can directly cause physical and physiological strain or damage. Among the known physical consequences of commuting by car are elevated risk for acute herniated lumbar intervertebral disk (Kelsey & Hardy, 1975; Kelsey et al., 1984), cardiovascular stress (Aronow, Harris, Isbell, Rokaw, & Imparato, 1972), and possible associations with various types of cancer (Gubrean, Usel, Bolay, Fioretta, & Puissant, 1992). We review the evidence for each of these consequences separately and then discuss both their implications for employers and possible prevention methods (see Table 4.1 for a summary of these effects).

Before delving into the details of the data, it is important to consider the type of evidence available for the commute–strain link. As we have already stated, only a few studies directly investigated commuting variables as antecedents of strain. However, there are studies that provide indirect evidence for the commute–strain link. A typical example of this type of study are cohort investigations of known occupational groups such as bus drivers, truck drivers, and so forth. If one assumes that the health risks found for these groups are a monotonic function of exposure to driving, than one can infer that commuters are also at risk for the diseases that professional drivers may develop, albeit to a lesser degree. In some other investigations, there is evidence for a monotonic, correlative relationship between exposure to driving and health risks, and therefore, we consider this type of indirect evidence as supportive, albeit not proof, of a

Table 4.1. Purported Associations between Physical Symptoms and Commuting

Category of physical symptom	Examples
1. Physiological measures	Heart rate, blood pressure, chemical secretions
2. Physical problems	Back pain, herniated disk
3. Chronic diseases	Cardiovascular problems, stroke, cancer
4. Other diseases[a]	Gastric disorders, visual impairment, hemorrhoids, accidents

[a]Data collected from transportation workers.

cause–effect link, especially since it seems to corroborate studies that directly investigated the commute–strain link. Finally, evidence can be found in studies of the links between population exposure to various risk factors and the prevalence of the diseases in those populations. Again, the pattern of results for various population risk factors is consistent with studies that have provided direct evidence for the commute–strain link. In light of the scarcity of controlled designs—direct or indirect—in this domain, we also include some references to findings at the population level.

RESEARCH ON THE EFFECTS OF COMMUTING ON PHYSICAL WELL-BEING

Commuting and General Physiological Indicators

Some researchers have examined physiological changes after a commute. Arguably, this is the most direct change that can be expected after a trip of any type to work (or home) and, as will be explained later in our proposed commuting model, is the link from the commuting experience to other individual and organizational effects.

The physiological indicators that have been suggested as relevant to the commuting experience include heart rate, chemical secretions, and blood pressure. Several studies have shown that commuting may be associated with angina pectoris (Aronow et al., 1972), increased heart rate (Simonson et al., 1968), and increased levels of catecholamine (Singer, Lundberg, & Frankenhauser, 1978). Results of blood pressure readings after long commutes are much more ambiguous and seem to be a function of the operational definitions used. In one of the better-designed studies in the field, Stokols, Novaco, Stokols, and Campbell (1978) assessed the effects of traffic congestion on different physiological indicators. Contrary to expectations, high impedance as a result of spending more time on the road and traveling greater distances was not associated with elevated blood pressure readings. In a more recent study, Schaefer, Street, Singer, and Baum (1988) reported that high impedance was indeed associated with increases in systolic and diastolic blood pressure. As the definitions of impedance differed somewhat between the last two studies, the findings are not directly comparable.

Novaco et al. (1990) examined the effects of objective and subjective measures of commuting on health items including self-reported chest pain and occasions of colds/flu. Two of the specific characteristics of the commute, number of freeways and number of road exchanges, were significantly correlated with occasions of colds/flu, and a subjective impedance index, as defined by the authors, was found to be correlated with chest pains.

Similarly, Evans and Carrere (1991) found that among bus drivers, the percentage of work time spent in congested traffic was correlated with both epinephrine and norepinephrine secretions. Further, unpublished analysis of Greller and Parsons of a published study (Greller & Parsons, 1989) indicates that the length of the commute time is correlated with the following self-reported symptoms: stiff neck, tiredness, lower-back pain, difficulty in focusing attention, tension, anger, and "flying off on a handle."

Novaco and Sandeen (1992) also reported on the effects of several moderators on various physiological indicators. Some of the more specific findings will be discussed later in connection with the influence of moderators on the stress–strain relationship; however, it does appear from their data that knowledge of the mode of transportation (generally, car drivers are more affected) and of gender (here it depends—on some measures women do worse and, on others, men) are essential elements in predicting reactions to commuting. In summarizing the relationship between commuting distance or time and physiological measures, the results are somewhat ambiguous. Generally, positive associations have been observed, but as Schaefer et al. (1988) indicated, intervening variables must be considered in trying to understand the impact of commuting on individual or organizational measures.

Car Driving and Back Problems

Many studies of the association between car driving and back problems reported a link between driving and lower-back pain. For example, in one study that contacted people twice within a year, findings indicated that "driving 10 hours a week or more, seat comfort, and psychosomatic factors were associated with first occurrence of low-back pain" (Pietri et al., 1992). However, most studies of the links between car driving and back pain can be criticized on two grounds. First, some studies employed methods that are statistically unsound. For example, Buckle, Kember, Wood, and Wood (1980) used a sample of 68 men and tested 126 variables as predictors of back pain. Second, since most people (60–80%) suffer at some time in their lives from back pain without any discernable precipitating event, the criterion—having back pain—is very suspect (Hadler, 1993; Kelsey, Golden, & Mundt, 1990). However, a minority of the population—around 1%—suffers from acute herniated lumbar intervertebral disk. This disease can serve as a pretty definitive criterion (N. M. Hadler, personal communication). In addition, it is the second most common reason for worker disability payment among people under 40 years of age (the first is schizophrenia) and is the third most common among all ages. As such, it represents an enormous cost for employers and the health care system.

In contrast to simple studies that linked driving with low-back pain, the work of Kelsey and her colleague demonstrated that driving a motor vehicle is a risk factor in developing acute herniated lumbar intervertebral disk. In one of the earlier studies, Kelsey and Hardy (1975) compared subjects with herniated (ruptured, bulging, extruded, prolapsed, or free fragments of) disks to a matched control group and to a second (unmatched) control group. In both comparisons, elevated risk for this disease was related to driving on the job (especially trucks), and to a lesser degree, to driving in general (versus not driving at all). The estimated risk associated with driving—versus not driving at all—was found to have an odds ratio of 2.16, that is, driving seems to double the risk for the disease.

Kelsey and Hardy (1975) controlled for several possible confounding variables, such as the amount of time one sits at work, and matched one of their control groups on other known risk factors (e.g., being a male, age of 30–39); they were able to show that even after controlling for these nuisance variables, driving still seems to be a risk factor.

A follow-up work of Kelsey and her colleagues (Kelsey et al., 1984) replicated the basic findings of Kelsey and Hardy (1975), and found a monotonic relationship between number of hours driven per week and elevated risk for acute herniated lumbar intervertebral disk. Subjects with the diseases averaged 10.2 hours of driving per week, whereas controls averaged 8.3 hours per week ($p < .01$). Furthermore, this study suggested that increased risk was not related to driving Japanese or Swedish cars but was related to driving any other car (mostly American). Specifically, those who used Swedish of Japanese cars in the 5 years prior to the study had a risk three times smaller than those who used only other cars in that period. In addition, the risk for the disease was positively related to the age of the cars across all car types studied.

The differences between car types in their risk for acute herniated lumbar intervertebral disk was hypothesized by several researchers to be a function of car vibration (Kelsey & Hardy, 1975). Specifically, cars associated with elevated risk vibrate with frequencies in the range of 4 to 6 Hz. On the other hand, cars that were not associated with elevated risk have lower vibration frequencies. Coincidentally, the resonance frequency of the spine is found to be 4 to 6 Hz. Furthermore, medical research on animals confirms that vibrations induce several changes in the biochemistry of the spine area that can reasonably explain back damage. The changes induced by vibrations include a deprivation of nutrients to the disk, disk degeneration, and in fluctuations in the levels of substances involved in nerve conduction in the spine (for more details, consult Frymoyer & Gordon, 1989). The effects of vibrations on experimental animals are consistent with abnormalities observed in injured people. Therefore, although the mechanism through which vibrations induce back injuries is not fully understood, the evidence for such a link is too strong to be ignored.

Other explanations for differences between cars were also investigated but did not yield any positive identification of risk factors. Most notably, medical researchers tested different driver seating positions. For example, in one experiment, drivers were tested for 3.5 hours of driving in different positions, and the electrical activity of their back muscles was monitored continuously (Hosea et al., 1985). Elevation in muscle activity would suggest that the back is stressed and is compensating with muscle activity. No meaningful effects for chair position were found. This finding is consistent with typical findings regarding nondriving seating positions. These findings show that there is no good chair position, and that in order to minimize the stress on the lower back one needs to change positions frequently.

Finally, at the population level, there are reports that in underdeveloped countries the incidence of low-back pain is lower than in industrialized countries (Wilder, Woodworth, Frymoyer, & Pope, 1982). The higher incidence of low-back pain in industrialized countries was attributed by several authors to the interface of people in modern societies with vibrating machinery (Wilder et al., 1982). At all levels of analysis (i.e., direct, occupational groups, and population level), the evidence suggests a link between exposure to driving and other causes of vibrations to back problems, in general, and acute herniated lumbar disk, in particular.

Based on the numerous reports using automobile drivers, it appears that vibration is the stimulus that has received the most attention and evidence in the field. However, the exact mechanism leading to various physical symptoms and its generalizability to other modes of transportation still needs to be investigated. Although some epidemiologic studies indicated that the risk ratio between driving a car and not driving is quite high (i.e., 2.16; Kelsey & Hardy, 1975), other studies suggest that the length of the commute, regardless of the mode of transportation, is related to acute herniated lumbar disk (Kelscy et al., 1984). Indeed, in one set of measurements, the vibrational frequency of a train (6.0 Hz) and of a bus (6.0 Hz and 4.25 Hz) were within the range of the first resonance frequency of the spine (approximately 4.5–6.0 Hz; Wilder et al., 1982). These measures seem to indicate that if vibration is a the major risk factor for the back, than the risk is not limited to car commuters. Therefore, it appears possible that, over a long period of time, individuals who have used a bus or train for much of their commuting life are also at risk. Unfortunately, because of low sampling frequency, this effect was not apparent in the data of Kelsey et al. (1984).

Besides the more observable and measurable problems associated with back pain, commuting, or just being a passenger in a car can produce various levels of discomfort. Leatherwood, Dempsey, and Clevenson (1980), using the findings from more than 2,000 subjects, reported on a model for predicting passenger ride discomfort. The stimuli in their study included the previously mentioned noise and vibrations that have been shown by environmental psychologists as producing negative consequences. The attributes of these stimuli that were found to have the greatest impact on comfort were amplitude and frequency. The output from the model consisted of a prediction of discomfort on a continuous scale based on the noise and/or vibration environment.

As serious as the risk of car commute may be for back health, as a more or less chronic problem or discomfort as an acute and temporary phenomenon, other less common difficulties have also been reported. A report of a few case studies suggest that "the ulnar nerve is vulnerable to compression and vibration injury in drivers who have the shoulder abducted and elbow flexed with the arm lying against the lower edge of the window" (Abdel-Salam, Eyres, & Cleary, 1991).

Commuting and Cardiovascular Risks

Many other health issues are associated with the drive to work. In some cases, especially when chronic medical problems are involved, it is hard to say more than the fact that commuting may have *contributed* to the problem. The examination of the cause–effect links associated with one particular environmental issue, air pollution and health, has been quite prevalent over the past couple of decades. As was mentioned in Chapter 3, air pollutants are frequently found in elevated dosages in the commuter's environment (on the roads, in subways, on trains, etc.). In one study, Chan, Spengler, Ozkaynak, and Lefkopoulou (1991) examined the effects of commuters' exposure to a set of measurements derived from six gasoline-related volatile organic compounds (VOCs): benzene, toluene, ethylbenzene, m-/p-xylene, o-xylene, and formaldehyde. The authors found that driving a car increased the exposure to VOCs and that for those commuters using urban roadways or car heaters, the impact was even greater. Incidentally, as compared to walking or biking to work, a prolonged subway ride was also related to increase in exposure to VOCs. It appears from their work as well as others in the literature that exposure of commuters to a high level of air pollutants seems to be a risk factor for many diseases including heart diseases and cancer (for a good explanation of mechanisms linking different social/psychological or environmental stimuli with heart disease and cancer, see Baum, Fisher, and Singer, 1985, pp. 461–466).

There is also some direct evidence for the negative effects of commuter-related pollution and physiological measures of cardiovascular performance, such as elevated heart rate (Aronow et al., 1972). Aronow et al. supplied a group of drivers—patients of coronary diseases—with fresh air, stored in tanks in the experimental car, and compared their cardiovascular performance to previous riders in control cars. Both trips took place along congested roadways. Aronow et al. (1972) found clear evidence of the effect of air pollutants on cardiovascular performance. Similarly, Robinson (1989) tested the changes that occur in the blood during driving and found a significant rise in blood glucose and cholesterol and a decline in triglycerides and coagulation time in the first 15 minutes of driving. Increases in several of these measures, individually or in combination, have been linked with cardiovascular disease.

Air pollution may not be the only source of cardiovascular risk for commuters. Simonson et al. (1968) reviewed and replicated earlier findings showing that even short distance driving increases heart rate by up to 40%, and blood pressure by approximately 10%, and introduces abnormal changes to EEG not observed in other stress situations such as exercise. These driving effects are found primarily in urban driving and immediately following road events, and they do not seem to be affected by speed of driving (of up to 85 mph). Incidentally, race drivers show much more intense reactions. The sensitivity to urban driving and road events may be accentuated among populations of patients with coronary diseases.

Novaco et al. (1979) found that using various parameters of the driving experience such as time, distance, and speed (distance/time) were found to be related to a series of physiological symptoms including heart rate. The procedure used in their study required commuters to enter in their log books mileage and time of their trip during each day of a work week. On those days that a log book was kept, measures of physiological functioning were obtained immediately after arrival at work. Regression analysis showed that heart rate, after controlling for covariates of age, cigarettes, and medication, was not related to any of the three objective commuting parameters. When blood pressure readings were used as the dependent variables, distance and speed but not time were effective predictors after controlling for the covariates. Also, the authors obtained a significant finding that they couldn't explain. When the measures of time and distance were taken together, referred to as *commuting impedance* by the authors, and its interaction with locus of control (internals versus externals) determined, a *decrease* in heart rate for increasing impedance levels was observed.

The above findings relating to the commuting experience are, at best, only suggestive as risk factors for heart diseases because many of the physiological reactions to driving reported in the literature may be within the normal realm of body tolerance leaving no long-term effects on the driver. Yet, all the authors concluded with a warning that the evidence is too strong to be ignored and needs further studies including longitudinal designs to affirm the inference of negative impact.

Another piece of suggestive evidence for the link between driving and cardiovascular problems can be found in an occupational risk study of Swedish professional drivers (Hedberg, Jacobsson, Langendoen, & Nystrom, 1991). In this cohort investigation, the authors reported that circulatory diseases and ischemic heart disease were significantly higher among professional drivers than in the relevant reference group of Swedish males. In other occupational risk studies (cited by Wilder et al., 1982), workers' exposure to vibration was linked to abnormal changes in the cardiovascular (and also the gastrointestinal) system.

In addition, Robinson (1989) presented correlative data from Australia linking driving with both ischemic heart diseases (IHD) and cerebrovascular (stroke) diseases (C/V). Robinson used an unusual correlative method (1989, 1991) to link driving with various diseases. It is worthwhile to describe this method so its limitation can be recognized, yet at the same time, it should be noted that corroborative data for some of Robinson's claims were reported by other researchers using different methods. In Robinson's studies, number of road deaths per year is used as a proxy for number of miles traveled (primarily) in Australia, and this measure is used to predict number of deaths from a list of given diseases. This method is further flawed because Robinson did not allow a lag time between the predictor measure (road accidents) and the criteria, nor did the studies account for population size. Nevertheless, the predictor measure was validated against consumption of gasoline for a period of 15 years ($r = .98$). Returning to IHD and C/V, the index of road death for 1960–1985 showed a close relationship (no actual r or standard deviation for the regression is reported) with both diseases. Recognizing that the inferences are solely based on correlational data, Robinson (1989) noted that "it is often stated that there are many things that are rising with the use of motor vehicles. However, a case has been put, not only for a rise with the use of the motor vehicle, but also a fall in IHD and C/V with the fall in the use of the motor vehicle in both males and females" (p. 103). Although Robinson did not explain the decline in use of motor vehicles (in Australia) and these diseases since 1970, we believe that one should not rule out these risks given the unrelated work of Aronow et al. (1972) linking experimentally controlled car driving with temporary cardiovascular stress, and the elevated risk of IHD for professional drivers reported by Hedberg et al. (1991). In conclusion, the link between commuting and cardiovascular diseases is plausible, although it is based on minimal scientific research.

Commuting and Cancer

In contrast to the findings regarding cardiovascular diseases, the effect of driving on cancer is better established. However, we did not find any study definitively linking commuters to cancer. The evidence that does exist comes from studies of occupational risk or general population risk and are reviewed below.

As an overview of the evidence for the link between car commute and cancer, it is useful to refer to the conclusion of the International Agency for Research on Cancer (1989) as cited by Gubrean et al. (1992):

> Recently, the International Agency for Research on Cancer (IARC) has critically reviewed evidence for carcinogenicity of engine exhaust fumes provided by epidemiological studies, experimental studies in animals, and other relevant biological data. In the overall evaluation it has been concluded that diesel exhaust fumes are "probably carcinogenic" to humans and petroleum fumes are "possibly carcinogenic." (p. 337)

Several recent studies reached similar conclusions. For example, a Swiss prospective cohort study of 6,630 professional drivers showed a significant excess risk—with a 15-year latency—for lung cancer, esophageal cancer, stomach cancer, rectal cancer, and cirrhosis of the liver (Gubrean et al., 1992). Importantly, in this study, a distinction was made between groups of drivers according to the likely level of exposure to pollution. The authors reported that: "A significant trend from the least exposed to the most exposed category was seen for mortality from stomach cancer and rectal cancer, and for the incidence of stomach cancer, rectal cancer, and lung cancer" (p. 340).

In their discussion, Gubrean et al. (1992) report that other studies (in London and in Sweden) found similar results for lung cancer, and that most studies—including studies that controlled for cigarette smoking— linked exhaust gases with lung cancer (six studies out of eight reports). Other diseases such as esophageal cancer and rectal cancer can be attributed to excessive drinking and smoking among drivers, but not in all cases. Stomach cancer was linked in some explorations with air pollution, and Gubrean et al. (1992) conclude that the link between driving and stomach cancer is plausible although inconclusive.

At the population level, the results are similar. As with IHD and C/V, Robinson (1991) found a relationship between road accidents (proxy for miles traveled) and cancer deaths from all causes. In one of these analyses, population size was controlled by establishing the link between road deaths and lung and breast cancer rate per 100,000. In addition, the ratio of road accidents and all types of cancer was strikingly similar for American (United States), French, West German, Italian, New Zealand, Norwegian, Japanese, and Australian data. In another paper, a link to leukemia was reported (Robinson, 1991). In what may be the most telling analysis conducted by Robinson (1989), data were presented for the link between lung cancer and road death. In that paper, Robinson reported that between 1940 and 1981, lung cancer deaths increased by 1,061% (one must assume that the increase is in reported lung cancer deaths), gasoline consumption by 909%, whereas the population itself increased by only 111%. For the period 1920 to 1972, gasoline usage grew by 2,840%, lung cancer by 2,810%, and smoking tobacco by only 69%. When considering these numbers, Robinson suggests (1991) that the predictability of the rate of lung cancer deaths from road accidents lagged for 1 year (probably an unrealistic lag) cannot be dismissed out of hand as a noncausative correlation. The implications are clear: the data may be only correlational, but the inference is that the variables are causally linked.

In summary, various studies with different methodologies—each suffering from its own methodological deficiencies, which at times are serious—point at a very plausible link between exposure to exhaust fumes and various types of cancer, and especially lung cancer. The question that these alarming statistics raise regards the destructive effects that driving has on the normal functioning of diverse biological mechanisms. At this point at least two mechanisms are offered as an explanation for these risks: air pollutants and the general reaction (strain and information overload) to the visual and cognitive cues present in driving, which is consistent with some hormonal changes found in drivers (Robinson, 1989). Further research is needed to understand better the relevant processes and, perhaps, to determine ways to weaken the linkage involved here.

HEALTH IMPLICATIONS OF COMMUTING

The above list of diseases that seem to be partly traceable to the commuting habits of employees is probably an incomplete list. Nevertheless, the hidden cost for employers and for modern economies seems to be staggering. Commuting by automobile, but not only automobile, seemed to be related to acute herniated lumbar disk, heart diseases, and several types of cancer (primarily lung cancer). The leading item for workers' compensation in the United States is back problem where herniated lumbar disks account for 80% of this cost (Hadler, 1993). In a 10-year period, back pain was responsible for 12.5% of all sickness and absence days in Sweden (Svenson & Anderson, 1983), and, in 1 year in Great Britain, 3.6% of all work days were lost because of back pain. Kelsey, Golden, and Mundt (1990) cite reports that 16% of the Swedish population had experienced incapacitating back pain for periods of 3 to 6 months, and that 4% have been incapacitated for periods longer than 6 months. Only about 7% of the people who suffer from back pain don't improve within 2 weeks of the start of the episode. However, these people—including the sufferers from acute herniated lumbar intervertebral disk—account for the lion share of the cost. For example, the Boeing Corporation reported that 10% of the back-injury claims account for 79% of the cost for worker compensation (Kelsey et al., 1990). The cost for the entire U.S. work force was estimated as $11 billion of lost wages resulting from back pain disability (Frymoyer et al., 1983).

Of course, the added *risk* for acute herniated lumbar disk *per person* accrued from driving is small relative to other risks such as lifting while twisting, and smoking (e.g., Damkot, Frymoyer, Lord, & Pope, 1982). However, the added negative *utility across all workers* must be much higher for driving than for lifting while twisting because few people do jobs that require lifting while twisting, but many employees have long car commutes. The same logic applies for the added risk of heart diseases and cancer.

SPECIAL PROBLEMS OF PEOPLE WORKING IN TRANSPORTATION

Although the focus of this book is on the commuter and the antecedent and consequent variables associated with the trip between work and home, there are workers in the transportation field who are exposed to many of these stimuli on a continuous basis, not just for a few hours in the morning or evening. We have already referred to some of the unique problems such as back pain and discomfort associated with all users of transportation.

When there is a potential overload in regard to such stressors, the problem may become chronic and much less amenable to solution.

As of 1985, there were 4.5 million people employed in the transportation industry moving or delivering people or goods in the United States (MacLennan, 1992). A close examination of the distribution of these workers showed that two-thirds were between 18 and 44 years of age, and 91.8% were male. Over 60% had at least a high school education, and 40% earned more than $25,000 per annum. According to data reported by the National Center for Health Statistics (1989), some categories of transportation workers had among the highest risks for cardiovascular disease (particularly high blood pressure), ischemic heart disease, hemorrhoids, deafness, and visual impairment. Nearly 30% of the workers reported gastric disorders, considerably higher than the national average. Each one of these health problems can be legitimately described as an occupational health hazard directly or indirectly related to various functions or activities involved in the transportation field.

More specifically, some of the conclusions concerning back pain and discomfort experienced by commuters have been shown to be particularly relevant for several types of transportation workers. For example, findings reported previously that vibrations and seating in a fixed position pose a serious risk for herniated disk are consistent with a study of occupational risks of bus drivers (Bovenzi & Zadini, 1992) and truck drivers (Piazzi, Bollino, & Mattioli, 1991). Bus drivers were compared to maintenance workers in the same bus company, and the results indicated that

> after controlling for potential confounders, the prevalence odds ratios for the bus drivers compared to the controls significantly exceeded 1 for several types of low-back symptoms (leg pain, acute low-back pain, chronic low-back pain). The occurrence of low-back symptoms increased with increasing whole-body vibration exposure expressed in terms of total (lifetime) vibration dose . . . equivalent vibration magnitude . . . and duration of exposure (years of service). (Bovenzi & Zadini, 1992)

The authors concluded that the increased risk for low-back troubles may result from "both whole-body vibration exposure and prolonged sitting in a constrained posture."

Findings regarding truck drivers are generally similar—although one should bear in mind that truck drivers are also engaged in other risky behaviors apart from driving, such as lifting with twisting and smoking. Specifically, "there was an elevated frequency of herniated disk and the risk was 4 times higher compared to the control population . . ." and the "disease of the lumbar spine leads in a very large number of cases to permanent working incapacity among truck drivers before pensionable age" (Piazzi et al., 1991). Similarly, some reports (cited by Wilder et al., 1982), linked workers' exposure to vibration and helicopter riding with abnormal changes in the musculoskeletal system.

In the next few pages, we cite some of the findings pertaining to long-distance truckers and Amtrak engineers, two groups who are particularly vulnerable to the effects of stress.

Long-Distance Truckers

According to data cited by MacLennan (1992), there were more than 425,000 truck and trailer operators in 1989. Most interestingly, according to a report from the National Safety Council (1988), these operators were involved in 20% of all road accidents. At the Regular Common Carrier Conference (1990), a survey of truckers arriving at three Florida inspection sites from all over the United States were asked to give the reason for accidents in their industry. Two-thirds stated that the cause was fatigue. The major contributors to fatigue, as reported in the survey, were working to meet tight schedules, loading and unloading trucks for inspection, road congestion, and having to travel at peak hours. For many truck drivers, especially the ones involved in accidents, substance abuse seems to be quite common. MacLennan (1992) cites the fact that more than 30% of all fatally injured drivers were on some type of drug or alcohol. It is possible that drugs are serving as an intermediate outcome caused by fatigue or other stress-related factors. But once the drug option is chosen to relieve stress, this "coping" mode may itself be responsible for accidents and, it would seem, for many deaths.

Railroad Engineers

In the past decade, high-speed trains have been developed in Europe and in Japan. This has had an impact on the behavior patterns of many commuters. In explaining the denouement of public transport policy in Europe, Jones, Bovy, Orfeuil, and Salomon (1993) describe a so-called stage process of commuting patterns where the car first increases in importance until it is realized (by individuals as well as companies and governments) that the roadways are so clogged that other means must be devised for moving people. In the last stage reached by the most advanced Western countries, rail travel, especially at high speeds, is seen not as a luxury but as a necessity. Although in the United States the image of train travel has turned more positive, the usage data do not yet show movement in that direction (Pisarski, 1992). The little data available relevant for our purposes come from AMTRAK, which runs high-speed trains along the Eastern corridor.

In the case of AMTRAK, switching over to high-speed trains allowed management to let go of about half of all the engineers in the system. The newer trains could run with just one engineer (MacLennan, 1992). Engineers remaining in the system complained of increased stress because in many cases a close partner of many years had left and was not replaced. Closer examination of the situation showed several interesting phenomena. First, the drivers complained of the need to have a partner, not only for emotional reasons, but for helping to identify potentially dangerous situations that were now left to the discretion of the lone engineer/driver. Unlike an airplane situation, engineers felt there would be no co-pilot to take over if the engineer suddenly became ill. Anxiety was created from fears of potentially poor equipment or vandalized rail lines that might prevent stopping the very fast trains on time. Overall, engineers in the new high-speed environment were facing situations that were untried in the United States and, as perceived by them, that were liable to lead to higher costs both physically and psychologically.

SOLUTIONS FOR VARIOUS PHYSICAL PROBLEMS

As the problems associated with the physical consequences of driving are rather unique and have only limited implications for the general coping strategies available to the commuter, we discuss some solutions for dealing with these effects here. Coping as it relates to the emotional, attitudinal, and behavioral aspects of commuting stress will be presented in much greater detail in Chapters 7 and 8.

Since the characteristics associated with each physical risk factor must be understood and analyzed separately, the suggested solution, in turn, is also a function of the specific reaction experienced by the individual. For example, back pain or discomfort was described previously as a problem often linked to driving a car. Surprisingly, given the evidence for the risk to the back caused by driving, investigators have identified only a few solutions and even fewer have been adequately tested: "dampening vibration . . . and improved seat positioning and lumbar support in automobiles would reduce frequency of low-back pain and prolapsed discs [sic], although no studies have been undertaken specifically to evaluate these possibilities" (Kelsey et al., 1990, p. 710). Other generic solutions include cessation of cigarette smoking, improved physical fitness, and avoidance of sitting in one position for long time. The latter implies—for car drivers—frequent changing of the position of the car seat, and stopping for short walks on long rides.

Many of the solutions available for the other driving-related risks (e.g., air pollution) are often impractical at the individual level. In one (problematic) survey study (Skov et al., 1991), Danish respondents (over 90%), who recognized the risk to their health from air pollution, indicated that they are unlikely to avoid using their car in the event of "above average" air pollution notification in the media. Only in response to a "pollution alert," approximately half of the respondents indicated that they would change their commuting pattern. In probing the respondents for the reasons for the unwillingness to avoid car travel as a response to air pollution notification, 39.3% said that public transportation was too inconvenient, 35.9% said that they needed the car to perform the job, and paradoxically 18.9% thought that by driving a car they personally would avoid the effects of the air pollution. Despite the shortcomings of this survey study, its conclusions are similar to those available from the United States.

The severity of the traffic-congested roads and air-quality problems in some regions of the United States have led both corporations and governments to actively try to change the commuting habits of the work force. For example, U.S. employers are being called by the federal government ["The employer requirement of the Clean Air Act Amendments of 1990" Section 182 (d) (1) (B)] to reduce the number of cars driven to their parking lots, increase car occupancy, increase utilization of public transportation, and take other measures in order to reduce both traffic congestion and emission of air pollutants. Many of these changes will have a direct impact on the link between commuting and physical consequences. Examples of programs designed to decrease the number of solo drivers to work include: employers paying a percentage of the cost incurred by riders of public transportation (Osborn & McCarthy, 1987); inducements for car-pooling and van-pooling (Cervero, 1986); and government subsidies for mass transportation (Cervero, 1985). None of these solutions is cost-free, and they often are accompanied by employee resistance or loss of organizational control over employees (Forester, 1987; Long, 1987; Turnage, 1990). These methods and several others will be discussed in connection with coping with the usual strain responses traditionally associated with commuting stress. For now, suffice it to say, solutions for many of the problems are still far away. But the fact that some of the problems resulting from driving and commuting are finally being looked at by professionals and experts who are beginning to offer serious programs for dealing with this question indicates that some improvement in the not-too-distant future at least possible.

Several of the solutions offered are not practical, especially if the person uses some form of transportation for performing his or her job, and the car or train is not merely a means to get to work. Thus, in the case of the trucker, railroad engineer, or even traveling salesperson, a solution cannot focus on alternative modes of travel. Rather, the way to reduce some of the potential physical dangers or fears associated with these jobs is to analyze the problems and suggest ways of reducing the negative consequences. This was tried with truckers and engineers with some success (MacLennan, 1992). For example, if fatigue is a cause of accidents for the former, then more rest stops and breaks between trips are needed for keeping the driver alert and reducing accidents. If the railroad engineer worries that the lack of a partner in the engineer's cabin or faulty rail equipment contributes to the engineer's increased reaction time, then the equipment must be improved, and management must be able to convince the employee that there are no existing problems preventing a stress-free and safe ride.

A METHODOLOGICAL NOTE

Before we conclude the chapter, it is worthwhile to discuss the pathways that lead from the commuting experience as a stressor to stress perception followed by physiological (strain) reactions of various types. The association is quite complex, and, although causal direction is often difficult to prove scientifically, data from several sources have indicated that direct and indirect linkages seem to exist. Several investigators have long suspected that the human physiological system is very sensitive to psychosocial stimuli (Frankenhauser, 1975). It is now well accepted that cognitive processes are at work wherein the brain translates stimuli from emotional effects to physiological effects.

Frankenhaueser (1975) writes that increased levels of catecholamines after exposure to stressful stimuli are a reaction that reflects the emotional impact of the environment. Many of the variables that are associated with stress including control, novelty, anticipation, unpredictability, and change may produce a rise in epinephrine output and, according to Frankenhaueser, the "amount excreted in urine closely reflects the degree of arousal evoked by the stimulating condition" (p. 214). The effect has been shown in the opposite direction, as well. The physiological sensation may sometimes be responsible for some aspects of the emotional state. Thus, Frankenhaueser and Jarpe (1963) showed that subjective response to infusions of epinephrine (a known heart-rate and blood pressure stimulant) was partially explained by the observed physiological reaction.

In the commuting situation, the complex relationship among stressor, emotional reaction, and some physiological effect is well founded. For example, reports of lower-back pain appear to be partly caused by psychological factors such as anxiety, depression, and stressful events and partially by the commuting position during the trip (Frymoyer et al., 1980; Hadler, 1993). Frymoyer et al. (1980) found a very significant association between reports of various emotional or psychological factors and complaints of lower-back pain. This suggests that commute-induced stress may have an indirect effect on back problem, in addition to the direct link between commuting and back problems (e.g., Kelsey et al., 1990). Of course, the direction of causality is not clear because the commute-induced back pain can also be responsible for feelings of anxiety and depression. However, other commute experiences that are believed to be psychological are known to have a distinct physiological consequence. For example, crowding on the train seems to cause an elevation in catecholamines (especially epinephrine) that corresponds very closely to self-reports of discomfort but not to trip duration or length (Lundberg, 1976; Singer et al., 1978). This finding of a commute–stress–strain link suggests, at least in principle, that a driving–anxiety–back problems link may also exist.

In conclusion, given the scarcity of research in this area and the complexity of the phenomenon, we can only suggest that whereas the negative effects of commuting on health are both serious and costly, the mechanisms involved in these processes are poorly understood, and, therefore, apart from completely avoiding the commute, empirical tests of the effectiveness of various solutions are sorely lacking and needed in the field (Kelsey et al., 1990).

5

Behavioral, Emotional, and Attitudinal Effects of Commuting

Investigators from disparate disciplines have employed various techniques to examine the behavioral and psychological effects of commuting. Traditionally, commuting time or distance has been viewed as an independent variable that is accompanied by or produces various effects or outcomes on the individual which, in turn, impact the organization. This linkage between the individual and the organization is a fundamental assumption of the negative repercussions resulting from commuting to work. Recent work has also focused on the family environmental consequences of the trip home (Novaco et al., 1991).

As can be seen in Table 5.1, the main types of behavioral outcomes or dependent variables that have been associated with commuting distance are absenteeism, lateness, turnover, and performance. Anxiety, tension, job satisfaction, and burnout are among the emotional and attitudinal measures that have been related to the commuting experience. Few researchers have studied both types of variables simultaneously and have linked one set to the other. One of the major theses in the present book and the basis for the development of a model to explain the consequences of commuting is the integration of the two streams of research. In particular, emotional variables play either the role of moderators or serve as an additional link in the chain that eventually produces behavioral changes. This chapter focuses on the studies that have dealt with the dependent variables of interest to commuting researchers. A summary of the findings will enable the reader to draw appropriate conclusions about

Table 5.1. Some of the Possible Nonphysical Effects of Commuting

Category of symptom	Examples
1. Behavioral	
A. Withdrawal	Lateness, absence, turnover
B. Performance	Vigilance, proofreading error rate, perceptual reasoning
2. Attitudinal	Job satisfaction, job dissatisfaction
3. Emotional	Anxiety, mood, hostility, overall feelings of health

the state of knowledge in the field and identify the issues that need clarification. In addition, at a later stage in the book, we try to integrate these summaries with some of our own research and build on them in order to develop a process model that links the various causes and effects of the commuting experience.

As several researchers have discovered in their work, intervening variables and moderators play a pivotal role in the size of the relationship between commuting and outcome. In some cases, after controlling, through analysis of covariance or multiple regression techniques, for certain key personal variables, the strength of the statistical association (as measured by functions of F and R^2) is found to be reduced or in several cases, no longer significant.

Just as important are the diverse *moderators* that have been suggested in the field. Meaningful inferences are possible only after the data, where available, on moderators are examined. Examples of moderators that must be considered include, but are not limited to, the nature of the independent variable, gender, and mode of transportation. In this chapter, we discuss some of the moderators that have been used in commuting studies. In the next chapter (see Chapter 6) where our model is presented, we introduce some additional moderators that are "borrowed" from the general stress literature and seem particularly appropriate for understanding the commuting process.

Methodologically, the field is quite immature. Much of the research has been conducted with superficial or cursory surveys that asked one or two questions about the commuting experience. Inferences that were developed from these studies are, at best, only clues to the true effects of commuting. Only recently have investigators resorted to theory-driven studies using extensive, well-planned surveys or, even, quasiexperimental designs to test their hypotheses. Structural equation modeling with commuter procedures such as LISREL have not been reported and are needed in order to develop an understanding of the linkages involved in the commuting process.

The lack of studies with precise data has prevented the application of meta-analytic techniques for quantifying either the size of effect or determining corrected correlations to describe the association between commuting and behavior. In the brief review of the field that follows, studies that we feel have wide ramifications for the field as a whole are discussed in greater detail.

After presenting some of the general findings in the field, we return to a more detailed discussion of several key moderators in the commuting process.

COMMUTING AND ORGANIZATIONAL BEHAVIOR

Absenteeism

Many of the original studies in the field examined the correlation or association between commuting distance and absenteeism without considering mediating or intervening factors. In one of the first studies to use statistical tests, Knox (1961) reported that among a group of subjects who had been absent frequently (more than 28 times in the past year), approximately 19% (or more than double the value for a control group) lived more than an hour from work. However, this finding can only be viewed as indicative, since the author did not control for any other demographic or psychological variables. The authors did examine the association between age, tenure, and absenteeism but not in combination with commuting time. In another study with similar findings but with several factors such as age and longevity controlled, Martin (1971) reported that, for male workers, absenteeism was related to distance traveled. The author indicated that, for female workers, the association between absenteeism and travel distance was not significant. Martin suggested that women may be more likely to find jobs closer to home, whereas men may be more willing to travel greater distances for employment.

Further support for the relationship between absenteeism and commuting time was reported by Taylor and Pocock (1972). In an analysis not broken down by sex, the authors reported that subjects who traveled more than 90 minutes to work showed a greater absence frequency than those who traveled less than 90 minutes. The authors also examined the influence of two other indicators on workers' absence: the number of stages involved in getting to work and the mode of transportation used. A stage was defined as the part of the journey to work where neither the method of transport nor the vehicle changed. People with one or two stages had significantly less uncertified or unexcused absences than those with more stages between home and work. Also, those who used their cars to get to work had 20% more absences than those who used public transport.

These latter findings supported an earlier work by Stockford (1944). In a study of 200 nonsupervisory personnel at the Lockheed corporation, Stockford found that subjects with frequent absences were more likely to drive their own cars to work. Two studies, one with negative results and the other with ambiguous results have also been reported. Popp and Belohlav (1982) reported no significant relationship between commuting and absence for a male sample. Novaco et al. (1990) found that high-physical-impedance subjects had the largest number of absence–illness days and low-impedance subjects the least number of absence–illness days. However, when covariates such as age, smoking, weight, and alcohol consumption were introduced, the effects were no longer linear.

Interestingly, Novaco et al. (1990) also corroborated Taylor and Pocock's (1972) concept of the influence of trip stages. Using some specific measures of the commuting experience as possible predictors of absence, the Novaco group found that absence–sick days were significantly related to number of freeways ($r = .37$) and number of road exchanges ($r = .47$) during a trip between home and work. When a subjective impedance scale, derived from a 17-item questionnaire scale pertaining to the subjective ratings of various travel constraints was used as a predictor of absence, a low, nonsignificant correlation was obtained.

Lateness

Besides absenteeism, lateness has also been examined as a potential consequence of a long trip to work. Nicholson and Goodge (1976) found that, among women workers, lateness was negatively correlated with commuting distance. Women who lived closer to the plant were more likely to arrive late to work. The authors explained these results by suggesting that a short commute on a public transportation system, which is often the case among women workers, affords more frequent opportunities for minor lateness as compared with infrequent schedules over longer distances. Using the survey responses of about 1,500 workers, Leigh and Lust (1988) found that commuting long distances to work, among other variables, was associated with lateness.

In a review of variables that influence the work environment, Gaffuri and Costa (1986) state, without any statistical evidence, that the mere fact of commuting often leads to late arrival at work. Lateness, according to the authors, is one of the many negative consequences of the commuting phenomenon, which affects workers' well-being as well as their productivity.

Turnover

Two of the principal studies in this area indicated that commuting distance was related to turnover. The study by Knox, cited previously, also showed that when compared to groups with average and high absentee rates, a third group who left the organization had the longest commute. In Martin's (1971) study of factors that influence absenteeism, the authors also examined turnover as a potential effect of commuting. She found that among those who leave an organization, the distance between home and work is greater. However, this finding seems to be confounded with the absence variable, and it is not clear what the relationship between commuting distance and turnover would be if number of absences were controlled.

As a by-product of their research design, Novaco et al. (1990) examined the relationship between job changers (the turnover group) and nonchangers over two time periods. (The second time period had been used as a validity check of the results in the first wave, as well as an opportunity to present some new items.) The study found that commuting satisfaction was related to job change. For those who left their places of employment, commuter satisfaction was considerably higher at time 2 than time 1. In addition, this latter group was considerably higher on commuter satisfaction than the group that did not change jobs.

The authors concluded that "change in employment was primarily associated with *commuting* [italics in the original article] satisfaction" (1990, p. 253) and not with several other indices of satisfaction measured in their study. These job changes were a major finding in support of the contention of Novaco et al. (1990) that there is a reciprocal relationship among many domains in the individual's life. In this case, the bidirectional effects are between the commuting domain and job domain.

In a major study of teacher attrition, Seyfarth and Bost (1986) reported that the relationship between turnover and commuting was mediated by salary level. Although the zero order correlation between the number of commuters in a district was positively correlated with the turnover rate, the partial correlation between them, after removing the influence of salary, was not significant.

Inferences derived from the latter results were confirmed in a study by Williams, Livy, Silverstone, and Adams (1979) on ancillary staff at two London hospitals. From a long list of personal factors including traveling distance that could impact turnover, only age was found to be significantly correlated with turnover. The lack of predictability of the distance variable was contrary to the authors' hypotheses.

In summary, it appears that the effects of commuting on turnover are probably moderated by other variables that have produced ambiguous and, somewhat contrary, results.

One other aspect of turnover makes it somewhat unique among the various dependent variables examined here. It is not only a response to commuting stress, but it may also be a method of coping. Although we have not placed it under this heading in our book, Novaco et al. (1990) see turnover as serving such a function for the commuter. This fits in with their concept that what happens in one area affects other areas. An individual who feels that the quality of his or her family relationships or recreational opportunities are such that they have been adversely affected by commuting may change jobs and see if that change improves all of the domains at the same time. In such a scenario, turnover, indeed, may have a positive impact on many outcomes including those that are traditionally viewed as antecedents such as attitudinal, emotional, or even physiological variables.

Performance

Performance decrement has also been examined as a potential outcome of commuting. Schaefer et al. (1988) found that subjects with high impedance or low commuting speed had lower scores on a proofreading task administered immediately after arriving at work than subjects whose average driving speed was higher.

Although not significant, scores on a discrimination task were also lower for the high-impedance group. Novaco et al. (1979) did not find any relationship between impedance and two task performance measures: (1) perceptual reasoning as measured by subject's ability to trace a diagram and (2) scores on the digit symbol subtest of the Wechsler Adult Intelligence Scale. Their measure of impedance involved a combination of travel distance and time as defined before.

In a laboratory study by Tainsh (1973), a measure of performance on a critical thinking test was found to be related to traveling "several hours" to work. Specific descriptions of the various measures in the study were not reported. Thus, of the three studies quoted in this area, two found a relationship between commuting distance and performance, and one study did not.

ATTITUDINAL AND EMOTIONAL MEASURES

Probably the most commonly used attitudinal measure in the industrial/organizational literature is satisfaction. Researchers have identified many types of satisfaction. These include, but are not limited to job, residential, and life areas. Stress investigators have looked into each one of these areas separately but also recognize the fact that the individual outcomes should not be viewed in a vacuum but rather as possibly impacting each other (MacLennan, 1992; Novaco et al., 1990). In the literature, measures of satisfaction serve as outcomes or as intermediary variables that lead to or are indicative of other dependent variables, such as performance or behavior.

Studies using attitudinal variables rather than the ultimate behavior such as absence or turnover have several distinct advantages. In some studies, it is difficult to measure the behavior, and, if the attitude has been shown to be a precursor of the behavior, examining the impact of commuting distance or time on the attitude may be adequate. Furthermore, some researchers recommend attitudes rather than behaviors as the appropriate dependent variable because whereas "behavior is often influenced by unmeasurable variables outside a person's control, intentions are determined by the employee" (McFarlane-Shore, Newton, & Thornton, 1990, p. 58).

Other attitudinal-dependent variables such as intentions to leave a job have often been proposed as the result of various antecedents and one of the variables immediately preceding turnover behavior (Mowday, Porter, & Steers, 1982; Williams & Hazer, 1986). Even within the attitudinal domain, relationships have been studied. For example, indicators of job satisfaction and commitment have been investigated as both antecedent and consequent variables with the direction of the causal link between them somewhat ambiguous (Bateman & Strasser, 1984; Curry, Wakefield, Price, & Mueller, 1986).

The relationship between the various measures of commuting and satisfaction has only recently been explored scientifically. Much of the research in the area of commuting and satisfaction focuses on the influence of the former on the latter. Nevertheless, an examination of the findings from some of the surveys of attitudes *toward* commuting are quite informative and very relevant here. In reporting the results of a survey in Orange County, California, Baldassare and Katz (1988) found that only 5% of the population in the county was satisfied with existing freeway conditions, and perhaps, more importantly, nearly 50% of the residents in the county considered commuting as the county's most important problem.

One of the few research groups that have looked at different types of consequences including attitudinal effects are the Novaco, Stokols group (Novaco et al., 1979, 1990). To a large extent their findings are a function of their criteria for defining travel impedance. Two approaches were used by the authors. The first, considered as quasiexperimental, was an empirical definition combining time and distance. For example, in their studies on the effects of commuting on home-related variables, high-impedance subjects were those who traveled 20 to 64 miles and spent 50 minutes or more on their trip home, whereas low-impedance subjects were those who had to travel between 11 and 15 miles and spent 30 to 40 minutes getting home. In their more traditional study on the relationship between commuting and the work domain, high physical impedance was defined as traveling between 18 and 50 miles in 30 to 75 minutes, and low impedance was defined as traveling 7.5 miles in less than 12.5 minutes. As the criterion was determined each time by the distribution of the time and distance variables in the sample, a variability was automatically created that limited the generalizability of the results. Nevertheless, some of the authors' inferences from the studies have important ramifications.

Novaco et al. (1990) found, among other influences, a relationship between commuting impedance and certain measures of residential satisfaction. In making a distinction between objective commuting characteristics and subjective commuting impressions, the authors found differential effects. Although both measures predicted various health-related outcomes, the picture as regard to attitudinal and psychological effects was not consistent. Whereas the objective commuting characteristics were predictive of job satisfaction but not mood after arrival at home, the subjective impressions were correlated with mood at home but not with job satisfaction or residential satisfaction. The lack of isomorphism in the effects of these two variables was explained, by the authors, as a function of confounding variables or moderators including cognitive appraisal/or stress-mitigating factors.

Further, the authors (Novaco et al., 1990) did point out that the psychological effects of commuting are accompanied by an interdomain effect. This implies that "the psychological consequences of environmental conditions in one life domain (home, commuting, work, or recreational) transfer to another" (p. 255). Although the findings in support of this contention were somewhat ambiguous, Novaco et al. (1990) argued that there was sufficient overlap among outcome measures in these various domains to indicate a possible transfer of the effects from one area to another. The significance of this is quite important for both the theoretician and practitioner. If it can be shown that commuting stress, as described in the Novaco et al. (1990) model, is one link in a chain of reactions, then it is likely that the individual is not the only one to suffer from the consequences of stress. The family, the work place, and eventually, the society are all potential domains that may suffer as a result of commuting stress. This theme is part of the general model of stress to be presented later and will also play a role in describing the various coping methods available in the various domains.

In his discussion of correlates and causes of strain in the work place, Frese (1985) made a distinction between psychological and physical measures of the stressful stimulus. Researchers in the field of commuting have also distinguished among the various indicators of the commuting experience. Thus, Schaefer et al. (1988) did not find any relationship between impedance or average traveling speed and measures of anxiety or mood. Interestingly, single drivers as compared to car-pool drivers, did have significantly higher scores on hostility and anxiety measures.

Novaco et al. (1979) tested the effects of travel time and distance on four measures of mood. They reported that high-impedance subjects were more tense and nervous than low-impedance subjects, but no differences between groups were observed for irritability and impatience.

Using a so-called "health" measure as an outcome variable, Novaco et al. (1990) found that subjective impedance was moderately and significantly correlated ($r = -.37$) with mood. Moreover, when several residential and job variables were entered in the first step and subjective impedance in the second step of a hierarchical regression analysis, the observed change in R^2 with mood as the dependent variable was highly significant ($p < .001$).

Stokols et al. (1978) studied the potential mediating effects of the two personality types, the so-called A and B syndromes, on the relationship between impedance and several dependent variables including a performance test measuring tolerance for frustration. Contrary to expectations, tolerance for frustration was lowest among high-impedance type Bs and highest among high-impedance type As. The authors had expected the naturally more anxious As to exhibit a lower level of tolerance to frustration. Several potential moderators to explain the findings were presented. In summary, the investigations cited here indicated that certain measures of psychological or mental health are related to commuting.

One other approach to the issue of the psychological effects associated with commuting between home and work is the anxiety cost involved. B. H. Smith (1991) asked bus and private car users how dangerous (i.e., the likelihood of accident or death) and aggravating (e.g., congested, noisy, and dirty) they found the various methods of getting to and from work? Alternatives ranged from 0 "not at all" to 4 "a great deal." The analysis of responses from more than 1,000 subjects provided formulas for deciding the likelihood of using certain modes of transportation. For example, a 100% per week increase in the cost of driving one's car to and from work decreases the probability of using a car by about 17%. Such data can be particularly valuable for urban planners responsible for deciding how to convince people to change their driving habits and decrease some of the negative psychological effects of commuting.

MODERATORS AND INTERVENING VARIABLES

Commuting Measures

One of the important moderators in the field is the commuting measure itself. Some of the general issues associated with defining the variable of interest were already presented in Chapter 1. Here, we try to cite some of the relevant findings and draw inferences concerning specific effects reported by researchers in the field.

Investigators have tended to use either time or distance as the independent variable. A review of the studies cited above shows that significant relationships between dependent measures and each of the two commute measures have been reported. Novaco, Stokols, and colleagues (Novaco et al., 1990) decided to use both in their formulation for commuting impedance. As used by the Novaco group, physical impedance is a relative concept with the definitions of high, medium, and low varying from study to study. If the purpose is to determine relationships, a relative measure is adequate. However, comparisons among studies are difficult to make and, more importantly, such a technique does not permit absolute statements to be made. For example, it would be practical for personnel managers to know when a commute becomes stressful (perhaps, after traveling 90 minutes or distances greater than 50 miles or, perhaps, a combination of both) before attributing to it negative consequences.

Another contribution by the Novaco and Stokols group (Novaco et al., 1990) is the *physical impedance index*. Although others had previously employed specific objective characteristics of the commute as causing strain such as Taylor and Pockock's (1972) concept of commuting stages or the Gulian et al. (1989) designation of frustrating incidents such as being overtaken on the road, Novaco and colleagues were the first to provide an index of potential noxious stimuli (1990, 1991). The items in their index can be divided into two subscales: one tapping route characteristics and the other measuring travel constraints. The first includes such items as number of freeways, number of road exchanges, percentage of time and miles on freeways. Constraints include route choice, traffic jams, being slowed by traffic accidents, and traffic as a frequent inconvenience. Both subscales were found to be correlated with the objective physical impedance scale (i.e., time and distance). As the constraint scale is actually a subjective measure that is assessing the commuter's perceptions, it is a potentially important mediator. In Chapter 6, the concept of perception as used in social psychology will form one of the main pillars of our theoretical model.

The analysis of the components of commuting allows the researcher to visualize the commuting experience as incorporating critical elements that, individually, as well as collectively, influence the individual's reactions. Based on some recent findings by Koslowsky and Krausz (1993), this approach does yield a better picture of the elements that are at play during a commute.

Mode of Transportation

The mode of transportation, automobile or mass transportation, is another moderator that may influence the effects observed here and must be considered in order to understand the commuting process. As was already pointed out in the discussion on environmental stressors, the ability to control certain facets of a noxious stimulus may very well influence the reaction to the commuting experience. In the commuting context, control is related to the conveyance used to get to work or back home. In a bus, the commuter's control of the situation is limited, whereas in a car, perceived, if not actual control, is potentially much greater.

The obvious attachment of the American, as well as many others throughout the world, to the automobile has been a point of discussion in many popular as well as serious magazines and books. A good illustration of the sometimes irrational dependence on the automobile for getting to work was the situation in California following the earthquake in January, 1994. Although highways were partially destroyed and the use of some roads was nearly impossible, drivers still longed for the "freedom" associated with a car. In a graphic description of the state of affairs in the southern part of the state (One week later . . . , 1994), U.S. Transportation Secretary Frederico Pena stated that "Driving alone in your car is going to result in major gridlock and probably a four- or five-hour drive to downtown"; others were reported to have portrayed a simple 20-minute drive as turning into a 2-hour journey. Nevertheless, residents in the area of the earthquake continued to come to work by car. Those who didn't or couldn't were quite upset. For example, a worker who, for the first time, came to work by train was quoted in the previously mentioned article as saying, that without a car "my wings had been clipped."

From an environmental psychologist's perspective, the two types of commuters have completely different experiences. The physical surroundings of the user of mass transportation often consist of crowds, noise, pollution, space problems, and so forth. However, there are advantages, as well. A train or bus is controlled by someone else, and, at least as compared to when driving a vehicle, the commuter is free to relax during the journey. Concentration is not required, and, in cases where the noxious stimuli are tolerable, even sleep is a possibility.

On the other hand, the driver, particularly if unaccompanied by other passengers, must concentrate and actively participate in deciding how to get to work. The solo driver, in the process of minimizing many of the more noxious stimuli of the bus or train, exercises considerably greater actual or potential control of the environment than the former. However, particularly during rush hours, this potential for control often turns into a loss of control (i.e., neither the commuting time nor driving conditions are in the driver's control) and may result in great stress. Support for this contention was reported by Taylor and Pockock (1972), who found that the negative effects of commuting were greater for workers arriving with private cars than for users of public transportation (Taylor & Pocock, 1972).

In a study by Novaco and Sandeen (1992), specific attitudinal and physiological effects were measured for 138 subjects divided into three groups: solo drivers, ride-share drivers (defined as those who drove either a car pool or van pool), and ride-share passengers (defined as those who were passengers in either a car pool or a van pool) were compared. Their data suggested that ride-sharing mitigated to some degree several of the strain measures in their study. For male subjects, mean blood pressure and arterial pressure were higher for solo drivers than for ride-share passengers. However, the ride-share drivers were higher on both measures than the solo drivers. Although this finding was not explained by the authors, it may very well be that the ride-share driver is doubly affected, once as a driver and once as someone responsible for the safety of other passengers. In addition, it is difficult for the rideshare driver, as compared to the solo driver, to tune out other stimuli such as passenger noise or even involvement in discussions, some of which may not be to his or her liking or interest. These circumstances seem to enhance the prospects of negative commuting consequences.

On performance indices of digit–symbol copying, proofreading accuracy, and errors in proofreading, the trend for male subjects was in the expected direction with solo drivers always performing worst and rideshare passengers best. For female subjects, the trends were often not linear, and inferences were not possible. The authors concluded that in addition to the moderating effects of sex (discussed below), other personal and demographic variables are probably at play here.

In a recent study by Koslowsky and Krausz (1993), 682 nurses from several large hospitals in greater metropolitan Tel Aviv (Israel) representing 79% of the population of nurses in the area were mailed a questionnaire that contained several types of attitudinal, psychological, and demographic questions. The index of stress symptoms used here was based on the work of Pines, Aronson, and Kafry (1981). Originally intended as an indicator of burnout, the 15 items used were particularly appropriate as stress reactions to commuting: feeling tired, empty, calm, angry, mentally exhausted, guilty, moody, on the edge, drained physically, satisfied, frustrated, worried, drained of resources, somewhat depressed, and sad. For each question, the alternatives ranged from 1—"very rarely" to 5—"very often." Reliability for the entire scale, as measured by Cronbach α was .90.

Three short attitudinal scales measuring job satisfaction, commitment, and intention to leave were also used in the study. Analysis of the data showed that the mean time between home and work for the entire group was 32.1 minutes (SD = 15.7), and the two most frequently used modes of transportation were driving a car ($n = 173$) and public transportation ($n = 214$). Nearly all other subjects either walked or used more than one method of transportation and were not included in the analysis. In general, the trends in the two major subsamples (car drivers and users of public transportation) were quite similar. For example, the same pattern of correlations including the relatively high negative intercorrelations between satisfaction and intention to leave as well as between commitment and intention to leave were apparent in each subsample.

For those who drove to work, the authors reported a correlation between commuting time and stress of .23 ($p < .01$), as compared with .15 ($p < .05$) for those who used public transportation. For the car and mass transportation subjects, the correlations between commuting time and each of the dependent variables commitment, satisfaction, and intention to leave were all somewhat lower. The results of a comparison t-test, however, were not significant.

From these studies, there appears to be some partial support for assuming that the commuting experience is more stressful for car drivers than for bus or train users. The effect, however, is moderate, and other variables need to be considered before a causal model of commuting can be delineated. One last theoretical word on this topic from a tangential area of social psychology may be informative. Conceptually, the solo driver's experience fits into a model of privacy as originally described by Altman (1975) and cited by Darley and Gilbert (1985) as one of the direct applications of social psychology in applied environmental concerns. When viewed as a goal, privacy implies a desired level of social stimulation. It is an active pursuit by the individual so as to obtain the appropriate amount of social interaction for him or her. For many car drivers, this is the reason, against all logical arguments to the contrary, to continue to drive to work when the alternatives are often cheaper, more efficient, more relaxing, and ecologically desirable.

Gender

It appears that for many investigations in the field, the gender of the subjects was a salient variable that likely influenced the strength of the association. A closer examination of some of the these findings may help in providing some clues to the underlying process. In their study of the influence of mode of transportation on performance, attitudinal, and physiological measures, Novaco and Sandeen (1992) also examined gender as an independent variable and in interaction with mode of transportation. When the dependent variable was job involvement, an interaction effect was found. As compared to men, women solo drivers were more job involved, whereas ride-sharing women were less job involved. Significant interactions were also observed when the dependent variables were mean arterial pressure, digit–symbol copying, and proofreading measures. Examination of the mean values showed that, generally, solo-driver women and ride-share driver women did better than men, but ride-share passenger women did worse than their male counterparts.

In the Novaco et al. (1991) study, gender was found to be a relatively strong moderator. For many of the emotional and attitudinal indicators in the study, women in a high-impedance group (long distances accompanied by higher than average traveling times) appraised their commute as being significantly more negative than men. When describing their trip to work in the morning, the women were delayed more often by traffic jams, felt less able to avoid traffic, and, generally, felt more dissatisfied with their commutes.

The authors used the literature from several different disciplines to help support their contention that commuting is experienced differently by women. Sociologists and personnel specialists assume that the trip to work for working women is more complex because of the need to juggle domestic/household duties with their activities outside the home. For example, picking up the children from school, dropping him or her (them) off at the dentist or at after school clubs must be coordinated with all other pursuits including a career. An interesting piece of work by Frankenhauser et al. (1989) showed that women managers took much longer to "unwind" after work than men. Whereas men's blood pressure readings reverted rather quickly to normal levels after a day's work, women's blood pressure levels tended to stay high for greater periods of time after work. Two other secretions also indicated greater strain level for women: (1) as compared to men, the cortisol level for women showed smaller increases, and (2) women showed a significant increase in norepinephrine excretion.

In trying to explain the findings, Novaco et al. (1991) stated that investigators in other contexts have also found women to be more reactive than men across roles (Bromet, Dew, & Parkinson, 1990; Eckenrode & Gore, 1990). For example, in a study using blue-collar women, Bromet et al. (1990) reported that their female subjects were exhausted after work, which the authors felt might lead to other negative behavioral effects such as difficulty in doing housework and cooking.

The reason for the greater level of strain reactions in women is probably confounded with several other observed relationships including the following: (1) as compared to the morning rush hour, the trip from work to home is longer (see Spyridakis et al., 1991); (2) the commonly held notion that women, even in the more egalitarian society that exists today, are still the ones generally involved with family chores; and (3) as a consequence of the above, time pressures are more a part of life for women than men.

There are women who have started businesses at home because they could not tolerate the long distance between home and work. In quoting from a federally sponsored survey of commuting conducted by Kathleen Christensen, professor of environmental psychology at the Graduate School of the City University of New York, Lawson (1991) found that many more women than men make job decisions based on accessibility to home. Her conclusions were drawn from a federally financed survey of 14,000 women working at home in New York, San Francisco, and Chicago in 1985.

Christensen added that commuting tended to be much more problematical for mothers than it was for fathers because women are still primarily responsible for the practical, logistical, and emotional organization of the home and family. For commuting mothers who are new in a community, with no support network, the family and working balance are especially difficult. This conceptualization of commuting for mothers is consistent with the suggestion that women may find not only the stressors associated with the trip to work or home as stressful, but just the very fact that they have to commute may in itself be stressful. The observed stress level of women commuters is thus a function of many personal and demographic variables separately and in combination. Further research disentangling some of these variables would help in explaining the moderating effects of sex on strain.

Commuting Couples

Related to the issue of gender as a moderator are the problems associated with commuting couples. Over the past decade, the professional, as well as the popular literature, have examined several aspects of this issue. The investigators in the field have tried to identify the characteristics of the commute that may have negative meaning for husband and wife, individually and as a couple. Commuting couples is the phrase that has come to describe the phenomenon. As defined in the literature (Gerstel & Gross, 1984; Winfield, 1985), the partners in a commuting couple are geographically separated from each other but do get together in a common domicile at various time intervals. It appears that the distance aspect of the commute is the causal agent here. The very facts that partners travel to different locations to work and may not see each other for a period of time (ranging from a day to a few days and, in some cases, even a few weeks) are associated with possible negative psychological and social consequences. The greater the separation, the greater the negative effect. In a study of commuting couples in Canada, Driedger (1987) found that some of the manifestations of this lifestyle were loneliness, guilt caused by being away from children during their growing years, and poor spousal communication as a result of the lack of understanding by significant others of the need to commute. In addition, exhaustion, an irregular sex life, and feelings of social isolation were commonly expressed.

An investigation by Govaerts and Dixon (1988) also showed that married commuters experienced more difficulties with affective communication and greater dissatisfaction with time spent together. This issue has now become a major consideration in determining job locations, transfers, and promotions. In a study of executive decision making regarding dual career couples, executives' reactions to job transfers were significantly affected by the couple's attitude toward the move and the presence of a commuter marriage. Taylor and Lounsbury (1988) inferred from their findings that the decision to transfer employees must take into account the fact that spouses may have to travel separately to work and be away from each other for extended periods.

A more direct impact of commuting for couples, in particular for those living in the suburbs, is the change that has taken place in the mother's role in the family. For many mothers, commuting has added a new and complicated dimension to their life. In the previous generation, mothers who decided to work lived near their place of employment. It is even possible to argue that the original suburban–urban distinction was based on a division of sexes: the mother would stay home and take care of the children, whereas the father boarded the train or got into the car and went to work in the city. As always, the suburbs require a car because some of the basic needs, including shopping, doctors and medical facilities, schools, and leisure activities or conveniences, are not within walking distance or a short train/bus ride away. As originally conceived, the space inside and outside the home, the fresh air, and the other amenities of a suburban lifestyle more than made up for the long ride to work of the father. The mother was around to take care of the family's needs.

Today, however, a great many suburban women who have children are working, and a lot of them are commuting to offices far from home. In order to survive, they leave behind a maze of car-pooling arrangements and appointments and contingency plans for their children to keep their busy lives running smoothly and to take care of the children in an emergency. Lawson (1991) states that some commuting mothers say their lives are not all that different from the lives of working mothers everywhere, with the constant pressures to schedule and juggle and oversee the daily details of home and families. But others, writes Lawson, complain that the distance factor makes life harder.

Working a great distance from home, and being dependent on trains or buses that do not always run frequently, can add all sorts of complications, big and small, to a parent's life. The distance factor also reduces time spent at home with the family, and it leaves little room for error when arrangements on the home front break down. Researchers say that some women find the combination of commuting to work and raising children (especially when the family has more than one child) so stressful and time-consuming that they eventually look for alternatives, such as part-time work or jobs close to home or located in the home.

Driving Stress as a Dependent Variable

Gulian et al. (1989) took a novel approach in their studies of commuting. Unlike most other researchers in the field, they considered driving stress as a dependent variable that can be explained by some of the variables discussed above. Although we have referred to the effects of commuting stress as strain, Gulian et al. wanted to understand what are the elements that comprise driving stress. Using factor analysis to examine the driving behavior inventory, they identified the following factors in their driving stress measure: driving aggression, dislike of driving, tension and frustration connected with successful or unsuccessful overtaking, irritation when overtaken, and heightened alertness and concentration. In addition, family problems, work-related worries, personal variables, experience, and life stresses are potential correlates or predictors of driving stress.

From their perspective, the driver's response to a particularly troublesome stimulus or situation is a function of personality variables (e.g., locus of control), life hassles (stemming from the job and from the family), and the appraisal of the unique environmental situation confronting the driver at the moment. In the latter category are behaviors such as tailgating or stop-and-go traffic, which interact with the other predictors to cause driver stress. Interestingly, it is the use of the term "driver" rather than "driving" stress that best exemplifies the Gulian approach. The latter term would indicate only an effect related to the experience in the car, whereas the former term refers to all possible influences that accompany the commuter on his or her journey to work.

Lifestyle

Commuting has many other effects that are difficult to quantify, and precise data concerning some of these variables have rarely been examined in the literature. For example, Borzo (1992) stated that, at least as far as physicians are concerned, commuting is an important element in deciding which home to choose and, indeed, which job to take. Leisure time, family time, and the hour that the physician rises for work are all a consequence of that "stretch of minutes and even hours linking home and office" (p. 30).

In a study of undergraduate students' reactions to commuting, Wilson, Anderson, and Fleming (1987) found that commuting subjects displayed poorer personal adjustment and greater overinvolvement with parents than their counterparts in residence halls at the university. The implications for these findings are quite important as they may imply that students who are commuting on a near daily basis between home and school are worse off socially, and, perhaps more importantly, this disadvantage may also lead to greater academic difficulties. Well-designed studies here may yield some conclusions that are potentially useful in deciding between a dorm life and commuting. In another study that examined the psychological effects of the transition to university for dormitory students and home-based students, the results were not as clear. Fisher and Hood (1987) reported that both groups had increased levels of psychological disturbances and cognitive failure following the shift to university life. In addition, subjects who reported to be homesick were particularly vulnerable to the emotional problems identified in the study.

Information Costs

A different and somewhat innovative approach to understanding the commuting experience, and, particularly, the reason why people choose one mode of travel rather than another was suggested by Flannelly and Mcleod (1989). They argued that the information costs involved in arranging a trip involve time and effort, which encourages people to use the means of transportation that minimize this variable. In areas of the country where a well-regulated mass transportation system exists, such costs are actually lower for bus or train users than they are for car users. This can be explained by the fact that a train that arrives at the station and at a destination according to a schedule actually involves less effort by the commuter than does using a car. In the latter situation, the commuter must often be aware of traffic patterns, the critical car gauges (oil, gas, battery functioning, etc.), and weather conditions. As compared to the bus passenger, the driver of the automobile must expend considerably more mental, if not physical, energy to arrive at work. In a sense, such information costs and expenditure of energy are contributors to the stress associated with commuting of any type, but, with the harried and forced deadlines that are so characteristic of arrival to work during the rush hour, a commuter may prefer to let someone else do the driving and worrying. (This is, in a sense, a paraphrase of the argument often stated by the Greyhound bus company in their advertising campaigns.)

Nevertheless, based on the data collected from more than 600 subjects, Flannelly and Mcleod (1989) pointed out that the commuting situation is in complete contrast to that of a regular trip such as to a leisure destination, shopping, or a visit to a friend. Here, the automobile turns out to be more efficient, at least, in terms of information cost. The solo driver just gets into the car when he or she wants, does not need to check any schedule or to determine times of departure, costs, and drop-off points. The hassle, in this case, is associated with taking a bus or train.

SOME RECENT STUDIES

The first two authors of this book have spent the last few years developing their theory of commuting both in Israel and in the United States. Several presentations and papers have resulted, and we now discuss the two latest efforts that have not yet been published in the professional literature. The basic premise of this body of work is that moderators as well mediators are essential in understanding the commuting process. As these studies were critical in developing the model to be discussed in Chapter 6, the method, results, and conclusions will be presented in some detail here. In many ways the studies are typical of ones done by others, but they also build on previous research so they can serve as paradigms for future investigations in the field.

The first study by Kluger (1992) was based on findings reported at the APA/NIOSH meetings and focused mostly on the question of operationalizing one of the important moderators in the field of stress, control, or the more appropriate term in commuting, predictability. The second study, based on a paper presented by Aizer and Koslowsky (1993), was concerned with several issues that were brought up by previous researchers and employed structural equation methodology to try to get at cause–effect models in the commuting process.

In order to understand the background to Kluger's work, we need to present the various perspectives of control in the stress literature, in general, and commuting, in particular.

Control of the Environment

When referring to control, we can distinguish between actual or perceived control. (Actually, the word job control is the more common term; however, we use the term without the adjective so as to allow a more general use of the term; see, e.g., McClaney & Hurrell, 1988.) Actual control does not need to be exercised, if the person feels that there is a possibility of control that may be sufficient to lower strain responses. Both have been shown to be significant moderators (Landy, 1992).

Interestingly, not all researchers hold the view that job control acts as a moderator variable in stress studies. In a focused study of the relationship between traffic congestion and measures of assorted physiological indicators, Evans and Carrere (1991) indicated that perceived job control served as a mediator. They argued that similar to the findings reported by others (e.g., Sauter et al., 1989), perceived job control is an essential variable in producing the impression of a stressful environment and yielding physiological changes. Thus, for bus drivers, perceived job control was reduced as a result of the environmental stressor, traffic congestion. Such traffic conditions curtail the driver's ability to adjust driving speeds as well as the ability to change lanes during driving. The bus driver may feel a loss of control in that staying on schedule becomes much more difficult even though its importance for the job is quite obvious.

Although it is possible to consider perceived job control or control of the environment as a mediator, the usual convention will be used here. Most theorists, including Evans himself (Evans & Cohen, 1987) in another study recognize the potential role of control as a moderator. In the discussion section of their carefully conducted study, after stating that psychologists, by and large, consider this variable a moderator, they assert that their findings indicate that control functions as a mediator without presenting statistical evidence that it is not a moderator.

Nevertheless, their inferences can easily be applied to the general commuter, not only the bus driver, and control of the environment can be shown to act as a moderator variable. In such a formulation, the stressor, in this case traffic congestion, interacts with control so that under conditions of low traffic congestion, the commuter is not even aware of the control (or lack of control) in his or her environment. However, when traffic congestion gets to be high, the commuter suddenly becomes aware of a lack of control, and the negative consequence is heightened. Thus, on the way to home or work, the commuter may have a time schedule self-imposed or imposed by others. During the rush hours, the driver may be in less control as the traffic provides a formidable obstacle that is difficult to overcome. Just as would be expected from a normal commuter's experience, the bus drivers in their study showed less job control during peak traffic conditions. As these are fundamental constructs, we now develop them by citing theories and findings in other contexts and see if they can be applied here.

Actual and Perceived Control

In making the statement that perceived control is a moderator, we are implying that high levels of perceived control change or modify the negative impact of impedance on strain. This is based on voluminous laboratory literature showing that perceived control often moderates the effects of a variety of stressors on strain (e.g., Glass & Singer, 1972; Thompson, 1981; for exceptions, see a review by Burger, 1989). For Murphy (1988), it is one of the critical ingredients in stress reduction or coping. Thus, control can be viewed either as a method for preventing strain or as a legitimate intervention (i.e., treatment) after negative consequences have already appeared. In this regard, Murphy argues that from the available data it seems that it is less stressful never to have had control over a situation than to have had it and then to lose it (p. 324). For many organizational intervention procedures, this is a cardinal proposition. When increased worker control is introduced, it should not be for a temporary period. Rather the organization that has decided to make changes for the purposes of greater worker control must make a long-term commitment and either give the worker actual control or perceived control.

In another context, Karasek (1979; Karasek & Theorell, 1990) formulated a job strain model that is particularly appropriate for commuting. In this approach, a combination of high demands (high stress) and low decision latitude (low control) causes strain, but either low decision latitude or high job demands alone do not cause strain. For our purposes, a simple adjustment must be made: it is not necessary to exercise actual control but rather perceived control is adequate to act as a moderator.

The research on the influence of perceived control in moderating commute-induced stress is mostly mixed. Several researchers have considered it a personality variable and others as a measure with objective criteria. Schaefer et al. (1988) conceptualized control in terms of choice of number of routes available (one or more), and in terms of control over the inside of the car (driving alone vs. car-pool situation). Their findings did not support the research hypotheses. Instead, the results surprisingly suggested that, under high impedance conditions, drivers who had more choice (control) had higher stress (i.e., poor performance) than drivers who had less choice, and that those who drove alone (more control) reported higher level of hostility and anxiety than those who had less control. These results indicated that those who had more control, which was operationalized in two ways, suffered more from a stressful commute. Yet, car-pool drivers (less control) had a marginally higher blood pressure in high-impedance conditions as predicted. In addition, Novaco et al. (1990) reported a preliminary analysis of the role of choices in moderating the effects of impedance but did not obtain the moderating effect. The inconsistency in the findings regarding the role of control could be attributed both to the operationalization of control and to the lack of statistical power. Each of these possibilities is discussed below.

Given that it has been reasonably demonstrated that commute is a stressor, it is surprising that perceived control was not found to moderate its effects. In research areas other than commute, voluminous literature has shown that perceived control moderates the effects of a variety of stressors on well-being, performance, and affective responses. According to the definition proposed by Karasek (1979), it is possible that the circumstances surrounding the commute were such that the combination of low control with high environmental stress had not yet reached the critical point where it would adversely affect the individual.

Another explanation for the poor previous findings may be related to the operationalization of the construct. Control is a construct with several components and, in practice, is often difficult to define (e.g., Seligman & Miller, 1979). The constructs that are typically associated with control are choice and freedom, actual as well as perceived. Applying these constructs to commuting is quite difficult. First, many commuters can exercise vary little control over the stressor, that is, short of not commuting, people have to endure the stressful situation without being able to terminate it. Second, commuters who *do* have a choice (e.g., of routes, as in Schaefer et al., 1988) may not really feel that choice helps very much, especially during the rush hours. In addition, Kehoe (1979) suggested that it is the quality of the choices that contributes to perceived choice and not the mere presence of choice. Therefore, it is reasonable to expect, as Schaeffer et al. found, that the ability to choose among unattractive routes or methods to work does not increase perceived choice. Furthermore, it is possible that the reverse may very well occur. The commuter put into a situation of choosing between undesirable alternatives may indeed experience more, not less, stress.

Given the lack of real control over the situation or the poor choices available to most commuters, individuals may still experience a sense or perception of control if they can predict the duration of the (aversive) experience. Seligman and Miller (1979) suggested that cultures do not emphasize the importance of personal control when the control of their environment is indeed not available to them. Under such circumstances, people opt for the second best, that is, predictability. In addition, it was observed in laboratory studies that human subjects threatened by electric shock preferred predicting its onset rather than receiving it unexpectedly (Averill, 1973), although this preference was moderated by personality in one study (Miller, 1987) and the amount of attention paid to the predictor in another study (Burger, 1989). (In contrast to human research, it should be noted that animal studies of predictability and stress have not yielded consistent results, and the role of several artifacts and moderators in the relationship is quite ambiguous; see, for example, Abbot & Baida, 1986; Arthur, 1986.)

This aspect of predictability (or lack of) has ramifications in many actual driving situations and is well illustrated in the commute confronting urban dwellers such as New Yorkers daily. Foderaro (1991) describes the problems associated with the drive over the Tappan Zee Bridge, one of the largest and most congested arteries leading into the New York metropolitan area. The commuter's daily trek to work across this bridge is responsible for anger and rage and is a major contributor to stress. In quoting an engineering expert with the New York State Department of Transportation, Foderaro cites unpredictability as the big problem associated with the commute. One day it may take 20 minutes to get to work, the next day it may take an hour, and the following day it may take 40 minutes. Crossing the bridge should take no longer than 5 minutes but has been known to take as much as 68 minutes. This variability associated with commuting prevents an individual from planning his or her arrival time at home or at work and leaves the control of the situation in the hands of another source such as the environment or fellow drivers. Unpredictability appears to be the manifestation of lack of control in the commuting predicament.

The converse of predictability is uncertainty. This latter concept has been invoked by several researchers to help explain the relationship between job environmental factors and strain. In an atmosphere where the organizational climate fosters uncertainty, perhaps resulting from a lack of information, strain reactions are a likely outcome (Carayon, 1992). McGrath (1976) has referred to the "uncertainty of outcomes" felt by workers as being partly responsible for negative physiological and behavioral consequences. To paraphrase what we have argued about predictability above, Carayon (p. 29) wrote that "experienced (what we call perceived) stress does not result from a misfit between the perceived demand and the perceived ability to cope with it but rather from the uncertainty of meeting the demand."

Furthermore, Jackson (1989) has contended that much of the stress observed in organizational settings is to a large extent a function of uncertainty. In their article on the relationship between managing stress and uncertainty, Schuler and Jackson (1986) cite environmental stressors as one of the main origins of uncertainty. Although they did not consider non-work-place variables such as the commuting experience in their catalog of stressors, Landy (1992, p. 125) feels that many of these other types of stressors can involve inadequate knowledge about an event.

Although traditionally the uncertainty referred to in organizational settings alludes to task clarity or job ambiguity, it can easily be applied to the case of commuting also. Here, the entry into the mode of transportation chosen to get to work is fraught with uncertainty and lack of predictability. The weather, new construction on the road, a sports event that puts any more people on the road than usual, a delayed or broken train are all quite unpredictable. As a matter of fact, the uncertainty in the situation is the most predictable part, and this is often the complaint echoed by many commuters. "The car ahead of me was in an accident" or "They canceled the 8:03 out of Huntington" are the typical complaints heard from the commuter. Such occurrences lay the groundwork for negative reactions by the commuter.

For the commuting situation, it is expected that perceived stress, as well as other attitudinal and behavioral consequences, are all functions of the interaction between the objective commuting parameters and its predictability. For our purposes, control will be defined as predictability. The more the commuter knows what's in store for him or her during the commute, the less likely it is to produce a perception of stress, even if the objective measures of the commute would indicate that a stressful commute is ahead. In other words, a commute that has all the characteristics of being stressful (i.e, long distance and excessive time) should result in fewer negative effects than that of an unpredictable commute with similar objective characteristics.

Besides accompanying the commuter at the outset of his or her trip to work or home, a relatively predictable commute may become less so in any particular situation. Thus, the commuter who knows that the car ride to work takes about 30 minutes each day, may suddenly confront a traffic jam that, for this commuter, is unusual. As time goes by and the commuter is not made aware of the reasons for the delay, let alone its expected duration, a stressor variable, so-called "state" unpredictability (borrowing the distinction popularized by Spielberger et al., 1979) is created. Unlike the consistent version of this moderator, "trait" unpredictability, an individual on any one day may be stressed, and it behooves the researcher to determine this in order to be able to predict reactions on any specific day.

Apart from problems with operationalization and conceptualization of the job control variable, past studies with the control variable as a moderator often suffered from one or more statistical weaknesses. These shortcomings include sample sizes that afford little statistical power, that is, $N < 100$ (e.g., Schaefer et al., 1988), statistical techniques that reduced power, for example, dichotomized measures of impedance (Schaefer et al., 1988; Stokols et al., 1978), and, as we saw in the previous chapter, failure to report statistical tests altogether. Statistical consideration of power becomes particularly important when testing a moderator effect (see Bobko, 1990).

Operationalization of Commute Predictability

The measure can be operationalized in several ways, and this was one of the major purposes of a study recently conducted by Kluger (1992). As with previous studies that have not yet been published in professional journals, the design and findings from the study will be presented in some detail.

In Kluger's survey study, questionnaire responses were elicited from 411 commuters, mostly from the New Jersey area. The following scales were included in their study: a perceived scale of commuting stress, commuter choices, commuter well-being symptoms, and commute predictability. The author argued that commute predictability, rather than choice, would correlate with symptoms. Also, predictability would interact with stress perception in predicting symptoms.

As the concept of predictability had not been examined in a commuter setting previously, Kluger (1992) developed three separate indices. First, each respondent was asked "On the average, how much time does it take you to commute to work? —— minutes." This question was repeated for less-typical days by asking "On a BAD day, how much time . . . " and "On a GOOD day . . . " This series of three questions was repeated for commuting *from* work to home, also. For each respondent, a mean and standard deviation for the response for each question was calculated. The within-standard deviation of time was one index of predictability: The higher the standard deviation, the lower is the predictability.

Second, respondents rated a list of factors that affected their commute time on a 6-point scale. These factors were extra heavy traffic, weather, time of day, day of the week, time of the year, accidents, choice of routes, school buses, and different destinations. There were other factors mentioned in an open-ended question (e.g., toll booths, traffic lights), but the items reported on this open-ended question were not answered by most of the respondents, and therefore they were not included in the second Kluger index. The other responses to this set of questions were summed to form an index where the more these factors affect the commuter's travel time, the lower is the commute predictability.

The third index consisted of one item that measured on a 6-point scale how badly the weather affected their commute. The author decided to combine these three indices by standardizing them and then calculating their average. This then was Kluger's measure of unpredictability. The Cronbach coefficient α for the scale was .71, which was quite acceptable especially since the scales were really measuring different aspects of unpredictability in the commuting experience.

As Kluger was mainly interested in examining the moderating role of "control" on the relationship between stress and strain, the author chose the traditional measure of "choices" to compare with "predictability" as defined above. As stated before, having more (bad) choices does not provide the commuter with a sense of control. The "choice" index was operationalized as the sum of "yes" responses to the following four questions: "I decide what type of transportation I use to commute"; "Other means of transportation to work is available to me"; "I can only take one route to work" (recoding required here); and "Do you have flexible hours at your job?" The score on the scale ranged from 0 to 4.

The symptoms scale is based on 15 common complaints that people report as a result of their commute: headaches; stiff muscles/neck; sleeplessness; irritability; increased heart beat; sweaty palms; feeling tired a great deal of the time; motion sickness; difficulty focusing attention; lower-back pain; tension; feeling angry often; upset stomach; nervousness; and other. An overall well-being measure was created by summing the number of symptoms checked as well as examining the effects on each item separately.

The major hypotheses of the study were examined by using moderated regression analysis with each of the 15 symptoms serving as a dependent measure and the addition of the interaction term (product of perceived commute stress and commute unpredictability) to the main effects as the indication of a significant interaction term. All regression coefficients for each of the interaction effects were significant. Not surprisingly, the composite measure of number of symptoms reported yielded the strongest effect (most likely the result of better distribution and reliability).

The findings showed that commute choice predicted in the direction opposite to predictability—the more choices the commuter had, the greater the perceived stress. More importantly, number of choices did not interact with perceived commute stress in affecting total number of symptoms reported. The interaction term was also tested against each of the individual symptoms and showed only two significant results (just barely), which could be attributed to chance alone. Finally, each of the choice items composing the index was tested as a moderator of number of symptoms reported. This was done to test whether the beneficial effect of some of the individual choices was masked by the choice index. Again none of these interaction terms reached significance.

Kluger (1992) concluded from his study that operationalizing control as commute choices does not moderate the effects of commute stress on well-being. This supported Kehoe's (1979) argument that, when the choices available (to car commuters) are poor, a sense of psychological control is not created. Indeed, the more choices the commuters had, the higher the perceived commute stress they reported (even when average commute time was partialed out). It appeared from the Kluger study that predictability serves as a cognitive control mechanism that protects the commuter from the ill effects of the commute.

In the Aizer and Koslowsky (1993) study, the investigators were interested in identifying several aspects of the links among commuting, stress, and outcomes. It was the first study in the field that used structural equation modeling to describe the directions and the values associated with each of the paths. As part of his M.A. thesis, Aizer developed a series of hypotheses that were based on previous research findings in the field. In addition, several new instruments that were necessary for examining the hypotheses were developed in the study.

The following hypotheses were tested: (1) The correlations between commuting measures and perceived stress will be greater than the correlations between commuting measures and attitudes or behavior. By commuting measures, the authors are referring to time, distance, and predictability. The latter was defined as the difference in minutes between time to work on a good day and time on a bad day. (2) Burnout is an intervening variable between perceived stress and outcomes such as work attitudes and intentions to leave. (3) The model of the effects of commuting stress on outcome variables, attitudinal as well as behavioral, must include intervening variables such as perceived stress, perceived control, and burnout.

In order to test the hypotheses, the authors obtained demographic, attitudinal, and behavioral data from 200 workers at a large service organization in Israel (Aizer & Koslowsky, 1993). The attitudinal data were obtained by questionnaire/interview. The experimenter (Aizer) administered each of the scales individually by waiting with each subject while the latter completed the questionnaire. This assured a very low rate of missing data (less than 10%). The sickness data were obtained from the personnel files of the organization. Cooperation was assured by first contacting head of personnel, then individual department managers, and finally each individual worker who participated. The goals of the study were explained, respondents were asked if they would be willing to volunteer, and only then was a meeting set up for conducting the interviews.

The scales used by the researchers included the following: commuting characteristics including: distance, time on a good day, time on an average day, and time on a bad day; stress perceptions about the commute; perceptions of control about arriving at work; job satisfaction; desire to quit; burnout; absenteeism; lateness; and demographic items.

Structural equation modeling with the LISREL program was used for analyzing the data, and findings were generally supportive of the study hypothesis. Results showed that the best model depicts a path that shows the influence of the commuting experience on worker functioning is generally indirect. The direct model did not provide a good fit, but the indirect model that included variables such as stress perception, control perception, and burnout did provide a good fit. Models were successfully formulated for job satisfaction, desire to quit, and absenteeism.

6

Theory and Model Development

Among the major difficulties with research in the field of commuting are the incompatible conceptualizations of the process that has spawned inconsistent or unstable findings. As we saw in the previous chapters, the independent variables, the dependent variables, and the linkages among them frequently differed across studies. This fact, more than any other, has contributed to the ambiguity in the field and has been partly responsible for the inherent difficulty in drawing definitive conclusions. The criticism leveled at social sciences that worthwhile inferences from the data available in a specific field are often nonexistent is an old one and is a legitimate frustration felt within and without the discipline. It is this (sometimes, sad) state of affairs, more than any other reason, that has been responsible for the popularity of techniques such as meta-analysis over the past decade (Hunter & Schmidt, 1990).

Hunter and Schmidt, two of the major methodologists in the field of meta-analysis, have stated that accumulating knowledge without some method of organizing the information intelligently leads nowhere in social science research (1990). The practitioner, as well as the researcher, can only implement previous results in the field or in the laboratory if the state of knowledge is such that conclusions have a relatively firm basis. Without such an approach, we are "just spinning wheels." Any advance in a discipline requires a stepwise approach where each stage is built on the previous one. Hunter and Schmidt (1990, p. 13) write that there are two ways of cumulating knowledge: "(1) the cumulation of knowledge across studies to establish facts, and (2) the formation of theories to organize facts into a coherent and useful form."

Commuting research is not yet at the stage where enough studies have been conducted to allow meta-analytic techniques to be meaningful (too many unique conditions with too few studies for any particular condition). However, the recent attempts by Novaco and colleagues (1979, 1990) to carry out a series of commuter-related studies have blazed a trail that should allow an integrative type of research to be possible in the near future. At present, we pursue the second mode suggested by Hunter and Schmidt (1990) for deriving inferences and develop a theory that is built on previous formulations, such as that set forth by Novaco et al. (1979) but also includes some new ideas for tying together some loose theoretical ends and for future empirical testing.

A general theoretical framework within which commuting research seems to fit is outlined. Afterwards, mediators and some new moderators, derived from theoretical considerations (many of them not examined previously) are proposed as possible aids in explaining relationships described in the literature. By including some fresh concepts, we will attempt to reconcile some of the previously reported inconsistencies. Also, these concepts may prove useful for generating studies along somewhat different lines than heretofore seen in the field. Finally, in Chapter 9, it is our intention to discuss some of the methodological issues involved with testing the model, and suggestions for operationalizing some of the new constructs in the formulation will be delineated.

As we have seen in previous chapters, the study of commuting stress is part of the general topic of environmental stress but contains many features that are unique to this area of research. Whereas the source of most stimuli in the traditional social/environmental context is outside the individual, the origins of commuting problems are, at least, partially within the commuter. Thus, the length of the trip, the time it takes to complete the journey, the mode of transportation chosen and its implications are controlled, to a large extent, by the driver or passenger. Obviously, the environment plays a crucial role in determining the type and amount of stimulus to which the commuter will be exposed. Nevertheless, it is clear that for a thorough understanding of the dynamics at play in the commuting experience, the personal variables, including demographics, personality, and perceptions, of the driver or passenger must be considered.

The approach that appears most productive and may very well allow for explaining a large percentage of the variance observed in commuter reactions is to examine the interface between environment and individual. Although the potential responses to a traffic jam in a polluted and noisy area or a long ride on a crowded train are typical of the descriptions found in basic studies on environmental stressors, the moderators and mediators characteristic of both the specific commuting experience and the individual play a crucial role in the process. Researchers who sometimes

THEORY AND MODEL DEVELOPMENT

reported nonsignificant relationships were actually dealing with only portions of the model. For example, one series of findings in the field of stress has clearly indicated that in order for a study to be complete it had to examine the affects of gender on the relationship between stressors and strain (Frankenhaueser, 1975).

In addition, newer and more sophisticated techniques for studying relationships cross-sectionally and longitudinally either not available or unknown to most researchers before the 1970s provide an opportunity to examine the links or paths leading from stressor to strain. Structural equation models with software programs such as LISREL or EQS provide an opportunity to study paths that lead to specific outcomes of interest (Bentler, 1989; Joreskog & Sorbom, 1989). As both indirect and direct effects are responsible for any observed findings, structural equations allow the investigator to obtain all the relevant influences that impact on a dependent measure. The structural equations technique, along with multiple regression analysis, will be used for testing the influence of intervening variables including moderators and mediators. In Chapter 9, several methodological issues pertaining to the analysis of parts of the model are discussed in greater detail, and the necessary cautions one should be aware of before drawing inferences are presented.

RELEVANT STRESS THEORIES

In order to understand the commuting process, the model presented below is built from several theories that are relevant to stress inquiry in general and commuting in particular. At this stage of research in the field, with only a few adequately executed studies available, it would be too risky to focus on only one approach. Rather, our comprehensive model integrates ideas from several theories. The connection between stress stimuli and strain responses is quite complex. Many of the concepts in the model are drawn from other contexts in social and industrial psychology, including environmental stress theories. They have met with some modicum of success in both the laboratory and the field, and by combining compatible features, a model relevant to the commuting process will be delineated.

Person–Environment Fit

One approach that seems particularly relevant to commuting, although it has generally not been part of other environmental stress theories, is person–environment fit. The concept of person–environment fit has been around for several years and has spawned many articles on the mechanism by which the interaction between these variables may be the cause of different types of strain response (French, Caplan, & van Harrison, 1982). As applied to the stress process, we can borrow the following notion: "[the] perceived substantial imbalance between demands and response capabilities under conditions where failure to meet demands has important perceived consequences" (Landy, 1985, p. 544).

The advantages of using such a theory here are obvious. It provides a very apt description of what takes place in a commuting situation. According to Edwards and van Harrison (1993), person–environment (P–E) fit can be looked at from two perspectives: "the extent to which the rewards and supplies provided by the environment match the needs and preferences of the person, and the other representing the extent to which the demands and other requirements of the environment match the skills and abilities of the person" (p. 628). In understanding the commuting process from the P–E perspective, the second definition applies. Because of the commute, many of the demands made on the commuter are often difficult to meet. Thus, a job requirement to arrive on time so as not to invoke the wrath of the boss or the multitudinous potentially noxious environmental stimuli during the trip, all require responses from the individual. When the individual has only limited ability to cope, a strain response of one type or the other may manifest itself.

However, the findings with person–environment theory have been mixed (Landy, 1985), especially when one tries to apply the French et al. (1982) model. In a recent article on the relationship between P–E fit and strain, Edwards and van Harrison (1993) went beyond the original French et al. (1982) approach to investigate the relationship in three-dimensional space. They argued that the relationship between P–E and strain may not be linear, and other functions must be considered.

In the field of commuting stress, it seems that the theory is too broad, and often specific hypotheses are difficult to prove conclusively in either direction. We have added several aspects to this theory to help specify those points of interaction that are particularly likely to contribute to strain response. In this larger formulation, these added considerations play the role of mediators and can be posited as explanatory mechanisms.

Expectancies

The expectancies associated with driving to work or being driven by someone else are a feature of the P–E interaction that is particularly relevant here. Such a variable may be considered as either the independent variable of a commute study or a mediator between other variables. In such a cause–effect model, the gap between expectation and reality may be one of the causal variables that influences the individual's reaction.

THEORY AND MODEL DEVELOPMENT

Although we are not referring here to the usual version of expectation theories of motivation as introduced by Vroom (1964) and extended by Porter and Lawler (1968), it may be possible to borrow some facets of their theory for our purposes. The latter authors assumed that a person's actions are rational and are directed so as to maximize the chances of achieving the most desirable goals. Their innovative conception of motivation theory in an organizational context analyzed not only what a person thinks but also how the work environment interacts with this thought process so as to influence job performance.

In the present context, we are referring to a person's mind set when a commuting experience is planned. The estimates and evaluations formulated by the individual are, to a large extent, a function of past events. Thus, a commuter who lives close to work expects that a trip will take less time for him or her than for an individual who lives far away. Another expectancy held by many commuters involves a self-comparison with one's own previous experiences. Thus, if a bus ride should take only 35 minutes and during a particular commute, it has lasted more than an hour already, this event has now turned into a stressful experience. Interestingly, a second bus passenger who normally commutes for an hour or more may not react at all to such a ride, even though in absolute terms the rides of the two people are the same.

Whether knowledge and failed expectations will cause a strain response is dependent on many other factors. Brehm and Kassin (1990) feel that the reactions to failed expectations are formed from attributions made by people about the world around them, are a function of individual differences, and are, by their very nature, situation-specific. For us, this implies that without specifying the appropriate moderators and mediators, predictions of who will suffer negative effects are inaccurate.

Following the approach suggested by Brehm and Kassin (1990), we further propose that expectation in a commuting context influences two other indicators: perception of the commuting experience and the actual or perceived control that the driver or passenger can exercise. The first of these includes the mediator variable, subjective impedance, and the second one refers to choice or the latitude that is available to the worker. This latter variable will be considered, in our context, as a moderator. To understand the role of these variables, we now discuss mediators and moderators in more detail. The statistical analysis that goes with each of the techniques, we leave for a later chapter (see Chapter 9).

MEDIATORS

Actually, in our model, all the variables between stressors and ultimate organizational responses are mediators. However, we will discuss variables separately as mediators only if, in previous research, the variable was considered as a mediator. Otherwise they will be labeled as intervening variables linking or leading to the various stages of the model.

Until the work of Novaco and colleagues (1979, 1990) the independent variable in studies of commuting stress was commonly understood to be an objective indicator such as time or distance. The subjective component was not implicitly measured. Their work, however, showed that subjective impedance was a significant predictor, and, when analyzed as a mediator, it helped explain some of their findings as well as those in the literature. The subjective experience may or may not reflect the realities of the commute. Thus, a person misinformed about road conditions may find any commute longer than the time he or she has allotted to it (perhaps, unrealistically) as leading to negative consequences. In fact, the objective experience, besides the overall dimension of time and distance required to arrive at work or home, contains many specific stimuli that may be largely responsible for some of the subjective responses as well as the behavioral and emotional effects.

Interestingly, even after considering the subjective elements involved in the commute, several anomalies were found. Novaco et al. (1991) reported that their subjective index was related to several affect variables but not to residential satisfaction variables. This finding was somewhat disconcerting for the authors, and they suggested that the relationship and the mechanisms that lead from stress to strain constituted a more complex phenomenon than their study was designed to test. One of their recommendations was to give more weight to direct physical, objective indices. For this purpose, a structural equation model, which was not employed by the authors, could have proved useful as it would have allowed the inclusion of direct paths, in addition to the indirect paths by way of the subjective indices, for predicting strain measures.

The perceived commute stress or subjective impedance used by Novaco et al. (1990) did not yield the anticipated interaction with perceived control expected by the authors. They speculated that there may be a confounding moderator in their measure. The Kluger (1992) results showed that their measure of subjective impedance confounded perceived commute stress and predictability. In our model, predictability serves as a moderator and is measured separately from perceived stress, which is considered a mediator here.

MODERATORS

We would like to suggest some additional techniques for improving prediction. What was missing from the Novaco et al. model was a greater emphasis on moderators. They did find gender as an important moderator but were unsure why this occurred. In order to understand the process, several other moderators, in addition to those already analyzed in the literature, must be examined. As has repeatedly been shown in the literature, control, and as applied to commuting, predictability, is likely to play a major role in the stress–strain relationship. The data supporting the definition of control as implying predictability have already been presented in the previous chapter (see Chapter 5).

Time Urgency

Over the past few years, organizational researchers have gone back to personality theory to help predict or understand individual responses in varying areas including job satisfaction (Gerhart, 1987), job choice or preference (Frese & Okonek, 1984; Zuckerman, 1979), and performance (Caldwell & O'Reilly, 1982). Recently, various aspects of life stress have also been related to dispositions (Depue & Monroe, 1986). We would like to examine one of these measured traits that seems particularly relevant to the commuter.

Several investigators have begun to look at a new aspect of personality that relates an individual's perspective about time as a potentially meaningful predictor of a range of dependent variables in organizational settings (Edwards, Baglioni, & Cooper, 1990; Schriber & Gutek, 1987). Of particular concern here is the element of strain responses resulting from time concerns. It is clear that for organizational researchers "the role of time in studies of stress in the work place is axiomatic" (Landy, Rastegary, Thayer, & Colvin, 1991, p. 655). Its influence can be viewed as double-edged. On the one hand, the environment or job demands often require an individual to consider the element of time, even if this is not the natural tendency of the employee. On the other hand, an individual's response to this demand is a function of disposition or personality. For our purposes, both aspects of time play a role in an individual's reaction to the commuting experience.

Although time urgency has not been investigated in a commuting context, a related concept, preferred arrival time (PAT) has been discussed previously. Besides the personality component, PAT appears to be a function of the reaction the commuter feels awaits his or her arrival at work. This latter measure has been called work-place tolerance by Caplice and Mahmassani (1992). In their development of a mathematical model for predicting PAT, they showed that work-place tolerance was an important moderator in their equation. As defined by the authors, PAT refers to the amount of time (in minutes) before the start of work that a person arrives at the job.

Other variables including sex and hour that the workday begins were also found to be important moderators in predicting PAT. In this regard the authors found an interesting work-place tolerance by sex interaction also. For women, PAT increases (i.e., they arrive earlier at work) with a decrease in work-place tolerance to lateness. This finding is consistent with the notion that women are generally more stressed than men after a commute. If it is true that the employer's possible negative response may cause a woman's behavior to change (i.e., contribute to an earlier arrival time at work), then it is reasonable to expect that attitudinal and emotional reactions would also be affected if the commute took longer than envisioned. For our purposes, time urgency will include the notion of PAT, with a moderate-to-high positive correlation expected between these two measures.

Time and the Commuting Experience

There are few work-related activities that are more dependent on time and schedules than the trip to and back from work. Interestingly, the trip home has several unique characteristics that may make some feel the pressure of time more than the journey in the morning. The trip to work is considered by most as part of the workday, and if one gets stuck in a traffic jam or a train breakdown, it can be rationalized as "company" time. However, on the way home, a person may view the delay as a loss to him or her personally. Except for the measure of evening congestion discussed by Novaco et al. (1991) in their concept of subjective impedance, researchers have not compared the qualitative and quantitative differences in strain between the evening and morning commute. It would be interesting to see if such a difference actually exists and under what circumstances.

Based on analyses from a combination of self-report measures, Landy et al. (1991) identified a multifaceted construct that includes the following factors: competitiveness, eating behavior, general hurry, task-related hurry, and speech pattern. For the commuter, the third and fourth factors are particularly relevant. Among the items with high loadings in the general hurry factor were "pressed for time," "in a hurry," and "never in a rush" (reversed scoring). The items with high loadings in the task-related factor were "slow doing things" (must be recoded), "works fast," and "work is slow and deliberate" (must be recoded). The items often sounded quite similar, as Landy et al. (1991) developed their scale by combining several existing measures, many of which had items that overlapped.

In order to determine whether they had covered the various facets of time urgency, Landy et al. (1991) decided to use another independent procedure that would either support the factor analysis described above or yield some new dimensions that should be integrated into the concept. They accomplished this by using the behavioral anchored rating scale (BARS) technique. One of the main advantages of the technique is the use of graphical rating scales that are not readily prone to many of the common biases found in performance appraisals.

The dimensions generated from the BARS method and short descriptions of them are the following: (1) awareness of time—extent to which an individual is aware of the exact time of day, (2) eating behavior—extent to which time is involved in planning or actual eating, (3) nervous energy—extent to which person is in motion, (4) list making—extent to which person maintains or keeps lists, (5) scheduling—extent to which person schedules activities and keeps to the schedule, (6) speech patterns—extent to which person exhibits rushed speech patterns, (7) deadline control—extent to which person is controlled by deadlines, (8) time saving—extent to which a person engages in actions directed toward saving time, (9) tolerance of tardiness—extent to which a person can tolerate tardiness in others.

It is our contention that time urgency is one of the most critical moderator variables in a commuting model. It interacts with the physical impedance scale and influences the quality of the subjective response. In the work of Schriber and Gutek (1987), the time variable was considered as part of the culture of an organization. Thus, the organization's response to an individual who arrives on time or its reactions to a late arrival are part of the normative expectations operating within that environment. Furthermore, Shriber and Gutek felt that satisfaction, withdrawal, and productivity may all be a function of the match between an individual's use of time and the organization's expectations. In developing the subscales of time urgency, Landy et al. (1991) felt that they could serve as a gauge for assessing the level of the variable in the individual and could be considered as a personality measure for predicting organizational outcomes such as the ones described by Shriber and Gutek.

For our purposes, then, this measure consists of both a state and trait component. Similar to the distinctions used by Spielberger et al. (1979), there are elements that are permanent and temporary to this dimension. Thus, some people may have a time-urgency trait that is a part of their perspective in all occasions. Work, recreation, family time, or just relaxing is done by consulting a watch. Awareness of the hour and minute is a natural part of such people's lives. They are always on time for meetings or celebrations such as weddings or going away parties, or at the airplane terminal at the beginning of a vacation. Others who are less conscious of time, may, nevertheless, be forced into such a "personality" state if the organization sets rewards, actual or real, as well as performance evaluations on the basis of arrival time at work, to meetings, or and, in general, not being tardy for all job-related activities. In this case, the individual, regardless of his or her inclination regarding punctuality, will be under pressure during the commute to arrive on time. Any impediment or obstacle resulting in delays during the trip will be perceived as a subjective impedance and is likely to result in some type of strain reaction.

In particular, awareness of time, which Landy has already shown to be associated with general satisfaction as measured by the Job Description Index (JDI; Smith, Kendall, & Hulin, 1969), scheduling, deadline control, and time saving are dimensions of personality that interact with the objective commuting experience. Thus, an individual who is constantly looking at his or her watch during the trip to work, who "fiddles" with the radio dial to pick up the news at the top of the hour, and who frequently asks a fellow passenger on the bus or train what time it is can be described as time aware. This commuter, if delayed beyond expectations, may be particularly susceptible to a negative subjective experience. For some, the whole commuting experience with its countless time deadlines or pressures, such at arriving at the train station in time, making the right connection at a specified minute and hour, is stressful even if these deadlines are just part of the normal commute.

For other commuters, not particularly bothered by time under normal conditions, the organizational climate with its expectations concerning time may also be stressful. Thus, regardless of whether using train, bus, or private car, the commuter often has limited control of the time element, and as the hours and minutes pass, stress is liable to build up. The greater the emphasis of time in the organization, the greater the stress. Although there might be some real differences between the state- and trait-time-aware person, our model will focus just on the degree of time awareness evinced by the individual. The nature or source of this disposition will not be considered here as we feel it does not have a major affect on the subjective impedance variable that will be described below in detail.

The work of Landy et al. (1991) has many practical implications for researchers of the association between time and stress. First of all, although correlating moderately with certain components of the Type A behavior pattern (TABP) scale of Spence, Helmreich, and Pred (1987), time urgency taps dimensions that are distinct from TABP. Whereas the latter can be viewed as a more general personality trait, the time-urgency items and factors generated from the factor analysis or the BARS technique form a constellation particularly relevant to commuting. Second, our approach, as well as that of several others who have investigated commuting stimuli, considers the whole discipline as part of environmental psychology. Landy et al. (1991) indicate that their subscales probably interact with environmental variables with the time-urgent subjects more likely to show greater discomfort and physiological arousal than the non-time-urgent variables. Finally, the development of reliable and construct-valid scales in the field should help in testing the concept in various settings. Landy et al. feel that future researchers may want to test the concept in computer or machine-paced tasks where time seems particularly important. Our own research program also includes several studies that will help identify which dimensions of time urgency are most relevant for commuting and how they differentially affect emotional and physiological reactions.

Other Personality Measures

With a few exceptions, it is our contention that most other personality traits play a relatively minor role in the commuting process. Two variables that should be considered, each somewhat differently, are negative affectivity and locus of control. The first, which will be discussed in greater detail in the methodology section, is really a nuisance factor and should be partialed out before doing any type of analysis between self-report stress and strain measures. The other variable, locus of control, has somewhat of a checkered past with the findings not really clearly indicating any one direction.

Several researchers investigated both the main effect and the moderator role of individual difference measures of locus of control (Gulian et al., 1989; Montag & Comrey, 1987; Novaco et al., 1979). Higher levels of external locus of control and lower levels of internal locus of control were found among drivers who were involved in accidents than among drivers drawn from the general population. However, Montag and Comrey studied only the main effect of locus of control. Novaco et al. (1979) studied locus of control as a putative moderator of the effects of commute impedance. Although they found a multivariate interaction between locus of control and impedance in affecting their dependent measures, the pattern they had obtained was not hypothesized. Gulian et al. (1989) did not find a main effect for locus of control on perceived stress and failed to test any interaction, although their rationale would suggest that locus of control should be studied as a moderator.

Therefore, only the Montag and Comrey (1987) study, which found driving internality to be negatively related and driving externality positively related to involvement in fatal accidents, could be considered as evidence for the contention that locus of control is related to driving behavior. They argued that this is consistent with the notion that the former types of individuals are more attentive and more adept at avoiding aversive stimuli. Its role in the commuting process remains ambiguous, and it is suggested here that like the work of Ajzen and Fishbein (1980) on attitude–behavior links, work with locus of control should include a commuting-specific list of items.

Even assuming that it were possible to generalize the positive findings by Montag and Comrey (1987), it is not clear how they would relate to commuting. Although the concept of locus of control has been around for many years, a major work on stress and work published recently by the American Psychological Association makes no mention of it (Quick, Murphy, & Hurrell, 1992). Also, it has been shown to be related to trait neuroticism by several researchers (Archer, 1979; Gemmill & Heisler, 1972). Assuming the veracity of this finding, negative affectivity seems to explain much of what is referred to as trait neuroticism (Watson & Clark, 1984). Payne (1988) reports that after entering trait neuroticism as the first variable in a multiple regression analysis, locus of control no longer predicted anxiety and depression symptoms significantly. Its effects can therefore be subsumed under trait neuroticism or negative affectivity, as will be used here. Recent work, however, has shown that negative affectivity may be a poor construct and may not adequately explain self-report measure overlap (Kluger, Levinsohn, & Aiello, 1994).

THE COMMUTING MODEL

The model of commuting stress contains several stages wherein each one influences and is influenced by the preceding phase. This is clearly shown in Figure 6.1, which lists the main categories of variables at each stage of the model. Briefly, the first stage describes the potential stressors (e.g., time, distance, etc.) that affect the second stage consisting of perceived or subjective stress. Afterwards, physiological reactions of various types are observed. The next stage includes emotional/attitudinal strain responses that are influenced by physiological response. This is followed by job-avoidance inclinations by the workers, which brings us to the last stage containing the behavioral/performance indicators. When stress is perceived and acted on, the individual, organization, and the society (acting through governmental processes) may attempt to dampen the stress by reducing perceived stress, cutting certain links, or providing alternative, more acceptable, paths for expressing the stress. The chapters of this volume devoted to coping (see Chapters 7 and 8) will describe some of

THEORY AND MODEL DEVELOPMENT

these techniques in greater detail. Several other general considerations concerning this formulation must be appraised. The predictability and personality moderators appear at the early part of the model, since they are expected to attenuate the relationships that lead to perceived stress. For our purposes, the stages after perceived stress are similar to those that have already been identified by many other researchers. We have included in the outcomes part of the model variables, such as lateness or performance, that may be influenced directly by commuting. However, as we get further away from the actual commuting measures, the objective as well as subjective impedance indicators, the causal links become weaker.

The levels of the path coefficients as a function of distance from the commuting measures were clearly shown in the intercorrelation among predictor and outcome variables in the Aizer and Koslowsky (1993) paper. For example, the correlations between the predictability measure and perceived control or between predictability and perceived stress were

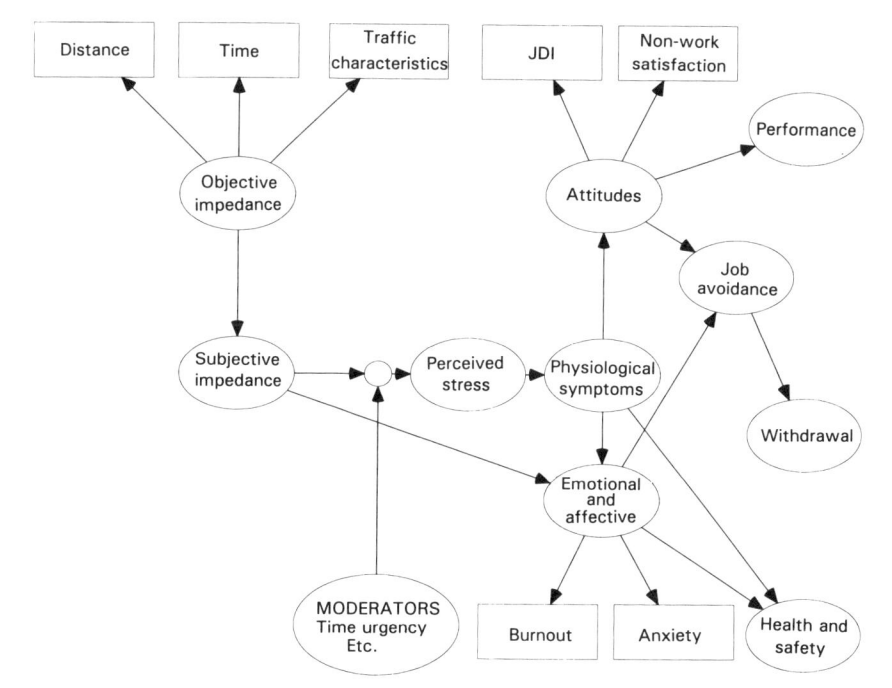

Figure 6.1. The commuting model linking stressor and strain variables.

significant (i.e., the greater the gap between a good day and bad day in travel time, the less the perceived control and the greater the stress), whereas the correlation between commute predictability and sick days was not significant. This would imply that whatever influence the commuting experience has on this outcome, it is mediated through other variables.

Besides the various statistical approaches for considering the influence of mediators and moderators in the model (some of which will be discussed in Chapter 7), it is also suggested that the models be run twice: once for high-time-urgent people and once for low-time-urgent people. Unlike the influence of other moderators, whose influence is at a particular stage in the process, we postulate that time urgency may affect several variables including emotional, attitudinal, physiological, and outcome indicators. As such, it would appear reasonable to expect that the strength of all the links would be affected resulting, in practice, with different coefficients. It may be assumed that some of the links may be altered, but until data are available, we will not hypothesize about any modifications in the paths among the variables.

A more detailed analysis of each part of the model reveals in the first stage a measure of impedance consisting of a latent factor derived from the measurement model of a confirmatory factor analysis. The objective measures of the commuting experience are the observed variables in the measurement model. These latter variables include but are not limited to time and distance of the commute. If possible, such objective commuting indicators should be obtained from non-self-report methods. For example, a stop watch or other timing device attached to the commuter can be used for obtaining this information. If collected from the subject through some questionnaire or interview, the data are no longer objective and may reflect perceptions rather than actuality.

In addition, other quantitative variables that can be included in this index are number of traffic lights, number of different stages (highways or changes in mode of transportation), and number of times brakes are applied (actually quite difficult to measure without some device attached to the car). Again, data should be collected from some source outside the commuter. Although Novaco, Stokols, and colleagues (1979, 1990) segregated the time and distance from the other variables, we have put them together and prefer resorting to a technique such as confirmatory factor analysis to determine the appropriate weights to assign to the various components of the objective measure (see Byrne, 1989, for a discussion of the topic in greater detail).

The use of confirmatory factor analysis allows the structural equations program (e.g., LISREL) to assign the appropriate weights between each observed variable and latent factor. Such a technique, as recently used by

Bretz and Thomas (1989) for defining the concept of baseball performance, allows an analysis that "avoids simple measures that may not have captured the multidimensional aspects of [the concept]" (p. 282). Rather than use any one of the six measures (such as slugging average or clutch hitting) individually or calculate a weighted sum to define the construct (i.e., total performance), the authors developed empirical weights from the results of the confirmatory factor analysis. This then served as one of the predictor variables in their study.

In the second stage, the subjective commuting experience is formed. This is a direct function of the latent factor in stage 1. Again, a latent factor is used to represent the underlying construct formed from the self-report measures of the commuting experience. The latent factor is an adaptation of the P–E theory and measures the reaction of the person to his or her perceptions of the environment. Although for the present we will assume that the two are related linearly to each other, it is possible that future research will show that the influence of the objective experience on the subjective experience is more complex (see the discussion of polynomial functions and other higher order powers in the P–E theory presentation by Edwards & van Harrison, 1993).

The issue of subjective and objective characteristics as necessary predictors in a stress model is the general assumption in stress models. Kasl (1987) and Fox, Dwyer, and Ganster (1991) have reported findings that support the notion that only by including the subjective measure much of the accuracy in strain prediction is reduced. For example, Fox et al., in a study of nurses, found that the objective stressors were related to physiological responses, and the subjective indicators were associated with affective outcomes. The authors concluded that both variables are required because the objective measures did not predict affect, and the subjective measures did not predict physiological responses. Taking an entirely different approach, Spector and Jex (1991) and Hall and Spector (1991), maintaining that the assumption of causality between the subjective–objective links is questionable, argued that other paths (sometimes through other variables) must be considered.

The third stage in the structural model is the first level of strain measure, perceived commuting stress. This construct is based on the first factor extracted by Kluger (1992) in his analysis of 31 reaction questions to the commuting experience. The items included here were: "I resent the length of my commute," "I resent the hassles my commute causes me," "My commute affects my productivity on the job by taking work time out of my day," and "In general, how do you feel about your commute?" All items were scored on a 7-point scale, ranging from "extremely negative" to "extremely positive." Kluger obtained an α value of .83 for these four items.

Between the subjective latent factor and perceived stress are the moderators in the model. Moderators include gender, mode of transportation, personality (e.g., time urgency), actual and perceived control (in the form of predictability). Predictability, which has been referred to as a substitute for control, can be measured in several ways. Besides the standard deviation of each of the objective commuting variables (particularly time and distance) as suggested by Kluger (1992) and the difference between a good and bad day as used by Aizer and Koslowsky (1993), prediction of outcome measures on a particular day may also require an estimate of the degree to which that day's commute deviated from the norm.

The next stage includes some type of physiological strain response (heartbeat, sweating, headaches, pain caused by discomfort, etc.). Here we have some of the physical symptoms that are commonly associated with commuting; they are generally acute and wear off over a short time, usually within minutes or hours after finishing the commute. However, over time, these symptoms may have a major impact on chronic measures of health, including cardiovascular disease, back problems, and so forth. The more far-reaching medical ramifications of these acute symptoms are observed in the last stage.

Following the manifestation of physiological symptoms, emotional and attitudinal latent factors become more prominent. The former include affective measures of mood change, fatigue, anxiety, depression, burnout, and so forth. These are all general measures of the distress level experienced at the job or at home. As with the physiological symptoms, they are temporary effects that over time and with continuous perceived stress caused by commute can become full-blown psychological problems. Of these variables, burnout, which has nearly become synonymous with stress, is particularly worth mentioning. For measuring this aspect of strain, the Maslach Burnout Inventory (MBI; Maslach & Jackson, 1981) is suggested. The MBI has been commonly used in stress studies and seems appropriate for our model, also. Examples of items included here are "I feel frustrated by my work" and "Working with people directly puts too much stress on me."

At the same time as the emotional effects are being observed, commuters may also experience attitudinal changes toward the job. The attitudinal variables of interest here are job satisfaction and non-work satisfaction. Often, organizational commitment is included as an attitudinal variable. As will be explained in the chapter on individual coping techniques (Chapter 7), commitment has been shown to be a "buffer" in the stress–strain relationship and is thus relegated to that role in our model. For measuring job satisfaction, the Job Descriptive Index (JDI; Smith, et al., 1969) is appropriate as it provides several subscores measuring reaction to the following: the work itself, pay, promotional opportunities, supervision, and people. The measure of non-work satisfaction needs to be constructed specifically for the objectives of the model. As was already mentioned by Novaco et al. (1991), the aspects of non-work satisfaction that are essential from the commuting perspective include residential satisfaction (dwelling, neighborhood, and location) and the home physical environment (noisy–quiet, pleasant–unpleasant, etc.). However, we feel that measures of non-work satisfaction must include the commuter's perception of spouse (significant other) and/or codweller's reaction to the commute. For example, items here would include "I find time for my spouse (partner) after a day of work," "I am so tired after the commute that I can't do anything but eat and go to sleep," "My spouse (partner) and I coordinate our activities according to the commuting schedule."

Extraction of the appropriate latent factor will allow us to use it rather than the individual subscores and/or items as the antecedents of the next stage. In the study by Schaubroeck, Ganster, and Fox (1992), the various indicators of subjective strain such as physical symptoms, depression, and job dissatisfaction were all seen as separate outcomes. We suggest here that they are linked, with the first of these preceding the other two. Although many theorists in the field do not make any temporal distinction between these last two phases and view the effects here as reciprocal and simultaneous reactions to the perception variable, we feel that the physiological response is the one most closely tied to subjective impedance (findings of Novaco and colleagues [1990, 1991, 1992] support this notion). Afterwards emotional reactions and attitudinal change can be expected.

Also, there is another element that makes this an apt link here. After some physiological response, such as a faster heart rate or excessive sweating, the individual may react negatively even if he or she is not aware of what was actually the exact cause of the physiological response. In our context, this can be illustrated by the relatively common occurrence in many urban areas of a particularly harrowing car ride to work. A feeling of subjective impedance is translated into a physiological response. The commuter may then have an elevated heart rate for a relatively long period of time, followed by some state anxiety as he or she becomes aware of the physiological response. The state anxiety can then produce job dissatisfaction or a lowering level of organizational commitment without the individual being aware anymore why he or she is experiencing greater anxiety.

At the next stage, we have placed job avoidance, a concept that has recently been shown as particularly relevant in linking attitudes or intentions with actual withdrawal measures. As was true in describing the concept of physical impedance, it appears that researchers may have identified a construct that describes intentions and attitudes related to missing days of work, coming late, or looking for another job (Hanisch & Hulin, 1991). A version of this construct was found to be highly related to job dissatisfaction (Fisher & Locke, 1992), one of the components of the preceding stage in our model. It should also be pointed out that the job avoidance measure is linked only to withdrawal behaviors in the final stage and not to the other outcome variables.

The last stage relevant for the commuter model of stress–strain linkages includes chronic medical effects or increased accident rate and actual behavioral and performance changes. Although the first of these effects can manifest itself at any time, at work or at home, the second criterion is exclusively an organizational measure, and the third one, if defined broadly, can include behavior at work (performance appraisals, productivity, or error rate) or at home (chores or activities, working alone or with a partner, etc.).

In actual practice, the entire model to this point can be said to impinge on the organization in several ways: the health/safety indicators that have implications for the efficient functioning of the entire organization, the worker's effectiveness demonstrated while performing in the organization, and the lingering effects of the home environment on the other two. It is, therefore, suggested that the outcomes also influence one another. In addition, the existence of both the individual attitude–behavior link, not always confirmed in the literature, as well as the emotional–attitude link, are quite meaningful for the organization. They provide an entry into the linkage scheme that may serve as an opportunity for the organization to sever a critical connection in the model and thus promote some form of stress control or management. As negative behavioral consequences are likely to have economic implications, the organization often sees its role as trying to offer alternative paths or to attenuate the attitude–behavior relationship. Some of these concepts will play an important part in our discussion of organizational coping methods (e.g., to provide special benefits for those commuting along modes of transportation preferred by the organization or to subsidize mass transportation fees on the basis of use or make it more difficult to find parking spaces at work resulting in the greater use of mass transportation).

Some Comments on the Model

The model as presented above is based on inferences drawn from a series of studies in several areas, including general stress research and commuting inquiries. Nearly, all the links have been shown in previous investigations as actual or potential cause–effect paths. It is also recognized that the model includes several new features not reported previously. This is particularly true with the application of structural equations to the variables. For this

THEORY AND MODEL DEVELOPMENT

reason, the model should be viewed only as a possible portrayal of actual relationships, and only by examining, testing, and confirming the different links can any confidence be placed in the formulation presented here.

The Attitude–Behavior Link

We need to devote a few words towards appreciating the attitude–behavior link that plays such an important function in our model. Social psychologists have always found the idea that attitudes are able to predict behavior a very appealing proposition. It provides consistency between a person's thoughts and actions as well as allows manipulations and molding of the latter through influencing the former. However, the work in this area has not allowed us to identify the exact relationship between the two concepts. Probably, the seminal work in this field was done by Ajzen and Fishbein (1980). Their study has generally focused on distinguishing between paradigms or situations that enhance the prediction of behavior from attitudes from those that do not.

Based on the theory of reasoned action and its recent revision, theory of planned behavior, several factors have been implicated as potentially enhancing the association between job avoidance attitudes/activities and withdrawal behavior (Ajzen, 1991; Ajzen & Fishbein, 1980; Fazio, 1986). First, the greater the similarity between the attitude and behavior, the better the prediction. Second, personal experience, rather than hearsay, forms a much stronger bond between the two (Brehm & Kassin, 1990; Koslowsky, Kluger, & Yinon, 1988). Finally, repeated encounters with the problem fixes the correspondence in the individual's mind and increases the probability that a relationship between the variables will develop. In our context, this would indicate the need to ask specific attitudinal/ intentional questions on the job avoidance scale that correspond to the behavior we propose to measure. For example, after a potentially stressful commute, the employee could be asked on a Likert-type scale: "Are you so tired of your long and difficult commute that you plan to look frequently for another job in the next month?" "Is your commute so long in time and distance that you expect to come late frequently in the next month?" The other conditions mentioned above, first-hand knowledge and repeated encounters with the stimulus, are features of any commuter's routine. Of course, the moderators and mediators in the model will also come into play and, possibly, influence the association.

The Outcome Variables

The objective measures in the last stage include some of the usual indicators in industrial/organizational psychology as well as measures unique for the commuting process. Major variables that are part of the model here are absence, lateness, and turnover (the so-called withdrawal indicators), productivity, and performance appraisal. In our model, withdrawal behavior has already been suggested as being a direct function of job avoidance, and the other outcomes are linked to attitudes and emotions directly.

Although withdrawal indicators remain the most frequently employed individual outcome variables in the literature (as evidenced by a short perusal of journals such as *Journal of Applied Psychology* and *Personnel Psychology*), they also are among the variables of special interest for the organization when working on the microlevel. The two major reasons for their importance are actually interrelated. Withdrawal behavior can be measured objectively and its economic impact relatively easily determined (Steffy & Maurer, 1988). Although less popular topics for research, such general measures of efficiency, health, and worker safety and methods for dealing with the problems originating in each of these areas, all have a significant place in organizational research and planning today. Their importance in formulations describing the effects of worker stress have already been pointed out (Landy, 1992). As with all these outcomes, the individual is the one most directly affected. Nevertheless, organizational efficiency and safety measures are, generally, viewed as macrolevel indices.

There are many ways for the organization to determine how well it is doing in these areas. Key indicators of absenteeism, lateness, or turnover for a specific company can be compared with those of other companies in the same industry or, by examining, intraorganizational data collected over the years. Keeping in mind the commuting problems faced by workers, comparisons on various critical criteria can lead to major decisions for the organization as a whole. For example, relocation, has been a very popular topic of discussion in many company boardrooms over the past decade. It has been considered a quick means for saving money (it's always cheaper in the suburbs) and, just as importantly, for improving working conditions such as the lateness frequency (it is easier to commute to the suburbs than it is to the city) in the organization (Hadad, 1991). Restructuring by building branches or regional offices may also contribute to easing up on some of the noxious stimuli associated with long commutes. In all these cases, Baron (1986) feels that the organization by taking initiatives and acting to protect its workers and reduce negative consequences is actually evincing control of the situation. And just as the individual does in stressful situations, the organization wants to control the environment and not be controlled by it. Other initiatives on the part of organizations for coping with individual stress are presented in Chapter 8 of this volume.

THEORY AND MODEL DEVELOPMENT

As the other behavioral indicators, worker accidents (the converse of worker safety) are not only caused by the stress (commuter or otherwise) experienced by the worker. Rather, they are a function and interaction of individual behavior and standards of safety maintained by the organization. When analyzing the commuting experience, we must be aware that the work safety issue is not really limited to the hours at work. For example, stress causing strain that influences or increases the likelihood of a threat to personal safety is part of the legitimate concern of the organization and has been cited as another reason for relocating from cities to suburbs by large and medium-sized companies (Hadad, 1991). Fears for the physical safety of a worker are not limited to the car driver. As we have witnessed so frequently throughout the world, commuters on trains or buses are not immune to threats or concerns about their safety. For example, in South Africa, commuter train usage has become so dangerous that many have abandoned this mode of transportation; others, who continue to use it, say that buying a ticket for the train is like "buying a ticket to heaven" (Wren, 1991). Finally, in New York City or London, where two of the largest and most sophisticated mass transportation systems in the world can be found, the situation has become almost intolerable with crime, bombs, and threats to personal safety, unfortunately common occurrences.

Direct and Indirect Links

Several features of the cause–effect chain presented here should be emphasized. Variables can affect each other directly and indirectly. For example, if perceptions about actual stressors are antecedent to certain strain responses, then the actual stressors may also affect the strain responses directly (e.g., the findings from Evans and Carrere, 1991 are a good example of these dual effects). A hot, long ride may be perceived as stressful but may also produce physiological reactions directly. Again, this argues for the use of more sophisticated techniques (e.g., structural equation modeling) in identifying the links between successive stages as well as across one or more stages.

Additional integral parts of the formulation proposed here are the feedback loops at various points. This would imply that variables at later stages affect those at earlier stages also. For example, satisfaction, the cause of performance in our model is, in turn, affected by performance. Of particular importance for commuting is the relationship between measures of strain and attitudinal variables. Although we indicated that the direction of the link is from physiological strain to attitudes, we must also consider the other path as a possible source for strain.

Support for a step-wise formulation as described by linkages among variables, that is, the effects of one stage are the causes of the next stage, is available from several sources. Novaco et al. (1991) concluded from the fact that subjective impedance often did not correlate significantly with certain effect measures, that the direct link between physical impedance and dependent variables must be included. In another context, Pierce and Newstrom (1983) showed that certain purported measures of job control (e.g., flexibility of work hours) were related to both strain and certain behavioral indicators. Although the authors did not examine the causal link among all these variables, the significant correlations did hint at a possible connection among the measures that could be examined with structural equation models.

Links in the Model and Coping Reactions

Coping is viewed as a process independent of the present model as described above. In our book, we have decided to take the approach that coping is a potential reaction to strain responses that may occur at any stage or between stages. In relationship to coping, all strain variables can be perceived as causal variables. If no active coping attempt is taking place, either because the strain does not exceed a certain threshold or because the person perceives that it will not help in any case, then the model flows as described. However, if an attempt to cope is taking place, then the various consequences in the model may be modified. It is not necessary for the commuter to do the coping by himself or herself; the government, community/region, or the company independently or working in tandem may be involved in modifying the elements that are responsible for strain reactions.

As the coping mechanisms increase in effectiveness, one of several new relationships among the stages can be expected. Either an equilibrium between strain and coping is achieved that allows the person to function at levels existing before the stressor was introduced, or the links in the model are altered. An example of the first case may be illustrated with an example from individual coping methods. A commuter who finds the drive to work stressful may decide to use the time in the car to learn a new skill. Many audiocassettes today are designed for the commuter and the ride to and from work. An example of an altered link in the model would be to take the advice of the company and switch from solo-driving to car-pooling or mass transportation. Here, the change of the mode of transportation, a hypothesized moderator in the model, interjects a new set of linkages that is expected to influence the outcome variables. In both cases, the person's strain levels, as a result of commuting, have been affected, and well-being, improved.

7

Individual Coping Strategies

The impact of commuting, as we have seen in the model, has negative implications for the individual, organization, and society. In order to minimize or, where possible, eliminate their occurrence, this and the following chapters (Chapters 8 and 9) suggest techniques for dealing with various consequences. Many of the recommendations are theory based, others empirically derived, usually from areas of stress research outside of commuting. Afterwards, some of the relevant inferences derived from the general literature are applied to our specific stress–strain relationship.

Among the approaches to be examined are techniques for altering or weakening links in the model, particularly at the earlier stages. In some situations, the manipulation and application of moderators are proposed. Although in a few cases, variables, such as commitment, could just as easily have been placed in the original model, it was decided to include them as part of the coping strategies. This decision was usually dictated to us by findings that had clearly identified a role for the specific variable outside the model configuration.

CONCEPTUALIZING GENERAL STRESS-COPING STRATEGIES

Diverse approaches have been recommended for developing coping skills in stressful situations. Examples of some of the strategies discussed in this chapter can be found in Table 7.1. Roskies' (1987) analysis of Lazarus and Launier (1978) divides coping techniques into two categories: instrumental or problem-focused approaches and palliative tactics that focus on regulating emotional distress. Instrumental coping includes techniques such as time management, organization problem solving, information

Table 7.1. Examples of Individual Coping Methods

Cognitive approaches and restructuring
  Relabeling, reframing, search for meaning
Self-control procedures
  Self-talk, self-monitoring, muscular relaxation, meditation, exercise at work and at home, meditation
Changing perceptions
  Changing environmental stimuli, challenging available information, changing or reducing discrepancies
Use of buffers
  Commitment, other moderators
Taking advantage of the commute
  Preparing for meetings and classes, learning new material, enjoying music or other diversions
Coping with specific environmental stressors
  Diverting the impact of crowding, noise, and heat
Instrumental approaches
  Time management, organization problem solving, information gathering, communication skills training, and buying time

gathering, and communication skills training. Essentially these procedures are employed to change the environment or remove oneself from it. Palliative tactics that focus on reducing emotional distress include techniques such as cognitive relabeling or reframing, relaxation, diverting attention, search for meaning, and positive thinking. Obviously, a more effective coping style might include a mastery of a variety of techniques. Here the person experiencing stress develops strategies for applying coping skills to fit the situation.

In a program developed for Type A behavioral syndrome clients, Roskies (1987) included the following modules: (1) Relaxation and learning how to control physical stress responses. (2) Control of behavioral stress responses that include self-monitoring of behavioral signs of tension. (3) Productive thinking that includes self-monitoring of self-talk and cognitive restructuring. This involves acting as one's own coach by formulating a game plan of what to say to oneself before, during, and after the critical commuting moments. (4) Preparation and plans for coping with the stress. Critical components are identification of stress triggers and stress inoculation training. (5) Learning how to "cool it," which involves applying physical, behavioral, cognitive, and emotional control in unpredictable stress situations. (6) Building stress resistance, which opens opportunities for rest, play, and pleasure. (7) Relapse prevention where the emphasis is on integrating stress-management techniques throughout one's life.

Paterson and Neufeld (1989) noted that when the degree of danger of a particular stressor passes an internally held threshold, the individual is motivated to engage in some type of coping. A secondary appraisal takes place in which the person assesses the stressor for opportunities where he or she can exert control and also examine him- or herself in an effort to harness resources for learning to bear or cope with the stressor. Different forms of control are possible. The most powerful form of domination is control over the stressor occurrence itself. In this case, the individual can prevent the stressor from occurring or avoid being exposed to it. A less powerful form of control involves reducing the likelihood that the stressor might occur or minimizing the severity of the stressor when it does occur. Paterson and Neufeld also discuss control over the appraisal of environmental events and stressors. These approaches include reframing or redefining the stressor in more positive terms (Sarbin, 1969) and utilizing verbal or imagery techniques that dilute or counteract stressor potency (Meichenbaum & Cameron, 1983). Somatic control includes techniques designed to reduce muscular tension and instigate stress-incompatible responses (one can't be relaxed and anxious or stressed at the same time).

Edwards (1988) defined stress as "a negative discrepancy between an individual's perceived state and desired state, provided that the presence of this discrepancy is considered important by the individual." Effects to reduce this negative impact on stress are classified as coping. Edwards points out that the success or failure of coping depends on many factors including the magnitude of the demands required for ameliorating the negative discrepancy, time, energy, personal ability, and individual resources, and other factors. When the discrepancy is resolved, stress will be reduced. For the individual who is unsuccessful at resolving the discrepancy, stress will persist.

According to this approach, coping is seen as influencing the determinants of stress in a number of ways: (1) changing aspects of the individual's physical or social environment, (2) changing a characteristic of the self, (3) challenging the available information upon which perceptions are based, (4) reconstructing or reframing by either denying perceptions or changing them, (5) adjusting desires or expectations to reduce the discrepancy, and (6) decreasing the importance of the identified discrepancy.

Edwards refers to some of the extant literature on coping and suggests that although it may be attractive to suggest that individuals under stress select from a wide variety of coping strategies, evaluate the efficacy and consequences of these alternatives, and rationally select the coping strategy that decreases stress and potentiates a sense of well-being, often, in real life, that is not the way it happens. Citing a number of research authors, Edwards offers a descriptive model for the selection of coping techniques in which an individual is more likely to rely on routine responses rather than implement a comprehensive decision-making process. He points out that available coping techniques are not always obvious.

Whereas increased stress tends to motivate individuals to generate a greater number of coping alternatives, it can also produce mental and emotional confusion. There also may not be enough time to generate coping alternatives, and the individual will then tend to use simple or superficial techniques. Also, coping techniques tend to be implemented sequentially rather than combined in a simultaneous manner. Essentially, in this descriptive model, people will consider a few coping alternatives, appraise the efficacy of these alternatives in a superficial or incorrect manner, and end up choosing an alternative that is not, necessarily, ideal. The factors influencing this process include levels of stress, available time, experience, available information and the accuracy of that information, experience with coping, and the ambiguity of the situation. These factors will result in cognitive limits to the rationality of the choice of coping strategies.

Edwards does not, however, take into account the fact that people can *practice* coping techniques, prepare for stressful situations, and increase their proficiency at selecting coping strategies most appropriate for individual stressors. His descriptive model argues for the implementation of stress inoculation at a preparatory stage or prior to the occurrence of the real stressful stimulus. In that sense, anticipating stressful situations and going through "dry runs" of coping with these situations may be the first step toward rational and effective selection of coping techniques. Bandura's (1982) self-efficiency model posits that the promotion of behavioral changes to secure a sense of well-being is closely related to the individual's belief that he or she has managed the skills necessary to engage in the new behavior. The individual can increase self-efficacy by engaging in participant modeling of those behaviors and acquiring positive feedback and by not attributing the results to external aids. This also helps limit the return to old, ineffective habits.

Till now, our discussion on coping with stress does not include a topic that, nevertheless, requires attention and understanding, and is particularly relevant for the main theme of this book—why is it that people sometimes submit to stressful situations and continue to expose themselves to continued stress without selecting coping strategies that might be helpful to them. There are many possible answers to that question ranging from a Freudian need and Oedipal models to Seligman's learned helplessness model of behavior. Health psychologists and the medical professions ask similar questions when trying to train patients and clients in adopting behavioral changes that will promote wellness and longevity. Personal motivation seems to be a clear prerequisite to implementation of those desirable behaviors. The process also demands a sense of self-awareness (this doesn't feel good or I could feel better), an opportunity to learn from models of desirable behaviors, a belief in one's ability to effect change, and the capacity to set goals and monitor achievement. The process implies unlearning of certain habits and acquiring new skills.

In the next pages, we offer suggestions for the individual in dealing with commuter stressors. There are, of course, a multitude of possible stressors and an equally large number of coping strategies. Although these strategies may be presented sequentially, we hope that readers, whether researcher or practitioner, will first experiment and then apply the various techniques individually and in combination so as to reduce their commuting stress.

COMMITMENT AS A BUFFER

Recent research by Begley and Czajka (1993) examined an interesting issue in applied psychology that has generally been overlooked in the field of stress. They tested the role of commitment as a moderator in the relationship between stress and several outcome variables. The authors compared two perspectives or commitment-moderating effects: the first posits that commitment increases an employee's vulnerability to psychological threat, and, consequently, according to this assumption, an individual so stressed may take these problems more to heart and show an increase in various negative outcomes. The less committed employees experiencing the same stress may find it easier to cope as the detachment from the organization may make it easier to block out or simply ignore the stressful stimuli. Although the authors did not specifically examine commuting as a stressor, this proposition can readily be applied to our case. Thus, the possible negative consequences of lateness from a lengthy and delayed ride to work may not really matter very much to the employee, and, emotional, or physiological changes would not be expected.

The second proposition states that commitment may act as a buffer by providing an individual with stability and feelings of belonging. According to this viewpoint, "employees committed to their company can be expected to benefit from the results of the tension resistance such commitment provides" (Begley & Czajka, 1993, p. 552). Here, stress will be correlated with negative outcomes for individuals with low commitment. Although this second hypothesis was never tested, indirect support for the protective aspects associated with commitment can be found in Antonovsky (1979) and Mowday et al. (1982).

The findings provided strong evidence that the second proposition was correct. For low- commitment people, negative outcomes increased as stress increased. For high-commitment people, the correlation between stress and outcome was close to zero. The authors felt that the results had implications for management and the individual employee. Organizations may want to create environments where commitment (or loyalty) is high. For example, in Japan the promise of continued, no-layoff employment has traditionally been viewed as an effective method for increasing commitment. From the employee's perspective, any activities that help to engender a feeling of commitment or belonging would also be likely to lessen the impact of stress on consequences.

A clear formulation for increasing commitment was presented by Rusbult and Farrell (1983). Using the investment model, Rusbult and Farrell showed that a blend of four variables can be used for predicting commitment:

$$com = (rew - cst) + inv - alt$$

where, com = commitment, rew = the rewards associated with the job, cst = costs associated with the job, inv = investment (resources inextricably connected to the job), and alt = alternative job opportunities. According to this formula, increases in rewards and investments as well as decreases in costs and the available alternatives, all have a positive effect on commitment.

Proper manipulation of the commitment variable or its antecedents can have a dramatic effect on commuter reactions to stress. Developing a high level of commitment can be used to buffer some of the negative stimuli facing the commuter each day. By making sure that there is a firm linkage between employee and employer, negative consequences may very well be held to a minimum.

METHODS FOR COPING WITH COMMUTER STRESS AND STRAIN

Organization and Self-Discipline

Coping with the commuting experience actually begins before the commute. An individual who is emotionally composed as the day begins (and actually at the end of the day, on the way home, too) is more likely to find the stressful stimuli that are encountered daily, or even less frequently, easier to absorb. The reverse is also true. As the individual confronts new stressors, even if the last one is not particularly more stressful than the previous ones, a point or level is reached where the pressure on the individual becomes so great that strain reactions are inevitable (Russell et al., 1987). In their analysis of coping with the consequences of more than one stressor, Greller et al. (1992) suggest that the overall effects may be cumulative or, possibly, interactive. An individual devising a coping strategy may need to take this fact into account and be prepared for such a contingency, that is, the strategy that is devised should take into account the possibility that two stressors may be qualitatively as well as quantitatively different from one stressor.

When facing the morning rush hour with its potentially noxious stimuli, an aware commuter can prepare for the trip to work (or home) by taking special precautions. Rather than trying to cope with a specific stimulus, he or she can try to cope with the commute as a whole. A less stressful commute begins the day or night before. Clothing, attache cases, lunches for the commuter or children in the family are prepared at night in order to avoid a morning rush. Diaries are consulted, papers are put in order, and an agenda for the coming day worked out in advance. Bedtime is declared at an hour that ensures enough sleep and wake-up time takes place at an hour that allows adequate time for morning toiletries, dressing, a good breakfast, and family interactions. This group of commuters will reduce time pressures by organizing their lives, taking care of physiological needs by getting enough sleep, maintaining proper diet and following recommendations for proper nutrition, and creating opportunities for dialogue with spouses and children.

These commuters can be viewed in contrast to others who wake up late, jump out of the shower into some clothing, and make a mad dash for the car, train, or bus. Breakfast may consist of coffee and a donut gulped rather than eaten. Such a life style permits little time for interaction with anyone. The image that is conjured up is of the harried or hassled commuter who is still eating as the door closes behind him or her. The commute begins with an already heightened stress level and the commuter waiting anxiously and, perhaps, in trepidation for the first stressful stimulus during the trip (an unexpected traffic jam, crowding, excessive noise on the train, etc.).

The factors that influence the allocation of personal resources for achieving a more organized, calm life accompanied by self-discipline are numerous. Often there is confusion between concepts such as organization, rigidity, and compulsion. An individual who is able to put the various components of his or her day into proper perspective is more likely to find that all facets or functions performed are synchronized rather than helter-skelter. For example, the events of the day or night before, in one sphere, should not be allowed to impinge on another sphere. Those workers who receive less fulfillment from their job or co-workers may find their time away from work as an escape or reward. Late-night television, and movies, or socializing with family and friends may be a primary method of unwinding. Here the work time has an impact on the time at home, and, the situation, as described, will probably have further repercussions the next day.

The idea of organizing one's self in preparation for the next day or making sure to get enough rest is often rejected because it conflicts with the recreational aspects of free time or the immediate needs presented by one's family. People who have difficulty setting limits for themselves and others or balk at authority may also have more difficulty with the concept of organizing their time. The consequences of this lack of coordination reduces the chances of effective coping with stressors and manifests itself in all activities including commuting.

In his discussion of work attitudes, Kornhauser (1965) states that "the unsatisfactory mental health of working people consists in no small measure of their dwarfed desires and deadened initiative, reduction of their goals, and restriction of their efforts to a point where life is relatively empty and only half meaningful" (p. 270). Kornhauser was writing about industrial workers with few options for significant advancement or meaningful work. In such situations, it is difficult to demand that any planning activities or job preparation take place before getting to work. The work experience may be so dissatisfying that very little of the time outside of the work place is spent organizing for it. When the individual is looking forward to the time spent at work, then it is easier to expect more appropriate behaviors for planning to get there. Locke (1976) identified a number of work conditions that provide greater job satisfaction and a desire to get to work. Among them are: (1) work situations that are challenging and tend to more job involvement and personal interest; (2) work that leads to self-esteem; (3) work situations in which performance is rewarded in a fair manner with accompanying feedback; and (4) work that is not too physically tiring accompanied by working conditions that facilitate work goals and are compatible with physical needs. When people experience their work life as rewarding and fulfilling, then it is more likely that they will organize their nonworking time around their jobs and face the commute with the least possible accumulation of stress.

General Exercise

The beneficial effects of exercise have been well documented. Exercise increases cardiovascular fitness, releases muscle tension, lowers blood pressure, and can help improve self-image and appearance. Each of these has been found previously to be affected negatively by the commuting experience. Although it is hard to say that the exercise will prevent any deleterious effects after the trip to work or home, it is not unreasonable to expect more limited damage for individuals who have prepared with exercise.

Exercise is an important factor in the voluntary control of adverse dietary habits and stress (Fremont & Craighead, 1987). Exercise should involve as many of the body muscles as possible. For example, aerobic exercises generally involve movement of large muscles and require moving the body across a distance or against gravity in rhythmic movement. Beneficial effects of exercise are often achieved at a frequency of three to four times a week at 30 to 40 minutes a session. Moderate intensity is generally required, and warm-up and cool-down periods should be added on to the 30 to 40 minute regimen.

Exercise conducted on a consistent basis can lead to a general state of fitness. Fitness is often described as producing the three Ss: suppleness, stamina, and strength (Powell & Enright, 1990). Suppleness allows a person to move more freely and reduces stiffness. Stamina enables us to resist exhaustion. Strength implies that muscles are working well within their capability. Ivancevich and Matteson (1988) cite research studies that indicate that about 15% of the adult U.S. population is actively involved in exercise programs. About 70% of these are classified as low active or inactive. Adults are generally not motivated to initiate or maintain exercise programs. (The junior author's experience with health clubs indicates that if all the people who acquired membership actually showed up, there would not be enough room in the clubs.)

Commuting by car, train, or bus often involves sitting for extended periods of time. This can cramp muscles and reduce overall flexibility. Standing in crowded public transportation can put strain on particular muscle groups and also reduce overall flexibility. Exercise can be part of an overall program of coping with commuter stress and can be integrated into the commute itself. The following are some ideas for implementing exercise programs to combat commuter stress.

Morning Exercise

Beginning the day with a series of stretching techniques and aerobic exercises can help a person achieve and maintain physical fitness and flexibility. Many people who begin their day with an exercise or stretching program report that they feel better physically and mentally and are more prepared for the day ahead. A sense of self-discipline, mastery over one's body, and achievement of exercise goals, all increase self-esteem and give a positive tone to the morning. With the proliferation of exercise and aerobic workout videos and home "gym" equipment, many people find that they can achieve an effective workout in their own homes, thus removing the excuse of inclement weather. Many neighborhood fitness centers cater to the early-morning commuter crowd, opening early in the morning and offering a nutritious breakfast. Walking, jogging, and running continue to be popular early-morning exercise programs as well. The drawback to an early-morning exercise routine is that the commuter must rise sufficiently early to implement his exercise routine. This may create additional time pressures as the morning commute draws nearer.

Exercise in the Workplace and during the Workday

More and more companies are making exercise facilities available to their employees. These facilities are generally used during lunch time and immediately before or after the workday begins or ends. Employees can enjoy the advantages of exercising without traveling to another site and can "work off" the tension of a morning commute or prepare for the evening commute to come. Lunchtime exercising helps break up the workday and often decreases caloric intake over the lunch period as compared to the intake of nonexercisers. Some fitness centers offer quick cardiovascular programs with the commuter or executive in mind. Turnaround time of an hour allows for a workout, shower, and change of clothing. Besides improving alertness and concentration, such a workout during the day is a positive means for preparing for the trip home.

Evening Exercise

Evening exercise allows for a beneficial "winding down" from the day's work and commute. It offers a transition period from the workday to home or family life. (The junior author has memories of getting off his train after a day's work and heading with a group of fellow commuters to a local fitness center before returning home. He returned home feeling relatively fit and at ease ready to wash dishes, give children baths, and be an active participant at home rather than an exhausted and, generally, passive partner.) Evening hours are often more flexible and allow for a successful implementation of an exercise program. Many people, however, report that it is hard for them to work up a desire to exercise after a day's work.

Integrating Exercise into the Commuting Experience

A small percentage of commuters walk or bike to work. Bike lanes are becoming a more familiar feature on streets and even some local highways.

However, it is obvious that most commuters do not live near their place of work. Nevertheless, exercise can be integrated successfully into the commuting process by doing the following: (1) walking or biking to the train or bus stop and reversing the procedure on the way home; (2) getting off a stop or two earlier and walking the rest of the way; (3) parking your car a distance from the bus, train, or workplace and walking the rest of the way; (4) using stairs instead of escalators or elevators; and (5) doing gentle stretching exercises during the commute.

Meditation

Research on meditation indicates that it can lower respiration rate, increase oxygen intake, reduce blood pressure, decrease tension, and initiate a state of calm, as well as create a sense of well-being. Although there are many meditation techniques, most seem to work equally well. Meditation is particularly effective at coping with stress and inducing relaxation. The relevant techniques can be learned relatively quickly, and they do not require special equipment.

In the first stage, meditation generally involves assuming a comfortable position. It should take place in a quiet environment. Regulation of breath and the adoption of a physically relaxed and mentally passive attitude is encouraged. Generally, the person meditating dwells upon an object that does not have to be physical. It can be a sound, an idea, a body rhythm such as breathing, or include the repetition of a word or phrase.

Similar to exercise, morning meditation can help prepare for the day ahead. Afternoon and evening meditation can help a person unwind and regain a sense of calmness and well-being. Some commuters meditate during their commute. Meditation audio tapes played through headphones can help create a meditative environment even on a train or bus. However, many people feel uncomfortable closing their eyes while others may be looking at them, and some potential mediators may be concerned with personal safety issues. Meditating while driving a car is generally contraindicated.

Cognitive Restructuring

Much of the field of cognitive psychology is based upon the idea that between every stimulus and response there is a thought process that takes place. For example, waking up to a rainy morning might elicit distinctly different responses from different people. A farmer might breathe a sigh of relief when he thinks of rain watering his parched fields. A college student might react with irritation at the thought of a canceled outdoor picnic with a girlfriend. The same stimulus evokes different responses because of the thoughts that precede these responses.

The work of Beck et al. (1979) on depression indicated that some people tend to think thoughts that reflect a lack of self-esteem and a sense of helplessness and hopelessness. When confronted with certain specific situations, this cognitive style tends to lead to depressive feelings. Beck also found that cognitive styles associated with work could be altered.

Albert Ellis' rational emotive therapy posited that much of our negative feelings are caused by irrational thought processes such as "I must succeed every time" or "Everyone should like me" (Ellis, 1962). Identifying the material thought processes and replacing them with a rational thinking style results in more healthful functioning. Interestingly, recent work has questioned some of Ellis' methods (e.g., Haaga & Davison, 1993), nevertheless, there is much to learn from its general guidelines. The commuting experience contains many potentially negative elements. There is generally a time pressure involved and an implied idea of "I must get to work on time." Monetary penalties or dissatisfied glances and negative feedback are often the costs associated with tardiness. Although there is a measure of control in the commuting situation (such as the time to leave in the morning), often things happen that are beyond one's control. Delays or accidents causing bumper-to-bumper traffic can cause the commute to come to a grinding halt. The delay may very well seem to be interminable. It is particularly at this juncture that one's thoughts assume a great deal of importance. Confronted with a lack of control over the situation, one has the choice of becoming angry or irritable or taking a more rational and positive view of the situation, accepting the reality and focusing thoughts in more fruitful directions. The learned helplessness model could be very appropriate for the commuter slowed to a crawl day after day. The cognitive literature posits that there is in fact a great deal of choice involved in the way one thinks about various stimuli, even when they are negative and repetitive.

Changing one's cognitive style and developing more rational and positive thinking skills require practice and self-awareness. As many psychologists point out, the inner dialogue that takes place between stimulus and response can occur so quickly that it may be hard to isolate and identify. Slowing down that process and becoming aware of intervening thoughts are of paramount importance. Changing behaviors can be addressed more effectively when all of the relevant information is available. With these ideas in mind, let's see how we can apply different cognitive- behavioral approaches to cope with commuting stress.

Powell and Enright (1990) have identified some methods that can be helpful in terms of the commuting experience. Donald Meichenbaum's

(1985) idea that self-speech can help us control our behavior is much the same as someone else speaking to us and providing helpful comments. First, the person is made aware of how much negative self-talk often occurs. The person is encouraged to conduct self-talk that inspires confidence, a positive attitude, and anticipation of success. In a sense, it is like having an inspiring coach on board who believes in you and in your capacity to cope (Let's do it for the Gipper). In the present context, before starting out on the trip to work, one might use self-talk along the lines of "The rush hour is horrible and I do feel awful now but I know the bad feelings won't last long and that I will cope." During the commute experience, the person might say, "I'm dealing with it; it won't get the best of me" or "This will all be over soon." Afterwards, the self-talk might include ideas like "I did well" or "I'm proud of myself; I coped with that train delay." For people who have difficulty remembering suitable self-talk statements, cue cards can be used or a prepared audiotape can be played at the appropriate times.

Beck and his colleagues (1979) have a five-stage program in their cognitive therapy techniques. The first step is for the person to become aware of his thought processes by identifying his thinking or images as a result of an anxiety- or stress-prevailing situation. Keeping a record of these thoughts and images is encouraged. For example, "This bus is late again., My supervisor is going to blow a fuse. I'll get fired, then I won't be able to make payments on the house. I'll lose everything."

The person then learns to restructure his or her thinking and imagery by asking three questions: (1) What's the evidence? (2) What's an alternative way of viewing the situation? (3) So what if it happens? In other words, the person is encouraged to challenge irrational thoughts, think of more likely alternatives, and even cope with a worst-case scenario. In commuter terms, "I've been doing a good job and I'm not often late. There is no evidence that I'll be fired for being late." "A more likely alternative is that I'll be noticed for my lateness or perhaps even be docked, but it's not the end of the world as far as management is concerned." "Even if my supervisor blows up at me, I still have recourse to others in management."

Stages 3–5 include strategies for testing out thoughts, reappraising initial negative thoughts and beliefs, and role playing irrational and negative ideas. In other words, self-awareness of negative thinking is fostered and alternative realistic and adaptive thinking is encouraged.

Similarly, Ellis' (1978) rational emotive therapy approach helps people to examine and readjust irrational thinking. Ellis' techniques include an almost philosophical argument technique that reveals irrational thoughts as false and unhelpful. Sentences that contain shoulds and musts often contain irrational thoughts. "I must be in control" and "I should be able to get to my desk by 9 A.M." may imply a tendency to deny that things are sometimes beyond our control and generate a great deal of pressure.

A somewhat similar approach, stress inoculation (Meichenbaum, 1985; Meichenbaum & Cameron, 1983), can also be used for dealing with stress. Here, the first stage is educational. The person is encouraged to identify the relationship between negative thoughts and negative feelings and behaviors ("There is no room on the bus again"; "I know this will be a lousy day"; "I can feel my stomach acid dripping already"). The second stage is acquisition of various skills and rehearsing them. The person is encouraged to learn new coping techniques or employ others already available to him or her. Self-instructional training, relaxation, and problem-solving skills are examples of skills to be acquired and used in various situations. The final stage is application and practice of those skills in the actual situation. Different stressors are anticipated. Strategies are formulated to bounce back from failures. Finally, confidence begins to build up.

Much less prevalent in the professional literature but more commonly found in religious, motivational, or pop psychology settings is the idea of positive thinking. People are encouraged to organize, act, do what they can, but remain flexible when things don't go the way originally planned. Religious/motivational spokespeople often go one step further by suggesting that maybe "this is the way it is supposed to be." Flexibility and looking for hidden opportunities are encouraged.

Most serious promoters of positive thinking emphasize the fact that it is a discipline rather than an expression of empty phrases. A positive thinking paradigm reflects the idea that thoughts can affect well-being and health, and that there is generally more than one way to perceive an event. Reframing, a technique used by many therapists, is utilized to help see events in a more positive light. A traffic delay may be an opportunity to review the day to come. A crowded bus may be an opportunity to strike up a conversation with a passenger.

Taking Advantage of the Commute

One of the major arguments for the use of mass transit rather than the automobile during the commute to work is the ability to take advantage of the time spent on the bus or train. Although some people may prefer to sleep, talk to friends, or read a newspaper, there appears to be at least one group of people that may be motivated to use any available opportunity for working, including the time spent commuting. Greenberg (1978) found that the degree with which individuals expressed support for the Protestant work ethic was correlated with the frequency of working while commuting and with the perception of commuting as an extension of work time rather than of leisure time. Commuters with the Protestant work ethic are characterized as industrious, ambitious, and condemnatory of sloth and laxity.

When Greenberg conducted his survey, he probably could not have envisioned the technological advances that are now becoming part of our everyday lives. For example, laptop or notebook computers, sophisticated audiotape systems, and cellular phones have dramatically changed our concept of usable time. It is interesting to note that the relationship uncovered by Greenberg was not due to the opportunities or requirements associated with the job. Rather, they were a function of the attitude the individual has about work. It may be possible to take advantage of this specific commuter need by providing more features or conveniences on a passenger train for the modern worker. A sort of moving office with computer supplies, phone hookups, and printing facilities could very well attract a new type of person to the train.

It appears that for those who have the need and are inclined to do so, commuting can be made a positive experience. For example, Borzo (1992) describes various ways for making the drive time a "prime time" for the physician. That means, says the author, increasing the physician's productivity and improving the quality of the commute time. Some of Borzo's suggestions include using a car phone (even bikers or joggers can get a mobile cellular phone), dictating notes and correspondence over the phone to a secretarial pool or into a portable tape recorder, and jotting down questions and lists of things to do after getting to work or home. In all cases, of course, the commuter using an automobile must take care and concentrate first on driving and only then on other activities.

Quoting experts in management, Borzo states that the most useful tool available to any commuter is the audio tape (or Walkman). The possible uses for this simple and relatively inexpensive device are nearly endless. Whether it is used to brush up one's French or earn CME credits, listen to Mozart or to review the latest findings in a specific area of medical research, a tapes is the answer. As anecdotal data, Borzo quotes from several physicians each of whom found the time spent traveling to the office much more productive and enjoyable after making the right decision regarding which audio tapes to play. Another machine that is becoming indispensable for some commuters is the laptop or notebook commuter. With the increased popularity of communication devices such as fax/modems and similar attachments, the commuter is now in direct contact with the office, clients, and data bases not just while in the office but also during the drive to work.

In concluding his analysis of the different options available to the commuter, Borzo writes that perhaps the best activity of all is thinking, planning, reviewing, and organizing the coming day or the one just completed. This is valuable time both for the car driver and the train or bus commuter. At least for those who want it to be, it is the part of the day with the least outside interference and provides the commuter with the opportunity to make critical decisions without being hassled or bothered.

It may behoove transportation authorities to advertise such facilities or to conduct surveys among motorists to determine what specific features would make them consider switching. In the chapter on organizational and industrial coping methods (see Chapter 8, this volume), we present other persuasion techniques for gaining compliance or behavioral change by the commuter.

Increased Control of the Commute

As we discussed previously, control or predictability of the ride is one of the most efficient methods for reducing the negative consequences of the commute. As more information becomes available to the driver, uncertainty is reduced, and our model predicts that such individuals would experience less strain. Recently, computer specialists and civil engineers have proposed mapping programs as part of the options available to car purchasers.

In the first case, software containing maps of specific regions can be bought by commuters who are in unfamiliar areas or by tourists renting a car. The coordinates of the starting point and the destination can be entered into the "dashboard" computer, and one or several routes can be printed out and used by the driver for making decisions on how to get to the destination. For example, it would be possible to provide routes that avoid troublesome roads during the rush hour but are perfectly usable during the rest of the day. Mapping options are already available from several automobile manufacturers.

A video system is another device that could help the commuter in navigating the route to and from work. Davis and Ridgeway (1991) have discussed the feasibility of using such location-specific information for reaching an unfamiliar location in the most efficient fashion. Such a video/commuter device may also be tied into traffic information from a central commuter that would integrate real-time data with information that is already available in the computer's memory. Davis and Ridgeway argued that traffic congestion, excess travel, fuel consumption, and air pollution would all be reduced by intelligent use of such a system.

Chores and Other Time-Related Activities

Although commuters as a whole listen to a good deal of music on their journey to and from work, it is clear that their favorite musical selection is not "Time is on my side." Often the commute does not take place in a vacuum. In the morning, there may be children who need to get to school or spouses who have their own commute to negotiate. Chores need to be done, the dry cleaning has to be dropped off, or a car pool needs to be rearranged. A child's shoelace breaks, there's a spill on the table, or the car engine won't turn over. The commute home may also include pick-ups, the need to get supper on the table quickly, or rushing home to a sick child who missed school.

One of the most direct pressures involved in the commute is related to work. Clocking in on time, making the morning meeting, seeing the first sales appointment are all different expressions of the same factor—starting work on time. The reality that the commuter experiences, such as train delays, clogged inner-city traffic, and gridlock and traffic jams can create a great deal of stress for the individual who is trying to start the workday on time. How does one cope with chore-related, time pressures?

Buying Time

It is true that everyone has the same 24-hour day. However, time is a commodity that can also be purchased and traded. In the case of the morning commute, one-half hour of time can be acquired at the expense of one-half hour of sleep. Rising earlier and leaving earlier can help get the commuter to work on time if not early. The extra time can also be put to use in terms of helping in the house, spending some time with one's spouse or children, or simply relaxing before the workday begins. Acclimatizing one's self to an earlier rising schedule can be accomplished in a period of a few weeks. Once it becomes a habit, the benefits that accrue will help maintain the practice.

Organization

Freud once said that the goal of therapy was to make the unconscious conscious. "Where id was, there shall ego be." One of the best ways of managing time pressure is to identify what those pressures are and where they fall in our list of priorities. Mumbling to one's self "I've got a lot to do tomorrow" is not as helpful as organizing a list of those things, prioritizing them, and planning how and *when* they can get done. There are things that need to get done before the commuter leaves the house, and most situations that arise can be anticipated. In a family situation, chores can be allotted, tasks can be shared, and older siblings can help younger ones.

Windows

Teachers sometimes use this word when they say "Yes, I have a window in my schedule." The commute can be a window when there is work that needs to get done. Reports can be read on the bus or train, figures on statistics can be worked on, and meetings with co-workers can be organized around the commute. Utilizing windows of time can help the commuter feel that the work trip is not his or her adversary as he or she struggles to start the day, rather, it is an opportunity to invest in the day before it officially begins. Similarly, the trip home can be viewed as an opportunity to assess, unwind, and learn from the experiences of the day.

Communication

Although there are those who argue that technology has increased the pace of things to the point where we demand instant knowledge and gratification, there is no doubt that if used intelligently, technology can help us stand up to the stress of time pressure. For many people, an acute source of stress during the commute is the inability to communicate about one's situation to the work place or home. Often, the capacity to inform others of one's status during the commute is sufficient to leave the commuter feeling more in control and to reduce stress caused by time pressure. A telephone call to advise others about lateness, a change in plan, or a delay can make the difference between a stressful commute and a calmer one. It is here that the mobile or cellular phone have made significant contributions in helping individuals cope with time pressure. Using this method, communication with others can assume a very flexible format. Besides the commuter's ability to contact the office or family, the commuter can easily be reached by others. The mobile phone enables the commuter to make appointments, conduct business, and communicate information throughout the journey to and from work.

It is interesting to note that whereas for many people the enlarged capacity for communication during the commute and outside of the work place can act to relieve the stress of time pressure, for some people the idea of being reachable outside of work hours can actually be a focus of stress. Although there has been little research conducted in this area, it is clear that many people prefer their privacy and the right to determine when they are available to communicate with others. The scenario depicted by some science fiction writers of a personal number ascribed to each individual that would enable others to locate and communicate with him anywhere on the globe is not far off. The accompanying stress associated with such a state of affairs has yet to be studied.

Optimizing Commuting Departure Times

One of the interesting contributions of mathematics to the commuting process is the development of commuter departure models. In these models, commuter response functions are devised that take into account such variables as driving time, on-route waiting time, and waiting time at the end of the destination (Mahmassani & Chang, 1986). In mass transit models, the operational features of the mass transit system, including vehicle speed and its fluctuations, regularity, frequency, and scheduled time of operation, are all parts of the equation (Sumi, Matsumoto, & Miyaki, 1990). An individual with the proper knowledge of the equations or built- in programs can plan individual departure times. If part of a network, each individual connected within the system can be assigned a departure time, and optimal efficiency of departure times can be achieved.

ENVIRONMENTAL COPING

We have already presented reasons for considering the environment as one of the major stressors during the commute. In the next few pages, we discuss some of the ways individuals can cope with specific environmental stressors.

Coping with Crowding

As Epstein (1982) points out, crowding is by definition a stressor that occurs in a group situation. To experience a feeling of crowdedness, one must share a space with others, and problems related to crowding imply difficulties in interacting and coordinating activities with others sharing the same environment. Epstein explains that in a crowded environment the activities of one person may interfere with the activities of another. There may be unavoidable interpersonal interactions and violations of spatial norms. In a commuting situation, perfect strangers may be crowded together in physical contact with one another and with their faces only inches away. There may be extreme competition for those seats that may become available along the way, or for positions near the exits of the bus or train. In a car-pool situation, passengers may feel that there is little room to maneuver or read a newspaper. For the driver, being surrounded by other drivers who are also attempting to get to work and may cut him or her off or move into his or her lane is likely to create a great deal of stress.

In Epstein's model, several factors are involved in efforts at coping with crowding stress. The first is the individual's appraisal of the severity of the threat to his or her attainment of goals by the crowded environment. Translated into commuting terms, it can be phrased in the following ways: "Will I get a seat?" "Should I stand near the door so I can get to work on time?" The second factor is the goal structure of the other people occupying the space. Are their goals cooperative or competitive? In commuting terms: "Will she take the seat first?" "Will he cut me off at the toll booth?" "Is this commuter going to give me room to read my paper?" The third factor is the interval resources that the person has available for coping with these problems. Epstein posits the following circumstances as causes of strain: thwarted goals that are considered important, a sufficiently severe threat, lack of cooperation from significant others, and, as we have stated several times before, a feeling of inadequate environmental control.

Using this scenario as a model of the crowded environment, we can identify a number of effective ways to deal with stress. Coping with crowding stress can then be implemented on many levels. A first effort should be directed at primary prevention, by trying to avoid the crowding phenomenon as much as possible. This may dictate making an earlier train or bus in the morning and taking a later return trip home to assure a seat and a less crowded environment. It may require picking up transportation at an earlier stop or choosing a point of entry onto public transportation that is less popular and consequently less utilized. In an automobile or car, crowding may be ameliorated by talking with the other participants in the car pool and agreeing to rules concerning rotation of seats, bringing aboard hand bags, attaché cases, and so forth. If problems do arise, they can be discussed by the group and corrective actions taken to reduce the stress. The fact that crowding is a group and social phenomenon also makes it particularly amenable to corrective action if the group is willing and open to changing its behavior.

Crowding on public transportation often means limited standing room not to mention seating room. This often leaves the commuter weary and frazzled from the trip itself. Unpredictable delays can increase the number of commuters waiting for a particular tram or bus and exacerbate the problem. Frequently, assertive action is necessary to establish norms in a situation where resources, such as space, are limited. Most trams and buses have specific seats reserved for the elderly and handicapped. Senior citizens and the handicapped should have full access to those seats, and if they cannot assert themselves, other passengers need to intervene. This action inserts a sense of control into the crowding situation and generates normative behavior and social rules in a stressful situation. Commuters should make every effort to extend the same courtesy to pregnant women and those who seem to be having trouble coping with crowded conditions. Being kind and courteous to others is not just "nice," it is an effective method of coping with crowding stress and allows commuters to exert control in a stressful situation. It might also have an effect on other passengers who will stop acting competitively for the limited available resources, space, seats, or the spot near the exit.

As mentioned before, self-talk and coaching oneself not to react to crowding stress in a negative way can also be helpful to the commuter. Realizing that the crowding stress is time limited and that it can be dealt with a rational/positive thinking process can be quite helpful. An appreciation of the fact that it is also all right to "bail out" and leave a crowded environment gives a person the option to exit from the stressful situation and helps ameliorate the feeling of being trapped.

The results of crowding can include the physical stress of standing for long periods of time or suffering discomfort from the heat and odors generated by many people crowded into a limited space. Comfortable shoes or sneakers may help a great deal in ameliorating physical discomfort. Dress during the commute may be less formal with a change of clothing effected at the work place. Adequate ventilation should be assertively requested. When crowding includes jostling and the possibility of physical injury, assertiveness skills have to be quickly brought into play in order to alert others to the serious nature of the situation. Of course, the possibility of exiting from the situation as soon as it is feasible should be seriously considered.

The psychological dimensions of crowding include many common reactions that are a function of body or eye contact at close range. Kutner (1973) found that the stressful effects of crowding can be lessened if these phenomena can be reduced. Commuters can create emotional and physical space for themselves even when surrounded by people. Observing rules of etiquette, in eye contact in public situations may be helpful. Not allowing eye contact with another person for more than 3 or 4 seconds is one way of keeping emotional distance. Closing one's eyes effectively signals to others that one is not interested in social interaction. Some commuters use headphones and closed eyes as a method of creating their own mental space even when they are standing in a crowd. When body contact is unavoidable, it is often helpful to depersonalize the situation by reasoning that there is no emotion attached to the contact. It is unavoidable and temporary. If there is any malevolent intent to the contact, such as groping or touching for sexual satisfaction, the commuter must feel secure in his ability to assertively put an end to the action by looking straight at the person, stating in a loud voice "Stop touching me like that," and not remaining in close proximity to that person. The knowledge that such assertive behavior could be expressed if needed can be helpful in ameliorating some of the stress that accompanies uninvited body contact.

In another approach, the commuter may try to clarify and perhaps modify personal goals during the commute. This cognitive approach involves some mental restructuring by the commuter. Obviously one wants to have a safe ride and arrive at one's destination, but within this limitation a great deal of flexibility may exist. Is it vital for me to get a seat? Is it very important to be able to read a newspaper? Must I locate myself near the exit? In other words, clarifying what is and what isn't necessary for the commute can be helpful in dealing more realistically with the commuting experience. If the 7:55 train is generally filled to capacity and getting to work is of primary importance, then one may have to switch to the 7:35 train. An understanding and acceptance of the fact that there may be no possibility to read the financial section of the newspaper and self- labeling that goal as desirable but not primary can reduce stress when the objective is in fact unattainable.

Coping with Noise

Noise is part and parcel of the daily commute. Commuting by automobile leaves the driver open to the sounds of blaring horns particularly when traffic is heavy. Motors being revved, truck and motorcycle engines, road construction, and blaring radios can all be part of the commute to work by car. Many of these noises are beyond the driver's control, and some are unpredictable as well, all characteristics of common stressors. On the one hand, the effective driver attempts to remain vigilant to sounds in his environment. Another car's blast on the horn may be an important signal to effect a particular maneuver—to slow down or move to the right for example. Hearing a car move up in the left lane may be the first indication that it is not an appropriate time to execute a passing maneuver. On the other hand, noise can stress the driver and render him less effective in terms of driving safely to work. What steps can be taken to reduce noise and its accompanying stress to the commuter in an automobile?

One of the primary techniques for coping with noise is to take the uncontrolled and sometimes unpredictable nature of the stimulus and try to insert some measure of control. For example, if the automobile commuter is familiar with events that generally occur along the route to work such as traffic congestion at particular points or intersecting a truck or bus route, the driver can begin to prepare himself for the accompanying noise events. Self-talk throughout the stressful event along the lines of "Another 10 minutes and these blaring horns will be over" or "Once I get through the tunnel these diesel truck engines won't seem so loud" can be helpful in controlling the effects of the noise stressors. Employing relaxation techniques such as deep breathing at the onset of the noise stressor generates a relaxation response in place of a stress or anxiety response. The driver can focus on achieving a sense of mastery over himself and his reactions to stressors even under conditions when they are in fact beyond his or her control.

A second approach involves exerting more control over the environment in the automobile itself. Closing windows of the car shields the driver from a significant percentage of noise from the outside. Obviously, the decision to close windows must take into account the need for proper ventilation and maintenance of a comfortable temperature, as well as the need of auditory awareness of the environment in order to maintain vigilance and the capacity for safe driving.

Alternatively, the creation of a pleasant and satisfactory auditory environment can also yield satisfactory results. Given the fact that most automobiles are equipped with radios and tape or disc players, this can be easily accomplished with minimum preparation. The driver can preset radio channels that broadcast music or other programs that are appealing to him. As mentioned previously, creating a pleasant sound environment has many beneficial features. For our purposes here, suffice it to say that the driver feels more in control if he or she determines the noises that enter the environment. The distraction benefit of on-board music or other programs can significantly take the edge off noise stressors from the outside. Focusing on other stimuli essentially reduces the noxious effects of noise.

For some, traveling with a companion is another way of dealing with noise stressors. Mutually pleasing conversations can be a powerful distractor, and the content of the dialogue can also be rewarding. The trick here is to choose a companion who is not a source of noise stress. Commuters using modes of transportation other than automobiles are exposed to a wide variety of noises that can include loud subway or train sounds, public announcements of all kinds, loud conversation from other passengers, construction noises, and emergency vehicles, to mention just a few. Many, if not, most of these noises are beyond the control of the commuter. The junior author remembers the audience's roar of approval at a *Star Trek* film when Mr. Spock rendered a punk rocker with a blasting portable stereo unconscious, effectively ending that noxious source of noise. In real life, this becomes somewhat more complicated, and some of the cognitive and motivational techniques for coping with unavoidable stressors mentioned before are probably more relevant in a mass commute setting.

Some commuters have taken to wearing noise filters of one kind or another. This reduces the intensity of the noise to which they are exposed. Again, it is important to take into consideration the necessity to be aware of important auditory environmental cues and not have them compromised by too much filtering. Wearing headphones while skating in traffic is an example of this.

The "Walkman" and portable disc players have contributed greatly to the commuter's capacity to cope with noise. Commuters can successfully shut out environmental noise and listen to a sound environment they create. Obviously care must be taken to observe a safe decibel limit with the use of headphones, but with proper use, music or words transmitted through headphones, can effectively block out or mask noise and successfully distract the listener's attention from environmental noise.

Commuters may need to assert themselves when the source of noise is the conversations of other commuters. Firm requests for quieter interactions may need to be made. The commuter may also need to be flexible enough to move to another subway car or wait for a different bus so as to maintain a sense of control in the situation.

Coping with Heat-Related Stressors

Listening to the weather report is part of our everyday routine. We are interested in knowing whether it will rain or snow, how to dress, and whether or not our date for a concert in the park might be canceled because of inclement weather. Commuters are exposed to the weather conditions in many different ways and in many different settings. Driving in foggy or snowy conditions can be stressful for the automobile commuter as he or she tries to focus his/her vision and maintain control of the vehicle. Physiological effects of heat and cold are part and parcel of the daily commute. Humidity, temperature, air speed, and clothing all contribute to a general sensation of thermal comfort or discomfort. The multiple transitions that a commuter might undergo from walking in freezing weather to the heat of a railroad train and then back out again onto a cold street on the final leg of the journey can induce a number of thermal stresses. Standing on a crowded bus on a hot, humid day or crawling through highway traffic without air conditioning can precipitate heat stress characterized by faintness, nausea, vomiting, headache, and restlessness. Moving through an icy wind without adequate clothing can tax the body's capacity as it struggles to maintain the appropriate core temperature of about 98–99° F.

INDIVIDUAL COPING STRATEGIES

Coping with thermal stress is a significant factor in the daily commute. Arriving at work or home feeling like a "wet rag" or "frozen stiff" can affect performance at work and behavior at home. Baron (1976) found that drivers honked their horns more frequently when the temperature was above 85° F than when it was cooler. This applied to drivers in cars that were not air conditioned. Most research on heat and social behavior has looked at anger, aggression, and violence (Sells & Will, 1971; Goranson & King, 1970). What steps can be taken to deal more effectively with thermal stress?

Preparation

Knowing what the weather conditions are going to be on a particular day is of great importance. Gleaning the information from the newspaper, the smiling weatherman on the morning news, or on the radio enables us to know how to dress, what extra equipment we might need, and what our commute to work or back home might be like. Special attention should be paid to information concerning humidity, wind chill factors, temperature-humidity index (THI), or other comfort indexes. Past experiences with similar weather conditions should be revived. An important factor, particularly in the wintertime is that the morning commute may take place during daylight hours, whereas the ride home may take place in the dark. For automobile commuters, in particular, this may have specific ramifications as road conditions change from wet to icy.

Preparation also includes the need to make sure that the proper equipment is readily available and is in good working order. In the car, air-conditioning, heaters, windshield wipers, and defrosters must work well in order to maintain climate control and proper vision under varied thermal conditions. Umbrellas, thermoses, rain outfits, gloves, and so forth need to be organized and easily found when their use is required.

Clothing

Bell and Greene (1982) emphasize that thermal stress is not just a function of ambient temperature. The most important factor is how well one's body can maintain core temperature. Factors that reduce the efficiency of homeothermic mechanisms increase thermal stress, and factors that increase their efficiency will reduce it.

If the air temperature is below body temperature, then increases in air velocity, that is, windspeed, will increase convective air loss. Stronger winds make people lose their body heat more quickly. If there is both high humidity and cold weather conditions, this also sets up a situation of increased heat loss through convection. As the body cools, the skin of the hands and feet shows the most dramatic cooling response. A great deal of heat is lost through convection in the area of the neck and head.

As temperatures rise, perspiration occurs so as to increase heat loss through evaporation. In high ambient temperatures, a high humidity will reduce the efficiency of heat loss through evaporation and cause the body to tax itself in an effort to maintain its core temperature. Proper clothing is one important way we can cope with the thermal stresses. Clothing provides various degrees of insulation and can retard or promote heat loss. Different fabrics with their varying insulation values make their contributions in terms of thermal regulation. Gaydos and Dusek (1958) reported that cooling of the surface of the body produces little performance decrement if the hands are kept warm. Since their research, it is a commonly accepted fact that the single act of wearing a cap and scarf can be a significant factor in preventing loss of body heat.

Layering one's clothing is probably the most effective way of dealing with the multiple thermal and climactic challenges of the commute to work. Having the flexibility of dressing warmly on the way to the bus, (and then "peeling off" layers as one finds that the bus's heating system and crowded conditions are generating a good deal of heat), can be an important factor in having a comfortable commute. In rainy or snowy conditions, maintaining dryness with the right apparel can prevent significant heat loss from evaporation and convection.

Hot weather and its demands can sometimes conflict with the dress requirements of one's work. Nevertheless adequate provision must be made for the wearing of comfortable, even loose-fitting clothing whose fabric will allow and even encourage evaporation and perspiration. Hats should be worn to protect the head from direct sunlight. If possible, comfortable traveling clothes might be considered for the commute, while another set of clothing could be waiting for the commuter at work. This would require preparation on the part of the commuter and flexibility in terms of the employer providing space and the opportunity to change clothing.

Hydration

An important factor in fighting thermal stress is adequate hydration, in other words drinking enough fluids. The average fluid requirement for an adult is about 8 glasses a day, or 2 liters. Much of this fluid is derived from the foods that we eat, but often we drink too little in any case. When thermal conditions prevail that include high or low ambient temperatures as well as high humidity or high air velocity, it is very important to increase our consumption of water. In heat exhaustion, for example, replacement of lost water and salt along with rest is often the most direct and simple antidote. Water is generally the liquid of choice. Coffee, tea, and other drinks can actually have a diuretic effect. In cold weather, warm drinks can replace fluids as well as aid in the maintenance of the core body heat. A thermos and water bottle should be part of every commuter's travel equipment.

Controlling the Temperature in the Environment

During the commute itself it may be difficult if not impossible to exert control over the climate. Commuters are well acquainted with the overheated bus or overly air-conditioned train car. One exception to this rule is of course the commute by automobile. Climate control is within the purview of the driver and his or her passengers. Despite extreme temperature conditions that may prevail outside, the climate inside the automobile can provide for a comfortable ride to or from work. Familiarity with the heating and air conditioning systems and their options is important. It is also important to remember that humidity control is not one of the strong features of an automobile's cooling or heating system, and ingestion of liquids needs to be taken into account.

DEALING WITH COMMUTING FEARS

For some commuters, fear of personal injury during the commute to or from work is a significant stressor. We discuss this topic from the perspective of government intervention in Chapter 8. Statistics of violent crime on public transportation are rising. For those commuters who work the evening and night shifts, there is an added factor of travel during less busy hours at a time when the opportunity for a mugging or personal assault is greater. Similarly, commuters whose route passes through high-crime areas often feel stressed until they arrive at work or home. Automobile commuters are also exposed to the threat of car-jacking and assorted criminal behavior. Some automobile commuters also report that they are concerned about becoming a statistic in a traffic accident particularly in inclement weather and during night driving conditions.

Commuters who journey to and from work by public transportation in the inner city are frequently exposed to high-crime neighborhoods on the way to their bus or train. Given the fact that tokens and tickets are often purchased with cash, they are likely targets for muggers and petty crime offenders. Limited police presence on public transportation and the feeling of being confined in a subway car or bus with limited options for exit can all contribute to an overall feeling of vulnerability and stress.

Coping with commuter-based fears must take place on a number of different levels. The first step is to realistically evaluate the risks involved and work to minimize them. Commuters who walk to their trains and buses should utilize well lit and populated streets on their way to and from work. Neighbors or co-workers can arrange to walk together. Waiting for trams or buses should take place in designated, well-lit areas. Commuters should make themselves familiar with the basic safety features of the public transportation conveyances they use. Bags and purses should be held close to the body, jewelry should not be flaunted, and eye contact with strangers should be held to a maximum of 2 to 3 seconds.

Cars should be parked in well-lit areas, and keys should be at the ready when one is returning to the car. A quick look at the back seat should insure that no one is in the car. Car doors should be locked and windows closed when one is traveling through high-crime areas. If hit from behind, drivers should continue on to a well-populated area where there is a police presence. Finally, automobiles should be maintained properly so that the chance of a breakdown is low.

INFERENCES ABOUT INDIVIDUAL COPING

There are times when things really are beyond our control. The commuting experience has its familiar day-in and day-out qualities, but there are many times that we are delayed and can do little to ameliorate the situation. Weather, mental fatigue, power failures, accidents, and so on are just some of the variables in play that can create unexpected circumstances and generate time pressure and stress.

It is here that personality factors and the effective employment of coping and cognitive techniques mentioned earlier come into play. Developing a rational approach, helpful self-talk techniques, and a relaxed attitude are not insignificant factors in combating time stress. The ability to put things into a proper perspective is a powerful method of achieving control in what may seem to be a situation in which one is powerless. With some foresight, planning, and, perhaps most of all, determination to control as much as possible the external stressors, the commuter can make the experience considerably more pleasant.

8

Government and Organization Coping Methods

In addition to individual coping styles, the government and the organization can help the commuter in solving some of the basic problems of getting to work and returning home. This intervention does not have to wait for commuting problems to manifest themselves. It can begin before any commuters have moved into a new area or residential development zone. From the government's perspective, an appropriate infrastructure is necessary so as to enable the commuter to drive or ride to work in the most efficient fashion. From the organization's viewpoint, determining the optimal location for an office building or factory must take into consideration traffic patterns, parking spaces, availability of mass transportation, and so forth. Often the accelerated growth of a community or the relationship between a rural and urban region is unforseen, and the problems begin to appear after the infrastructure is already extant; nevertheless, even under such circumstances the government and organization can still do much to alleviate potential sources of stress and the ensuing negative consequences. The major techniques described in the chapter can be found in Table 8.1.

The added risk incurred by commuting at the individual level may be too small for people to notice in their personal lives, and therefore any campaign for behavioral change may lack "social validity" (Stokols, 1992). Yet many health risks that are small at the individual level may be enormous at the aggregate level because of their prevalence in large segments of the population. Therefore, an action at the societal level, such as legislation, ordinances, or legal action, may be much more effective (Stokols, 1992). Requirements by employers (where legal), such as making

Table 8.1. Government and Organization Coping Strategies

Urging switch to mass transit
  Urban planning
  Subsidies
  Tax breaks
Marketing to the individual
  Better road and transit conditions
  Improving mass transit access
  Selling car-pooling
  Government–corporation cooperation
  Using social psychological and learning principles
  Reducing fares
Technology
  Mapping
  Special toll booths
  Smart highway and sensors
  Personal mass transit
Company methods
  Relocation
  Flexible working hours
  Telecommuting

residence within a short commuting distance from the work location a condition for hiring, may be much more effective than simple persuasion or attempts at convincing people first, that commuting is bad for them, and second, to change their commuting habits.

Such practice is already part of the understanding, written or unwritten, that can be found in municipalities where employees are required to be residents of a specific area or areas. In Israel, academics in universities, all of which are public institutions supported in most part by the government, are asked to live within certain city boundaries. This is done for noncommuting-related purposes. It is hoped that short distances between home and work will increase the likelihood that lecturers and professors will work in their offices on days in which they are not engaged in lecturing.

Only recently have the problems associated with the mass transportation system in the United States become a central item in government planning and budgeting. Some of the proposals are new, have not been tested, and are based on ideas generated by community planners, urban specialists, and personnel managers rather than social scientists. The suggestions by such experts often do not appear in the professional psychological literature but rather in the publications of these specialties or the more general, popular periodicals.

Recognizing the need to suggest practical solutions, we have combined the two types of reports so that the theoretical perspective comes from professional sources in the psychological stress literature and the practice from more generally available periodicals, such as *The New York Times* or *Personnel Journal*. On many national topics in organizational matters, the latter two are up to date in their reporting as well as objective, in most cases, in their discussion of the benefits and drawbacks of new schemes and solutions. The gap between finishing research and seeing it in print, especially in the professional/scholarly press, is considerable (Campbell, 1982), and, sometimes, publishing in more popular media provides outside and objective input. Many advantages can be cited for airing and discussing either controversial ideas or innovations as the literature is developing, not only after it has been published in final form. Besides presenting the latest relevant demographics on commuting-related themes, the reactions of individuals, organizations, and government officials to proposed changes can be found here and only much later in the industrial/organizational literature. In the following presentation of coping strategies, methods for solving the existing problems, derived either from laboratory studies or the field will be suggested, and an attempt to blend the theoretical and practical streams from the various approaches will be made.

THE BASIS OF GOVERNMENT COPING STRATEGIES

Although individuals and organizations are the ones most directly affected by the commuting problems in the urban areas of the United States, only the government can provide the global perspective needed for solving problems over wide geographic areas. One approach that has been shown to be ineffective is to continue building, whether it is more roads or more mass transportation alternatives, without careful planning and analysis of present needs and future requirements. The situation has become so critical that today the entire urban area is being overwhelmed by people on the move in both directions during the mornings and evenings. In areas such as Houston, Texas, the number of cars coming in and leaving the center city are now about equal (Orski, 1985).

The sprawling metropolitan areas that now include the city, suburbs, and, in many cases, rural locations that are well situated for highway access present a new trend that has wide-ranging implications for the future. Some feel that the problems of regional transportation will be among the most important issues facing planners in the future (Conte, 1985). To deal with these issues comprehensively is beyond the scope of this book, but by citing ideas recommended by Cervero (1986) in a review article on traffic congestion and urban sprawl, some of the major directions and possible solutions can be identified.

The first aspect of commuting that must be gauged is the design and physical layout of the land used by various employers. For our purposes, density is the key variable here. When a firm building in a corporate park decides that it is more important to have wide-open spaces than high density construction, then auto utilization will continue to dominate the mode of transportation used to get to work. Only by coordinating building plans with other companies or agencies and, more importantly, considering travel patterns in planning and developing a site, is there a chance to introduce some type of mass transit or paratransit into an area. Such integrated and coordinated complexes can include walkways, internal escalators, private buses, and other means to move people around and to direct them to central pick-up points where mass transportation is available.

A related issue is the amount of parking spaces in corporate or office parks. Studies have shown that the available area for cars is much more than is practically needed (Lenny, 1984). The effect of building and providing large open spaces in relationship to the available work space has both economic and psychological implications. Generally, parking is free to workers and their guests making it a very strong incentive to use the car even if other modes of transportation are accessible. The psychological message here is quite obvious: Bring your car, space is there for the asking, and don't worry about such things as pollution or the environment—others will take care of these problems. The solution, according to Cervero, is the creation of higher-density work settings that would go a long way toward attenuating the auto's dominance.

Another feature of these corporate parks is the attitude expressed by the designers towards public transportation. In many, if not most cases, the average walk from the office building to the parking lot is but a fraction of the walk from the office building to the nearest public transportation stop or station. In a survey of 32 centers, the average walk for the former was 116 feet and, for the latter, 480 feet. One way of partially solving this problem involves the introduction of internal private or public transportation. With the aid of subsidies by corporations and municipal authorities in the area, this convenience can be a strong incentive for individuals to give up their cars for commuting. In places where high levels of bus service are provided and amenities (for example, convenient bus shelters) maintained, these services become attractive alternatives.

Another trend that is picking up momentum in the last few years, and on the surface seems an ideal solution, is to build residential/office complexes. Here, the employee literally rolls out of bed and into the office. Vehicular traffic, of all types, is reduced. There is an increase in walking or cycling to work, as these can be efficiently accomplished if travel distances are short. New York City with its Battery Park complex is an excellent urban example of this type of construction. Although located in one of the busiest areas to be found anywhere, several esthetic components (gardens, atriums, etc.) were integrated into making life for the local resident/commuter more pleasant. However, Cervero feels the future for these large developmental projects will be set more by the marketplace than government intervention. Incidentally, housing prices, whether in the city or suburbs, are quite high and not easily afforded by most workers. This argues against this concept as a panacea for all urban transportation problems.

Many of the ideas for new projects require government involvement, although not necessarily additional taxes. A more efficient approach is to make the community wherein the development is taking place responsible for the required changes. Thus, property owners, individuals and corporations alike, finance the construction of roads or mass transportation expansions within their district through some levy on the basis of appraised land value. Such benefit assessment districts get the local people involved in both identifying their needs and recognizing that they are a logical source for the funds required to solving the problems. Variations of this method include traffic impact fees and road districts, both of which, according to Cervero, have adherents around the country.

In some cases, where some of the transportation issues have been particularly intractable and difficult to solve, government ordinances have been tried with some success. These can take many different shapes. A popular one is trip reduction schemes where companies are fined if a certain level of ridesharing or mass transportation usage is not achieved. Such ordinances have several advantages in that the corporations are given quite a degree of leeway in determining how to achieve their goals. The main disadvantage is enforcement and monitoring the progress. It is hard to know who is and who is not complying, and the effort and bureaucracy necessary are sometimes quite formidable. Similarly, parking reduction ordinances and traffic-induced growth moratoriums have supporters and antagonists for reasons similar to those of trip-reduction schemes.

FOCUSING ON INDIVIDUAL COMPLIANCE

In each of the last cases, the government is using legislation, fines, or active monitoring to obtain corporate compliance for behavior designed to reduce traffic congestion. Social and environmental psychologists focus on changing the individual, sometimes with government help. An example of this are the possible effects of train stations and bus-stop locations on individual's attitudes and stress reactions. In many situations, the government has invested resources in spreading out the distance that people have to travel. Thus, instead of having large numbers getting on at a station in the middle of the subway's journey to midtown or downtown and pushing on to the car, there are advantages for the commuter to be one of the first to enter the train.

There is some empirical evidence for this contention from a study conducted by Singer et al. (1978). The authors reported that commuters who had boarded their train at its first stop experienced less physiological strain as measured by epinephrine excretion (urine analysis) than commuters who boarded the train at a midstation. Although on the surface this negates some of the notions associated with commuting stress, namely, a longer trip implies more strain, it is consistent with the notion that subjective impedance mediates between stressor and strain. It would appear that a commuter who gets on a train without pushing, gets a seat, and is able to relax on the journey to work will perceive less stressful stimuli in the environment.

Often, governments will encourage and/or subsidize construction and use of new train stations or terminals further from the city so as to allow people to leave the crowded city or its immediate suburbs. Although, in the short run, the number of commuters coming to the city during rush hour stays approximately the same, over time, and especially if the housing is in newly developing areas, they will be able to explore more job opportunities. It may be hard to believe, but even in the crowded Northeast, there are places that have not yet been developed fully, and, with the help of government planning and encouragement, mass transportation can be an attractive selling point and inducement for potential buyers wanting to leave the city.

In 1991, *The New York Times* reported on a successful new housing development where actual and potential residents expressed satisfaction with their new homes even though their commutes were as much as 65 miles. The housing developer reported no difficulty in finding buyers for new homes which were as much as 71 to 87 minutes from work by train. Richard Birch, the planning supervisor for the Dutchess County Planning Department, was quoted as saying the location, despite its distance, was considered very attractive to commuters traveling to a wide area around the new housing development. The average number of peak-hour (i.e., rush-hour) passengers traveling from Beacon, where express trains start a nonstop run to Manhattan's Grand Central Station, has almost doubled from 1985 to 1990. Of course, for many families, the lower prices and the better environment for raising children were important selling points, but it would appear from the speed and interest expressed by buyers during the selling campaign that the absolute distance did not deter many would-be buyers. Consumers' reactions would likely have been different if there were no train station near the development and if the only way to reach mid- or downtown Manhattan business districts was through one of the infamous traffic-congested highways in and around the New York area.

GOVERNMENT SUBSIDIES

Direct governmental subsidies have been suggested as a means for getting people off the roads and onto trains and buses. From the perspective of Peter Gorgon, an associate dean of urban planning at the University of Southern California, government aid for transportation spending, including highway and mass-transit items, should consume over 100 billion dollars of the federal budget in the early 1990s. It will be wasted unless the government adopts a policy that exploits opportunities to privatize and subsidize needy transit patrons (Passell, 1991). He believes that unless a transportation policy exploits opportunities to privatize, asks most users to pay their own way, and subsidizes needy transit patrons rather than the empire-building of transit bureaucracies, the alternative will be gridlock.

The decision to spend on highway construction, road repair, and billions on surface transportation over the next few years will, according to Gorgon, simply mean more interest monuments to transit engineering. At the same time that government refuses to charge road users according to the congestion they create, some of the new transit systems carry far fewer passengers than expected and require enormous subsidies to operate. The Miami heavy-rail system is moving only 15% of the forecast traffic and at a cost of $16.77 a ride. Even Washington's much admired subway system costs the taxpayer almost $9 a ride.

Trollies are not much cheaper to operate. A relatively new system in Portland, Oregon carries just half the number of passengers projected, at a cost of $5 each. The reason for such an absurd situation, argues Gorgon, is that in most cities there are not enough commuters living along narrow corridors to support rail transportation. Also, where commuting density is too light, it is difficult to justify the use of regular bus schedules. But transit authorities keep investing in steel and concrete because the alternative is a loss of influence and employees.

At the same time, highway policy is ambiguous. Users of private cars, which are the backbone of transportation in the United States, are paying only a small fraction of the upkeep required to maintain and run an efficient highway system. According to Gorgon, one innovative way of dealing with this morass of problems is to phase out mass-transit construction subsidies, convert operating subsidies to vouchers for low-income families, and make all transit aid contingent on breaking local transit monopolies. The vouchers, modeled after food stamps, would support service for people who could not afford to commute by car. Just as important, they would create demand-driven transit systems—which Gorgon expects would evolve into flexible van and jitney networks operated by workers paid competitive wages.

He would also chip away at policies that encourage profligate use of roads. It may not be possible to eliminate existing tax-based subsidies for employer-provided parking. But one could even the playing field by allowing employees to receive transit vouchers in lieu of free parking without incurring added tax liability. By the same token, Federal rules prohibiting tolls on "currently free" parts of the interstate highway system may not be the only reason local governments balk at imposing congestion fees. Nevertheless, elimination of the prohibition would certainly do away with one good excuse. John Kain, a transportation economist at Harvard University, estimates that 90% of urban road congestion is caused by the underpricing of a key 5% of road capacity (Passell, 1991).

These are radical reforms that would alter the entire thinking about transportation, both in the eyes of the government and the consumer. Although it is unlikely that many of these changes are in the offing soon, such proposals do have many attractive features. If the poor and indigent can be taken care of and the rest of the populace be subject to the marketplace with competitive pricing, there may be some aspects of the present commuting situation that may indeed improve.

The greater use of transportation modes other than the solo car would have a major impact; however, as we have seen, the commuter's love affair with the car is quite resistant to change and this attitude is even voiced by bus riders (Flannelly & Mcleod, 1989). As yet there are too many uncertainties connected with Gorgon's plan, and it still seems hard to imagine that at any time in the future, government intervention in the commuting process could be left only to foster competition and not to as an active player in social policy making.

CAR-POOLING

Indirectly, the government is also responsible for the subsidies that many corporations mete out to their employees. For example, Osborn and

McCarthy (1987) reported that many suburban municipalities are considering or already have forced companies, through legislation, to reduce single passenger trips. The authors believe that the new attitude towards pollution can be brought into play here and be used to convince the employer and employee to subsidize certain forms of transportation at the expense of others.

We have already pointed out that mode of transportation, specifically car-pooling versus solo driving, may serve as a moderator variable (Novaco & Sandeen, 1992). Novaco and Sandeen showed the impact of gender on attitudes related to ride-sharing with regard to commuting stress. For males, mean systolic blood pressure and arterial pressure were higher for solo drivers than for ride-share passengers. Also, measures of performance including proofreading accuracy and errors in proofreading showed that performance for males was higher for car-poolers than for solo drivers. For females, significant differences were also observed, but the trends were not linear.

At least for some portion of the population, driving in a car with others produces lower levels of strain after the commute. Society, in general, and communities, in particular, are most interested in expanding the numbers of car-poolers. The advantages are clear: less air and noise pollution, less traffic congestion, and, if enough people change over, a faster commute. The problem, however, is convincing the individual car owner that the advantages are worth the perceived benefits that the solo commuter gets from driving his or her car to work.

Sims (1991) has discussed how difficult it is to get the American to switch from the private car to car-pooling. In examining survey data from the Commuter Transportation Service, a nonprofit transportation management company, responses showed that in 1980, 33% of commuters who drove to work participated in car pools, compared with only 22% in 1990. In the New York metropolitan area, data from local transportation agencies showed that, after decades of persuasion campaigns to switch away from the private automobile, more than 85% of New Yorkers still prefer to drive to work alone rather than with someone else. This confirms the inferences from a questionnaire study of commuter attitudes: Americans just love their cars (Flannelly & Mcleod, 1989).

Car-pooling, long viewed by governmental agencies as a possible remedy for worsening traffic, has simply failed to catch on in metropolitan areas around the United States. Despite a decade-long effort to persuade people to double, triple, and even quadruple up in the interest of reducing traffic congestion and pollution, the campaigns are not heeded by the public, and little behavior change is observed. Some commuters drive alone because they want to be able to leave work early or stay late and not be bothered by someone else's schedule. Others want their own cars on hand so that they can run errands at lunch, or depart immediately in case of family emergencies.

From the present book's perspective, it is not at all clear whether car-pooling should always be recommended. In many cases, it can engender its own stress. For example, commuters have to be ready at a specific hour in the morning, often quite early, especially if several people must be picked up. Although the time pressure may be somewhat less intense in the evening, the commuters still tend to wait longer than would be the case if they were driving by themselves. With midlevel managers or higher, whose working hours are often hard to pinpoint, working hours of members in the car pool may not coincide. At the end of the day, some of the car-pool members may have to wait untill the last one finishes his or her work day. When alone, the commuter can choose his or her favorite music station or put in a musical or information audiocassette. Many commuters insist that the ride in to work listening for pleasure or possibly learning some new language or business skill is a high point of their working day. The thought of car-pooling is, for such people, very unattractive, especially in light of the independent and self-reliant American life style that encourages freedom and taking advantage of every opportunity, even the car ride to work. The cellular phone has also brought a degree of freedom that fits into the solo car rider's needs. The delay on the road is not of (his or her) concern; the workday, if the commuter so desires it, begins upon entering the car in the morning.

As populations in the suburbs soared in the late 1970s and 1980s, creating traffic tie-ups on highways and back roads that were not designed to handle the sharp increase in cars, transportation officials looked to car-pooling, van-pooling, and mass transit as ways to help relieve congestion. The changeover from solo driving to some other form of group travel to work did not take place. According to Sims (1991), one partial explanation for this immutable commuting pattern is the lack of significant incentives for people to switch; i.e., research is needed to identify the specific incentives that can be used to persuade commuters to give up the convenience and flexibility of driving their own cars to work. "The jury is still out on car-pooling," said Jeffrey M. Zupan, a senior fellow at the Regional Plan Association, a nonprofit research organization. "It can work and help reduce traffic, but not until we come up with new ways to make it more appealing to the average commuter" (Sims, 1991).

Recommendations for Overcoming the Difficulties of Car-Pooling

Although comparative research on incentives and their effect on persuading people to change does not exist in the literature, some suggestions, derived from empirical and theoretical sources, can be offered.

Economic and Logic Incentives

A recent study by the Regional Planning Association found that many car pools are disrupted when riders change jobs or residences (Sims, 1991). Half of all Americans change jobs or move every 5 years, the planning association said. Starting a car pool, which requires identifying the appropriate potential members and coordinating the schedules, is often difficult and takes time. In large companies, computers are necessary and often helpful in this task. A new person may not fit in right away. Nevertheless, despite all the odds and the widespread preference for riding solo, not all commuters are averse to car-pooling. Some say it saves them money on parking, gas, and tolls. Others, worried about air pollution, say ride-sharing is simply the right thing to do. And still others say they enjoy the company and conversation. Promotions that emphasize some of these advantages need to be communicated to all potential users.

Eric B. Langeloh, Commissioner of Transportation for Westchester County, has said that at present there are few local economic incentives to car pool. Langeloh says that economic incentives such as cheaper tolls for group riders are needed. Dee Angell, president of Metropool Inc., a nonprofit company that helps commuters and companies form employee car pools, says a significant increase in car-pooling will occur when we make driving alone so costly and unfavorable that people only do it in extreme circumstances. Car-pooling already has many advantages that are often discounted or go unnoticed and must be publicized both for the individual and public good. For example, Metropool estimates that a person driving alone pays about $300 a month (1991 dollars) in driving costs to travel 55 miles round trip. The same commute would cost the members of a two-person car pool about $150 each. Car-pooling also reduces the stress of daily commuting and saves on personal car maintenance and insurance. Metropool operates a referral service for commuters who wish to form car pools and distributes a registry of commuters looking for car-poolers.

Some practical rules for increasing the usage of car-pooling are suggested. The pools sometimes have very complicated rules concerning whose turn it is to drive. By eliminating this as an issue, for example, hiring a student to drive, perhaps, with a leased van (paid for by the commuters in the van or through the student's own investment which is reimbursed over time) may make the trip experience more palatable. Costs ideally should be split among workers, companies, and government. Only when a real partnership by all parties in costs and commitment is evidenced can commuters be expected to change behavior.

Applying Psychological Principles

Does psychology have anything to say in a case like this? Phrased somewhat differently, can theory contribute to an increase in car-pooling? Based on the work in learning and social theory, it may be possible to apply some of the lessons gleaned from these areas here, too. Most of the government experts presently in the field have backgrounds in economics, planning, and urban affairs; few social scientists are involved. For example, techniques developed in the subspecialties of persuasion and power may be able to contribute to procedures for changing people's attitudes and behavior.

We would like to suggest a joint government–corporation campaign to increase car-pool usage. At the first stage, municipal authorities and company officials need to sit together and set goals that are reasonable given the demographic and geographic make-up of the workers in a particular geographical area (Landy, 1985). Thus, if workers from a particular organization all come from within the boundaries of the city, the possible number of car-poolers seems to be less than if they are more spread out throughout the greater metropolitan area.

Although the goals that are established must be realistic, they can be set at somewhat higher levels than would be warranted from previous experience. The relationship between goal difficulty and high performance has been considered by some as something close to a law in psychology (Mento, Steel, & Karren, 1987). The implication is clear, if we set lower goals, we will not achieve much more than lower goals in the long run.

In addition, rewards or incentives can be established for the specific goals decided on by both sides. The combination of goals and incentives has been shown to be quite effective as a motivator of several nontraditional performance measures including prosocial behaviors and extra-role behaviors. At the governmental level, the government can calculate what would be saved in subsidies on mass transportation as more riders joined the system. The money saved could be returned to company management and then shared with all employees whose behavior has changed during the campaign.

Although punishment is generally not the best method for attaining desired goals, it does have the positive effect of getting quick compliance. After behavior has changed, positive incentives can then be applied. One of the popular techniques for punishing drivers during an effort to get people to switch to car pools is to fine those who drive to work with less than three people (Weisman, 1991). There are many ways to mete out such negative reinforcements including charging more for parking spaces to solo drivers in the morning rush hour, requiring higher tolls on bridges and highways for solo drivers, and, in more extreme cases, having a special highway "pool patrol" at major intersections, entranceways, and exits to highways with the authority to issue computer-generated tickets for those not following rules for multipassenger driving during the rush hours. A system of punishments can also be applied at the company level. During the construction stages, taxes or subsidies can be adjusted to take into account the number of people the new building is expected to bring into the community during the day.

At the worker–company level, "power" tactics such as information, reward (both personal and impersonal) can be used to show the workers the potential psychological, economic (to the company, in higher efficiency and to the individual, as savings in commuting expenses), and social benefits of car-pooling versus automobile usage. The campaign needs to be very intensive in a particular region so that familiarity with the subject matter can be expected at the outset. The tactical aspects of the procedure (i.e., how it should be done, who should switch over to carpools, how to divide up the rewards that will be available) should be left to the workers to determine in a participative decision making (PDM) process. The PDM has been shown to be particularly effective when used for tactical rather than strategic decisions (Sagie & Koslowsky, 1993).

Other examples of government–company interaction are the various air pollution bills passed at the federal or state level that generally require the company to comply by altering previous behaviors or activities. Again, the incentive principle with preset goals can lead to major modifications in behavior. This is well illustrated by the program installed at the Farmer's Insurance company in Southern California in the early 1990s. As theory and practice were combined so well here, we describe in some detail the methods used to gain compliance with the California Clean Air Act of 1989.

The law requires companies with more than 100 employees to attain new average-rider-per-vehicle ratios. In the southern California district where the company is located, a value of 1.5 was set as a goal for companies operating in that region. Stuart (1993) reports that incentives were used very effectively to raise the ratio from around 1.06 to 1.30 in just a few years. This was quite an achievement given the "independent" solo-driver mentality whose ideology, according to the author, can be traced to the original settlers in California whose beliefs of self-reliance were difficult to modify.

The company called in a consultant who advised management on how to set up a campaign for increasing ride-share employees. A fair was held where the people were shown the environmental need for changing one's commuting behavior, and incentives were attached to the change for employees at the firm. The prizes were clearly shown to everyone and employees were told that in the future, a catalog would be available in each manager's office. The incentive system included a bonus-point system for joining the ride-share program and for each day of use. From their experience with the incentive campaign, the company coordinator for this program suggested the following points for others interested in adopting such a scheme for expanding car-pooling: (1) Promotion campaign must be constant and all-embracing. A gimmick or slogan is worthwhile—in this case appealing to the individual's environmental conscience was useful. (2) The incentive should be of high quality and be perceived as something of value. (3) A full-time transportation coordinator should be appointed with complete responsibility for implementing the incentive program. (4) The new workers must be introduced to the system as soon as they are hired, even before actually starting to work. A detailed, personally oriented explanation for the purpose and procedures involved in the campaign is highly recommended. The point of the last suggestion is to influence employees before undesirable habits, such as solo-driving routines, are formed. Again, this is one of the basic principles in educational psychology.

One of the major implications from the findings of recent researchers (Kluger, 1992; Aizer & Koslowsky, 1993) is the relationship between predictability and the degree of strain experienced by the commuter. Applying this concept may have some very positive effects on both choice of transportation and feelings of well-being after the commute. Although Kluger did show that choice among different routes does not decrease stress, especially, if all choices are bad, no clear data of the effects of choice of transportation mode are available. Thus, if commuters are convinced that the ride on the train or bus is highly predictable, both in regard to environmental variables and punctuality, then these alternative means of transportation will become a viable option, if not every day, at least, on some occasions. Spending money on infrastructure or expansion may not be as worthwhile as trying to improve the perceptions concerning the present system.

Just the fact that such a choice is available to the commuter may help reduce stress. This is particularly relevant in trying to convince more people to switch to mass transportation. When time is of the essence, a commuter who feels that the train will get him or her to the office more promptly than a car may very well use the train on those days when time is essential. This may be a positive inducement as well as provide real, attractive alternatives as well as the feeling of being in "control." Investment in punctuality, eliminating dilapidated trains or buses that are responsible for delays, and most importantly, getting this information across to the commuter is essential in altering perceptions. Thus, if a commuter has an average ride of 45 minutes to work with a 10-minute standard deviation by bus, it should be more attractive than a car ride, even of 45 minutes, with a 25-minute standard deviation.

As we have shown already, the commuter is quite reluctant to give up the use of a car for all days of the week, but if the arrival time is more predictable or less expensive with the mass transit system it may be possible to convince the commuter to do it once or twice a week. Perhaps Mondays when traffic is notoriously congested or Fridays, when leaving the car at a convenient out-of-the-city location near a train station may allow the commuter a faster get-away for the weekend, could be proposed. In any case, the campaign should focus on two aspects of control: choice between modes of transportation and the predictability afforded by bus or train.

From a somewhat different perspective, the same conclusion could also be drawn. We have already mentioned the fact that lack of information leads to uncertainty, the converse of predictability, which, in turn, can bring about stress. For many commuters, the schedule of the train or bus may very well be known, but they are not aware of the commuting time with each of these conveyances. This information is essential for the individual in making a decision in favor of public transportation. If the lack of punctuality prevents transit officials from promoting their mode of transportation, then this is where the money must go. If the on-time record is something to be proud of, then they should play that benefit up in the advertising campaign. To paraphrase a common aphorism: an informed commuter is a satisfied commuter.

SOME NEW IDEAS

Perhaps, the hardest aspect for the urban planner or transportation expert is to identify the changes that would be required in order to convince people to give up their cars during the daily rush hours. In a survey of residents of a Honolulu suburb who used their car to get to work, many expressed an interest in using paratransit rather than their automobiles (Flannelly, Mcleod, Behnke, & Flannelly, 1990). The interest was highest when the change offered better service and decreased sharply with an increase in fares. Interestingly, better service can compensate to some extent for higher fares. The authors also attempted to develop formulas for translating interest into actual demand. One of the main tenets in social psychology is the recurring finding that interest or attitudes do not always indicate or predict behavior. That is, when it comes down to giving up the freedom associated with the car, albeit with its concomitant disadvantages, the commuter may say yes, implying that he or she may want to give up the car but not change behavior when confronted with the actual situation. (The classic study in the field was done by LaPiere, 1934; updated by Ajzen & Fishbein, 1980, and Ajzen, 1991. Implications of the theory for the commuting process are discussed more thoroughly in Chapter 6 of this volume where our commuting model has been presented.)

Even in the Los Angeles area, which contains the busiest highway in America, the Santa Monica Freeway, efforts are under way to convince people to switch to alternative means of travel. Whether they will work is hard to know, but the serious earthquake in January, 1994 was a major impetus for change. What is planned in the area is still at the infant stage, but urban and transportation planners are hard at work. Egan (1994), in discussing some of the ideas being bandied about, lists the following as possible changes: car-pool lanes, bike lanes, and revamping the commuter train system. Immediately after the earthquake, ridership on the latter was up to 30,000 passengers a day, a 200% increase (Egan, 1994). However, a month later the increase was down to less than 100% increase. Good—but not good enough. Of course, some of the original increase was due to the closure of alternate routes.

Is there a subway system that works and is also profitable in the United States? The answer is yes, and it may be worth looking at some of its characteristics to see if it can be applied in other communities. Finder (1991a) calls the Newark, New Jersey subway system clean and safe. It runs like clockwork—every 2 minutes during rush hour—manages to please passengers and even turn a profit. Part of the secret, writes Finder, is related to the scale or the extent of the system. The single-car trains travel a line that is 4.3 miles long, has just 11 stops and is used by 14,000 people a day. The seats are cushioned in beige and blue. Two sets of windows line the sides: one row for seated passengers, and above them another for those who must stand.

There is also much for the rider to see. At each of the first four stations, striking tiles that date from the Depression depict scenes of the history of the area. The ride costs $1, and after stepping out of the subway, the passenger is confronted with clean white tiles and glass-enclosed waiting areas. Buses wait at the last station to take passengers to the surrounding suburbs. A sense of both cleanliness and small-town friendliness pervades the system.

Since the state pumped money into rebuilding the subway in the early 1980s, the 55-year-old line has not shown a loss. It costs about $2.8 million a year to operate and takes in about $3.4 million in revenues. The profits go to New Jersey Transit to help subsidize other bus and railroad lines. The cars used by the system were bought in 1953 from the Minneapolis streetcar system, and similar ones are still in use in Pittsburgh, Philadelphia, Boston, Toronto, and San Francisco.

Although it is not reasonable to expect to apply such a system in all urban areas, it may be possible to set up small suburban lines of this magnitude in several communities around the country. The point is that, where possible, subway commuting can work, and efforts must be made to determine where it is most appropriate. One of the major issues in mass transportation is the amount and proportion of the total bill that should be born by the public and the amount that should be carried by the government. It is recognized by all citizens and lawmakers alike that it is impossible to require passengers to pay their way, as this would probably mean the end of mass transportation as we know it today. However, many experts feel, and rightfully so, that a service is appreciated and valued to the extent that the individual feels responsible, economically as well as morally, for its sustenance.

Every few years there are discussions in one urban community after another to raise the fares so as to, at least, keep up with inflation and increases in some of the costs. Ketcham and Konheim (1991), who head an environmental and transportation planning company in New York, contend that instead of always discussing increases, a decrease in fares is not only preferable but required. They base their calculations on the fact that for every 10% increase in fares in New York, there is a 1.5% loss of subway riders and a 3% loss of bus riders. Of these last two groups, 40% would be expected to turn to cars. Of this amount, 70% would use their cars during the rush hours or commuting period. This can be illustrated by the debate in 1991 on whether to increase the fare in New York City by 25¢ from $1.15 to $1.40. Ketcham and Konheim (1991) calculated the economic and social costs for such an increase.

First, the new fare would cause 108,000 hours of delay each workday. The total time lost, with an average of 1.3 people per car, multiplied by employee costs of $10 an hour, would amount to $1.4 million each day—$350 million yearly. Second, the authors argued that the added cost to drivers would exceed the $240 million the Transit Authority would gain from a 25-cent fare increase (after factoring in the loss of 200,000 riders resulting from higher fares). Added to all these are the grimmer figures relating to driver accidents, which impact both drivers and nondrivers. Each year, the added trips would cause almost 1,300 personal injuries, 375 incidents of property damage, and 7 deaths. This translates to a cost of $132 million per year. From an environmental perspective, all New Yorkers will pay additional health premiums and expenses associated with infrastructure physical wear and tear because of added air pollution and noise—another $20 million a year. (The authors did not take into consideration the element of psychological and behavioral costs to individuals and the organizations they belong to, probably because it is much harder to give an exact figure to these consequences.) Adding up the various factors, it can be shown that for every dollar the Transit Authority raises in revenues from a fare increase (of 25¢), New Yorkers will suffer a loss of more than $2.

A method that seems fairer and more equitable for all citizens, users and nonusers of mass transportation alike, is for the committed auto commuters to make up the transit deficit and keep new drivers off the roads and in public transit. Such a system can help preserve roadway space and make sure that public transit remains a viable option for a large number of people. It is consistent with the economic principle that those who benefit from using a scarce resource should pay its true cost. That method, which could be instituted through the state's annual vehicle inspection system, is to extend the weight-distance tax on trucks to passenger cars licensed to operate in the state. The weight of a vehicle and the mileage it travels indicate the pollution it produces and the damage it causes to the infrastructure.

At a penny a mile per thousand pounds of vehicle weight, such a tax could generate $4 billion for the state of New York—enough to balance the state budget, rescue Medicaid, improve our schools, rebuild our infrastructure, and, most importantly, finance transit. Such a tax is also equitable. Lower-income people have fewer cars and drive fewer miles than upper-income households. The cost to a middle-income, one-car household would be about $400 a year, considerably less than the $575 each subway rider now pays to commute, and far less than the $1,400 a two-commuter household would pay with a $1.40 fare hike (or the $2,800 for a two-commuter family in a two-fare zone). The tax would have truckers pay a fairer share of the cost of repairing the damage they do to roads.

The $650 million that would come from vehicles operating in the five boroughs of New York City would easily cover the $251 million transit deficit. It could also generate $166 million that could be used to reduce the fare to $1, and a further $160 million that could be used to eliminate the double fares that exist for some zones.

A rollback to a $1 fare would attract many more people to public transit. More people in the subways during off-peak hours would make the subways safer. Empty buses would be filled. It would cost less to deliver goods and services. More visitors would be attracted to shops and the theater district. Currently, they argue that a conventional fare increase makes little sense economically or socially because it actually has negative repercussions on both the subway user and car driver. Thus, a system of financing that reduce car use makes sense all around.

Similar calculations for taxing drivers have also been proposed by others including legislators and environmental groups. The former are always looking for more revenues, particularly when it is possible, to tax "bad" guys (i.e., car drivers) and leave the "good guys" alone. Typical of the suggestions that have been made recently is the program designed by the World Resource Institute, an environmental group that is interested in making sure nature is preserved by keeping air pollution at a minimum (Passell, 1992). As a major contributor to air pollution, the automobile should bear some of the costs for polluting the environment. The pollution associated with driving can be measured in many ways. For example, 19 pounds of carbon dioxide are released for every 1 gallon of gas burned, and waiting in traffic wastes approximately 17.3 billion gallons a year (Passell, 1992).

The incentive for much of the enthusiasm to tax comes from the Clean Air Act of 1990 that mandated outlays of billions of dollars annually to clean up waste, brighten urban skies, and eliminate emissions of toxic gases. One of the methods that has been suggested by many different people is very fundamental: tax the burning of carbon. This is preferred to legislating limits on its use or directing which substances should or should not be used. Even among those economic professionals in the field who recognize the need to do something in this area, artificial control of resources violates some of the basic rules of the marketplace. Rather, writes Passell (1991), charging a carbon fee that is based on the amount of undesirable emissions is much more acceptable to public and industry alike. Passell cites experts who consider "traffic congestion" as one of the major external difficulties in modern life, and a way of dealing with this problem must be developed. The way America rations space on the roads is through waiting on lines, which is counterproductive as it just causes more pollution with its accompanying expenses. Today, technology exists to calculate gasoline usage by time of day and location, which would allow the government to tax drivers on the basis of wasted carbon usage. Even more importantly, argues Passell, the commuter would be able to decide which is the best way for him or her to get to work. Thus, if the individual feels that driving in the rush hour remains essential for the particular job performed, then the tax would pay for the environmental damage caused by that decision.

An estimate of the effects of such a tax are quite persuasive. Fees ranging from 1¢ to 36¢ per mile could induce enough drivers to change their behavior so that up to $21 billion could be saved by 1999. Using 1989 as a guideline year, such a tax set at reasonable levels would also bring in $98 billion in revenue to various governmental bodies, depending, of course, on the specific fee and method of administration instituted by the collection body. Most importantly, writes Passell, the commuter paying the fee would be mollified as the roads become less congested and car-pooling becomes an attractive alternative both from an economic viewpoint and from the perspective of the environment.

Making the Best of Car Driving

As the situation on the roads is getting worse very fast, experts have started to examine various aspects of the automobile commute. One of the major causes of delays on our roads are traffic accidents. It is a rare commuting rush hour that does not include at least one accident causing tie-ups for miles and miles. In 1992, the cost to the nation of traffic accidents was nearly $275 billion (Passell, 1992). The stressful effects of the time spent on the road are not only a function of the time it takes to clear up the accident but also, as we have postulated, the uncertainty in that specific commute. As these two factors, time and uncertainty, are potential moderators of the stress–strain relationship, a method of reducing the causal or moderator effects would be beneficial.

In the early 1990s, a truly innovative procedure was introduced in South Korea that could have a dramatic impact on the commuting experience in that country as well as in many other places (Weisman, 1991). In an effort to combat the country's growing automobile traffic problems and resulting traffic snarls, helicopters are being used to swoop down and pull out cars that have stalled and blocked the highways for miles. If the feeling in the United States, often expressed by commuters and government officials alike, that the roads are becoming unusable during the rush hours is accurate, then the situation in countries like South Korea may provide a lesson for all of us.

In Seoul, it can take hours to cross town or commute to work. It is not uncommon to see fist fights or loud arguments erupt in traffic that remains frozen for long periods of time. To get from one side of town to the other side in Seoul, one must travel across the city. Weisman (1991) reports that the transportation situation is so bad that commuters can expect traffic delays wherever they go. In 1990, the traffic accident data were quite grim. The record of 325,962 traffic injuries and 13,102 fatalities, may make the Koreans the world's most unsafe drivers. The use of helicopters in particularly sensitive locations, such as where highway service roads do not exist, can solve a very bad problem in a matter of minutes rather than an hour or more. Although in an ideal world it would be better to put all the efforts into preventing accidents, clearing up swiftly after an accident and unclogging roadways expeditiously is second best and, truly, essential. Besides the importance of providing the necessary aid to victims more quickly, allowing traffic to begin moving freely can be of immense benefit in reducing the negative effects of commuting stress.

Government and Technology

Besides implementing taxes, providing subsidies, and trying to encourage certain desirable behaviors and reduce undesirable behaviors, the government has recently attempted to implement modern technological tools to deal with the problems caused by transportation demands. Although this sometimes seems like an admission that the car is here to stay, improving the quality of the automobile commute is highly desirable. Science fiction readers are familiar with the scene. You enter the vehicle, punch in the coordinates of your destination on the computer, and sit back to enjoy the ride as you are automatically whisked away to your destination. This is not likely to occur for a while, but advanced technology does offer techniques for reducing traffic congestion. The GAO (1989) report of several years ago identified five specific techniques in the area of advanced technology: (1) advanced control systems; (2) advanced motorist information systems; (3) highway navigation and guidance systems; (4) vehicle location and identification systems; and (5) automated highways.

Today, we can see the changes taking place in front of our eyes. We can tune into traffic reports and rely on traffic helicopters to supply us with information we need for choosing the less-congested routes. Some mobile phone companies provide a traffic advisory service free of charge. In the near future, advanced technology can contribute significantly to the development of "smart highways" and begin to make a real difference. Sensors located throughout the highway can be set to determine vehicle speeds and traffic density. Computers, digital maps, and telecommunication equipment could convey this information to motorists through an onboard computer in their cars. The feedback would include suggestions for alternate routings. Ultimately, as in the science fiction scenario, the vehicle could be guided to the best route automatically. At the same time, advanced traffic systems could reduce congestion by recalibrating traffic signals and rerouting automobiles and trucks to less congested roads. A precursor of this advanced system is the flashing sign that is already seen above some of the major thruways electronically indicating that there is a delay and suggesting an alternate route.

We now discuss some of these innovations, particularly the ones that show the most promise or have been investigated under the close scrutiny of scientific inquiry. One of the more ingenious uses of the computer is the concept of flexible routing. This concept is based on the well-accepted notion that commuters reject mass transportation because of the inflexibility inherent in the system. Traditionally, the vehicle arrives at a station or bus stop on the basis of some prearranged schedule—not when the commuter needs it. It is perceived as being unresponsive to personal demands. O. L. Smith (1991) suggests and describes the use of a system whereby the bus routes can be made more flexible.

According to his concept, buses would be assigned a set of potential route segments that are assembled in various ways, depending on demand. Either through phones or modems located at bus stops or the commuter's home, individuals would transmit requests to the commuter system, perhaps as part of a network, via call boxes located at the bus stops. By dialing a unique number associated with the stop, the commuter enables the system to identify where the user can be picked up. Similarly, information concerning the destination can be sent to the computer. The control system then merges various requests and schedules a bus to pick up the customer within a specified time and deliver him or her to a given destination within a specified time. Confirmation by the computer informs the potential passenger when to expect pick-up and arrival. The system incorporates all types of environmental data including weather, traffic density, and any other problems that may be encountered.

There are several advantages to such a system. First, from the perspective of transportation authorities, the entire transit system becomes considerably more efficient. Instead of sending buses along a route with a predetermined schedule often to find few or even no passengers at a particular point along the line, dispatchers can now have buses arrive only when there is a demand. Incidentally, in this system, it is possible for different bus lines to pick up a specific individual. The bus that is sent to a particular stop is the one that makes the most sense for the passenger and the system. A second advantage relates to our concept of control as allied to commuting. Since the commuter has been informed of the scheduled arrival time, that individual feels that the predictability of the entire journey has increased considerably. Strain reactions that are moderated by predictability in our model should decrease. In actuality, the control expected here is even greater than when one is driving one's own car where critical information available to the flexible bus route (through the commuter network) is not known by the solo motorist.

Examples of several more mundane solutions for dealing with various transportation problems can be seen in the case of the Tappan Zee Bridge near New York City. Of all the arteries into the city during the rush hour, the drive over this bridge has always been particularly troublesome (Foderaro, 1991). Across this one bridge, traffic has increased from 10.5 million vehicles in 1960 to 39.5 million in 1990. This fourfold increase in 20 years has put transit officials on the defensive, and they are most eager to discover creative approaches that might prevent a potential gridlock. Engineers see the need to speed traffic across the bridge as one of the major directions for transportation investing in the coming years (Foderaro, 1991). Along these lines, several mechanical solutions have been suggested for easing the traffic congestion. One of these is a moveable barrier across the bridge to improve traffic flow. A movable barrier makes it possible to respond to the changing volume of traffic so that more lanes are opened toward the city in the morning and just the reverse in the evening. Adding more lanes to a bridge crossing, though quite expensive, might also help in moving cars along.

As part of a coordinated effort with regional authorities and large companies in the area, transportation officials are trying to make the drive in by car pool more attractive. In the case of the Tappan Zee Bridge, an effort is underway to create a reversible or two-way "high-occupancy vehicle" lane starting in the highway's median and continuing on to and over the bridge. (Incidentally, with much fanfare, the infamous Long Island Expressway began a high-occupancy vehicle [HOV] lane in May, 1994.) The New York State Thruway Authority is also adding electronic toll collection so that cars can breeze through the bridge's toll barrier on the eastern leg. Commuters would buy stickers, embedded with computer chips, for their windshields; an electronic device at the toll barrier would let the car pass after reading the sticker.

Additions that have been with us for a few years that can be seen on different roads around the country are high-tech traffic control mechanisms including electronic information "billboards" on expected delays, alternative routes, and helpful hints on getting to one's destination. In some cars, devices for informing the commuter which way to drive can be linked to a central system. Such a system, often with a mapping software, has a dual role in the commuting process: It informs the driver and the central computer about the status of several key driving indicators including speed, road conditions, and alternatives that can be tried. Although all of these systems are designed to get the commuter to his or her destination faster, it is clear that they are also stress-reducing as they help in making the trip more predictable by reducing some of the uncertainty.

COMPANY COPING STRATEGIES

Over the past decade, several new organizational coping strategies have been formulated for dealing, primarily, although not exclusively, with the effects of commuting. Often, a specific strategy such as allowing employees to work at home, part-time or full-time, has other desirable benefits for a firm besides the reduction of commuting-related stress. Thus, by allowing people to work at home, it is possible to draw from a much larger pool of potential employees. The work force may even include people from various states or nationals from other countries. Although many of the strategies discussed in the chapter were actually designed for other purposes also, in general, we emphasize the advantages that relate to the commuting experience.

Before introducing new coping strategies for mitigating the negative effects of driving or riding to work and back, the organization must first recognize that certain workers are experiencing or may experience some form of physiological or emotional strain related to the commute that needs to be treated (in the widest meaning of the word) in some way. According to our model, the strain response has implications for individual and organizational outcomes including arriving at work on time (or not at all), performance, and safety.

Management that is not attentive to a worker's emotional state may only see a red line or warning signal when productivity or safety (with its concomitant medical and economic costs) is affected. Many investigations have shown that stress beyond a certain level, regardless of the model or theory underlying the relationship, influences organizational effectiveness directly or indirectly (Arsenault & Dolan, 1983; Landy, 1985; Spector, Dwyer, & Jex, 1988). With the stress attributed to the commuting experience only becoming prominent, at least from a research perspective, in the past decade or so, governments, companies, and even the individual employees are beginning to realize that organizational intervention is necessary for either preventing or dealing with commuting stress. According to our approach, the model provides a technique for providing assistance to the commuter: Anywhere along the model's paths intervention can prove useful. The organization that waits to the end of the process before deciding to act may actually have missed an earlier opportunity that would have minimized any damage.

For the rest of this chapter, we discuss some of the different techniques that are available for organizations interested in reducing the aftereffects of commuting. In most of the cases, the relationship to the model is straightforward. Several of the methods are actually connected to theories of stress in general, and a few are answers specifically to the problems of commuting stress.

Avoidance or Fleeing

One method that has been shown to have immediate financial implications for an organization is for it to move or relocate to another site. This may be referred to as the basic and first reaction by many inside and outside an organization to the problem of a large number of workers who must commute to work. Typically, but by no means, always, a large corporation with its headquarters in a downtown or central area, is confronted with the dilemma: to leave or dig in and try to make the situation more comfortable for the employee. Among the main disadvantages cited for leaving the city is the distance between customers of the company and management that a move to a rural or suburban area would be likely to create. However, with the introduction of such sophisticated tools as telecommunications, teleconferencing, and computer messaging, distance no longer has the same connotation as it did in the past.

As such relocations involve moving out of the city to suburban or even rural sites, headquarters staff, rather than manufacturing or line people are usually involved. The senior author worked for one of the large corporations in the United States in the early 1980s when a decision was taken to move from New York City to the southwestern part of the United States. By selling the corporate headquarters building for quite a substantial sum and paying a portion of this amount for constructing a new central office building, the organization was able to realize a very handsome profit.

Although the motivations for leaving the city are many, and "life style" is said to improve after such a move, transportation concerns are clearly a part of the picture. The decision is a difficult one, as many employees have formed attachments over the years, children must be uprooted, and the needs of working, as well as, nonworking spouses, must be considered. As Pearson (1989) writes so clearly, the alternative sometimes comes down to either moving the work or the people. A middle approach, intervention, of different types, has a laser or surgical quality associated with it, and is appropriate in many cases.

Assessment and Intervention

When discussing the organization's role in reducing stress, the concept of assessment of the stressors in the environment is essential. The first step involved in arriving at an estimate of what the stressor is and how much of it is actually affecting the employees, involves an analysis of the objective characteristics of, as well as the subjective reactions to, the stressor. In our model, both objective and subjective impedance are included because the objective experience affects later stages directly, in addition to the direct and indirect effects attributed to the subjective experience. A worker who feels that the commute is stressful because of the long trip or excessive time involved may actually experience physiological reactions (e.g., sweating because of the crowded conditions or high temperatures in the subway) because of some other stimulus. Intervention then would only be focused on the problem causing the strain if all the significant aspects of the trip had been determined and their impact assessed.

Assessment of stressor stimuli is also important for another reason. Without knowledge of the relevant stimuli and consideration of certain moderators, the links that lead from stressor to strain cannot be analyzed and studied. As the manifestation of strain in work has many origins, untangling them is one of the major goals in personnel and industrial settings. The employer and employee are both interested in the same thing: quality of the work life and high productivity. Maximizing well-being and reducing negative effects associated with any stressor can be viewed as values for the organization in letting the worker know the organization's concern is important in helping to get the message across that the employee is not alone but that the company will work with him or her to solve all outstanding problems.

Not all of the methods are available to each organization. For some people within an organization many of the coping techniques are not appropriate, and for still others, because of various individual difference variables, the methods will not work. Nevertheless, it is critical for the organization to investigate various coping strategies or intervention techniques for the purpose of coming to grips with the relevant issues. The following discussion is based on empirical as well as theoretical findings that have recently been adopted by various companies.

Before we continue, a word of caution must be emphasized. Murphy (1988) in his article on workplace intervention states that the decision to implement a specific strategy is rarely based on scientific inquiry and evidence; rather, it is generally a function of the nature of the stress and costs or economics involved in implementing the specific course of action (p. 302). Thus, the problems associated with commuting will more likely be considered if objective data can be provided that workers have been affected and that productivity has been reduced. Applying our model to various settings may provide a method for the organization to determine the percentage of variance for any of the outcome variables that can be attributed to the commute. An estimate of the actual cost, in dollar and cents, can then be made by applying utility analysis formulas. Although originally applied to personnel selection decisions (Schmidt, Hunter, Outerbridge, & Trattner, 1986), "recent work in the area of utility analysis suggests that human resource policies and interventions can have a significant influence on business organizations" (Becker & Huselid, 1992, p. 227; see also Boudreau, 1991). A detailed model of the causes and consequences in the stressor–strain relationship in a particular situation can provide a better understanding of the particular changes that will make the most sense.

Flexible Work Arrangements

From the available data, it is clear that a major change in the 9-to-5 way of working is taking place in America today. In a recent survey reported in the *Personnel Journal* (More companies . . . , 1993), employers are beginning to change over to more flexible work arrangements. This includes telecommuting (working at home), flex-time work, part-time work, and job sharing. Catalyst, an organizational survey outfit, found, that compared to 1989, one-third more firms in 1993 were interested in using flexible work arrangements. Also, as compared to 1989 when only a few firms reported that such a possibility even existed at their place of work, in 1993 nearly 40% of companies offered such an option to some of its employees. Much of this change is based on a theory that supports the notion that flexibility at work can lead to many positive consequences for the worker and organization.

Alternative work schedules are potentially an ideal solution to the problems of commuting stress. It is during the rush hour in the morning or evening that the environmental stressors are most noxious. Crowding, noise, traffic jams, and time delays—these are all characteristic of the those few hours in the morning or evening when everyone is suddenly on the road. The requirement to arrive at the company's offices at 9:00 A.M. contains the ingredients so clearly described by our model as leading to strain reactions. It is at this hour when environmental stressors (noise, air pollution, crowding, etc.) are potentially at their peak. The commuter feels that little control, actual or perceived, is available to him or her. Restructuring the work schedule in such a way so that place of work or arrival time is not a given imposed by management but is open to input by the employee adds the element of control that is necessary for stress reduction.

Flex-time and the Concept of Control

Flex-time allows employees to vary (control) their work arrival and departure times. Landy (1992) defines the concept as permitting the worker quite a bit of discretion about the workday schedule as long as he or she shows up for a core number of hours during the day. Actually it is difficult to get people to change their behavior, and, at first, at least, there is little change as to the average time of arrival or departure. This resistance occurs because habits are often determined by outside variables including personal obligations, school times, and transportation schedules (Ronen, 1981). However, the fact that the individual is given the possibility of changing the start of the workday as well as the end of the workday is an adequate basis for achieving a feeling of control.

The organizational issues that were the forerunners of flex-time were problems related to motivating people to arrive at work punctually and the difficulties of transportation in many urban settings (Krausz & Hermann, 1991). Over the past two decades, many organizations have moved over to this new type of work schedule. Murphy (1988) says it is likely to provide a most effective organizational intervention technique.

In reviewing the findings in this area, we find much of the available data are anecdotal, and few investigators have actually studied the effects of flexible working hours on stress. Of the better evaluative studies in the field (Narayanan & Nath, 1982; Orpen, 1981), employees were generally found to be happier with their lives after changing to a flex-time system. The benefits of flex-time go beyond the workplace. For example, personal and family obligations may be more efficiently performed by starting the day later than usual. Landy (1992, p. 142) feels that even the possibility of change may be stimulating in that the organization is telling the person he or she may alter the routine when it is needed.

One of the more comprehensive studies in the field, though somewhat flawed methodologically, was conducted by Pierce and Newstrom (1983). They studied several aspects of flexible work schedules and found that psychological strain symptoms correlated with most of the flexible work schedule characteristics. Methodologically, according to Murphy, the Pierce et al. study was weak because the data were collected from one group in a posttest design. It is hard to draw any inferences about the effects of intervention in such a case, as the observed results may be caused by many other external stimuli. However, the study did yield important findings in that work schedules were perceived by employees as contributing to strain. The study also showed that behavioral outcomes (absenteeism and performance) were related to the flexible work schedule characteristics.

The organization should maximize the information relating to flex-time by providing a detailed description of how it works and what is expected from the employee (Landy, 1992). In Chapter 5, on studies relating to control and stress, we pointed out that leaving the worker in the dark by not clarifying specific information creates uncertainty and is stress producing. Workers who have to arrive on time at rush hours or be penalized, formally, according to organizational rules, or informally, by the cultural norms that exist, may very well experience stress. Flex-time is a method of reducing this potentially noxious stimulus.

Does Everyone Like Flex-time?

The advantages of flex-time are clear. However, are there some disadvantages also? Are there people who don't like it or prefer not to use it? In a study by Krausz and Hermann (1991), some of these issues were reviewed and discussed. For some people, to change habits even if offered an opportunity to do so is difficult and is resisted. Also, workers report being disturbed by the comings and goings of their colleagues as well as the strict system of accountability that goes with the flex-time. It appears that as with the other suggested solutions to commuter stress, flex-time can work in many circumstances, but not all, to reduce the effects of stress.

Telecommuting

Probably, the best way to reduce the negative consequences of commuting is to stop going to work. In many work settings, this technique is available for various job titles. Although some cost savings are also involved, these are, probably, of secondary importance in deciding to let workers stay home. Often referred to as telecommuting or teleworking, this new phenomenon has become increasingly popular over the past decade. Today, the numbers of people it involves are truly impressive. According to some estimates, the number of people doing any type of income-producing work at home may be as high as 20 million people, about 20% of the total U.S. work force (Shamir, 1992). Whereas in the late 1980s the number working at home for a corporation or true telecommuters was only about 1.9 million people, or less than 2% of the U.S. labor force, by 1992 the number had swollen to 6.6 million people, over 6% of the total working population (Catching up on . . . , 1993).

In a survey reported in *Home Office Computing* (Espindle, 1992), a periodical aimed at the telecommuter, data showed that the telecommuter group is growing faster than any other segment of the work-at-home force. The rate has been higher than 20% annually through the early 1990s. Reasons given for this change included those we have become familiar with in discussing stress in a commuting context: air pollution, traffic congestion, and ability to supervise children. The survey also indicates that the corporate workplace has become more flexible in allowing workers to opt for working at home.

The so-called computer and technological revolution as manifested in the recent talk of an information highway has produced major changes in the way we work. Once the image of work and home were distinct and comprised, basically, of a man or woman leaving home in the morning for a day of work at the office or factory and returning in the evening. Today, the trend at many work places is to decentralize various types of work and allow both the employee and organization to benefit. This major transformation of the work place is probably the main antecedent to teleworking (Collins & Heywood, 1992).

Although telecommuters are generally assumed to be doing their work at home, there are many types of activities that allow or require the employee to work outside the office. People who are sales representatives, utility meter readers, and insurance agents all do some of their work "on the road." Shamir (1992) refers to this type of employment as remote work. The fact that they do not have to be at the office at specific times and that they have little contact with other workers presents some major problem for the individual and for the organization. In particular, loyalty, organizational commitment, and job involvement may be hard to develop under such circumstances.

For the commuter, the alternatives seem clear. The disadvantages of commuting have been described through much of the book; for them, telecommuting removes some of these stressful stimuli. The opportunity to work at home is not possible for everyone but when and where it is available, an employee decision must be made. Is the trade-off worth it? Each individual must evaluate for himself or herself and determine the costs associated with each alternative: giving up the corporate culture, some promotion opportunities, and role/identity by working at home versus the strain reactions including psychological, physiological, and behavioral consequences that result from commuting.

In a report of a comprehensive survey of over 4,000 readers of *Home Office Computing* conducted in 1992, several reasons were cited for working at home (Espindle, 1992). The one that was listed first was "I feel more relaxed." About 98% of subjects are happier working from home, 96% would recommend working at home to others, and 88% would never return to the corporate world. The mean age of responding subjects was 43.4, 61% were males respondents, and 75% were married, with an average of two children each. Although the sample was probably biased in that we do not know the characteristics of readers who didn't respond and how representative of all telecommuters the readership of the periodical actually is, it does provide some insight into the phenomenon. It appears from the trend of the data over the past few years and the satisfaction expressed with working at home, that the numbers are likely to increase in the future.

If technological advances such as telephones with television capabilities and the establishment of a universal information highway (including the use of living rooms or basements in private homes as "control centers") continue at the present pace, the home should take its role with the office and factory as a routine work place. Although the trend is up, a plateau will eventually be reached. Staff functions such as supervisors or managers and line jobs at factories will always be part of the corporate scene, but with the new possibilities they will be part of a rich fabric of flexible work places in the future. Shamir (1992) feels the jury is out on the merits and demerits of telecommuting. Future investigators must examine the whole area from a social psychological perspective. Their role must be not to report on the trend but rather concentrate on how it can be made more agreeable for employee and organization alike.

SUMMARY REMARKS

From the above discussion, it is clear that a model such as the one presented in the book provides a particular advantage to management. The usual research designs applied in the field of commuting, including much of the research reported in the book, employ correlations or multiple regression analysis for drawing inferences. They do not permit the personnel manager or human resource specialist to make sophisticated economic calculations concerning costs of adopting certain coping strategies. However, our model, which includes indirect effects, provides a much broader perspective of real costs. The changes that result from trying to meet some of the problems faced by commuters can be compared to leaving the situation unchanged. With the inclusion of all, or at least most, variables described in the model a more accurate picture of the value of one or more intervention technique can be obtained.

9

Methodological Issues in Commuting Research

The area of commuting research is one of the most difficult for the social and/or environmental psychologist to examine scientifically. Although we can often simulate many aspects of the field in the laboratory, the commuting experience is a rather complex social phenomenon that must, at some point of a research protocol, be studied in a natural environment. As we have seen in the previous chapters, the constellation of variables at play here are too numerous for the researcher to manipulate in a laboratory, where only a limited number of independent and dependent variables can be manipulated and tested. Nevertheless, the laboratory can play a critical role in commuting research. By allowing the researcher to isolate one or two variables with the intention of studying them methodically (i.e., a series of controlled studies with each new study building on the previous one), the laboratory may help in identifying the qualitative and quantitative nature of specific links and for developing more comprehensive theories (Monahan & Loftus, 1982). Yet, one should not underestimate the difficulties present in commuting-related laboratory research because such research has not always yielded clear results (Aiello et al., 1977).

As interactions are very common in the field, it is important to remember that the sum of the individual effects is probably not equal to the overall effects of several variables acting together. Thus, a significant link found in the laboratory may be attenuated or even disappear completely when examined in the field. This is particularly true in an area such as commuting research where multivariate relationships are the rule and not the exception.

Although it is difficult to find many true laboratory investigations in the commuting literature, studies such as the one conducted by Novaco et al. (1979) on the impact of traffic congestion (referred to as impedance by the authors) attempted to focus on very specific hypotheses for selected participants. Novaco et al. found that impedance predicted subject mood but not task performance. The authors reported that locus of control interacted with impedance and helped in predicting some of the tasks but not all of them. Many other potentially critical variables discussed previously in the book, such as the quality of the trip (traffic lights, etc.) or personality indicators (time urgency), may have improved prediction in the study but were not included by the authors. A well-designed study such as was conducted by Novaco et al. (1979) focuses only on a few variables at a time, and only after a series of these studies with their positive and negative findings can some meaningful inferences be drawn.

A few more words from one of the better social researchers about the distinction between laboratory studies and field research as well as the implications of the latter for the former may be appropriate here. Rodin (1985, p. 862) has stated very succinctly that the applied researcher must not give up theory for social relevance. Even when the situation does not lend itself to explaining all the linkages in a process, it does not preclude the researcher from trying to explain as much as possible. Intervention, for example, even when based on only partial knowledge or "some" of the truth, may still be effective. In any case, when completely accurate information is not available, repeated attempts may yet reveal useful, practical, if not, theoretically precise information. This does not mean a person should go fishing for significant relationships, or phrased slightly differently, conduct research that is not hypothesis driven. Rather, the opposite is true. The researcher should base his or her attempts on theory (e.g., in the Novaco et al. [1979] study, traffic impedance was expected to serve as a constraint that is likely to have negative consequences on the individual) while recognizing that each trial is somewhat faulty and incomplete.

ISSUES RELEVANT TO FIELD STUDIES

The fact that the commuting process involves field research and uses, in most cases, correlational data endows the whole area with certain features. Although many rich statistical techniques are available for analyzing such data, the limitation as regards cause–effect statements implies that the researcher and practitioner must proceed cautiously before making any inferences. As it is hard to isolate the link or set of linkages responsible for a specific response, statements concerning the nature of the theoretical model as well as the best intervention technique are often difficult to prove. A partial solution and relatively new approach to this predicament is the formulation and testing of structural equation models.

After presenting the setup of the structural equation model, which has already been suggested as the preferred method for testing the relevant linkages in our formulation, we discuss several methodological issues that are particularly relevant to commuting and demonstrate some of the ways for dealing with each of them.

THE STRUCTURAL EQUATION MODEL

The precursor of structural equations, path analysis, allows the researcher to use multiple regression techniques along with information on temporal order to determine the linkages and sequence in a set of variables. For example, in commuting research, certain demographics, such as educational level or age are postulated as preceding the measure of time or distance between home and work. In turn, the latter variables are hypothesized as preceding the two main types of strain measures, namely physiological and psychological responses. Within the set of consequence variables, our model suggests that the former precede the latter, but this is not obvious and is a statement that can be tested with path analysis.

Besides the usual advantages of path analysis, structural equations or the analysis of covariance structure allows for the inclusion of latent factors as the relevant variables. Thus, it may not always be clear which specific variables are causally related, but it is possible with the structural equation technique to show that an underlying factor is actually responsible. Let us illustrate with an example from commuting. We have stated previously that the various obstacles perceived by the commuter during the journey to or from work must be considered in any comprehensive model. Novaco et al. (1990) referred to these constraints on the journey to work as subjective impedance. Examples of items included by the authors were: necessity to apply the brakes often, traffic accidents along the roads, numerous traffic lights, yield or stop signs that force reduction in speed, etc. When applying structural equations, these items need not be considered as individual variables, rather latent, underlying factors can be extracted from them (similar to traditional factor analysis), which, although not observed, are the basis for the cause–effect links in the model. Thus, instead of considering the list of individual items, their latent factors (which are, generally, much fewer than the original number of individual items) appear in the model.

Similar to factor analysis, the technique uses the common elements of the individual items to form latent factors that are considerably more reliable, and probably more valid, than models based on individual components and, invariably provides the researcher and practitioner with a more integrated and comprehensive model.

DETECTING MODERATORS AND MEDIATORS

As we saw in the commuting model, variables such as mode of transportation and sex serve as moderators, whereas perceived stress or job control may act as mediators. These variables are referred to as intervening variables, and their effect may be such as to modify, reduce, or even vitiate the relationships in our model. Over the years, multiple regression techniques have been devised for dealing with these types of variables, and the inferences drawn have been considerably more sophisticated than the traditional examination of the relationship between one dependent variable and one (or more) independent variable(s) (Cohen & Cohen, 1983).

Moderators are said to change the empirical relationship between independent and dependent variables (Frese & Zapf, 1988). The moderators do not have to be correlated with either variable, and their effects are determine by either looking at the relationships for different subgroups or by examining interaction terms in multiple regression analysis. In the commuting literature, gender is a good example of this phenomenon. As we have suggested before, female commuters may experience more of a strain response than male commuters after a long commute. A simple examination of correlations between time and strain response for male and female commuters separately would indicate whether moderators are present. According to our hypothesis, the correlation for the latter group should be significantly higher than for the former group. A more rigorous technique often referred to as moderated regression analysis has become the method of choice for detecting the significance of hypothesized moderators (Cronbach, 1987; Russel & Bobko, 1992). As presented and discussed in detail by Cohen and Cohen (1983), the method is quite simple in practice. With the usual multiple regression problem, independent variables are entered into an equation one at a time for purposes of predicting the dependent variable (in statistical terms "explaining the variance" associated with the dependent variable). An interaction term serves as an indicator of the presence or absence of a moderator when it serves as a significant *additional* predictor of the dependent variable. There are several different procedures for determining the order of entry that are not particularly relevant for us here.

In the commuting example mentioned above, this implies that in predicting a strain response such as heart rate, the variable time (or some other impedance measure) is entered first, followed by gender, and then the interaction term, gender by time. If the prediction afforded by the last term is significant, then we can assume that a moderator exists.

Techniques for increasing the strength of the moderator effect have also been discussed. One way for accomplishing this is to make sure that the observed variable contains as many response options as the theoretical construct (Russel & Bobko, 1992). Thus, a continuous measure or any scale that is behavioral is preferable to a Likert-type item (or items) that has been squeezed into a "manageable" format such as five or seven alternatives but is, in actuality, not representative of the latent construct. In most studies, where Likert-type moderators are used, the interaction obtained is an underestimate of its true value. In our model, gender of the commuter or even mode of transportation (mass transportation vs. other means) are moderators whose construct can be considered as equivalent to their observed variable and should not be subject to any significant attenuation.

Mediator variable analysis serves a different purpose than the identification of moderators. They account for some or all of the observed relationship between the independent and dependent variable. Although they can also be identified by using multiple regression analysis, the procedure is actually quite different. The multiple regression is first determined by using the independent variable as a predictor of the dependent variable. In a second regression analysis, the dependent variable is predicted by the hypothesized mediator. Finally, in a third equation and the critical step here, the dependent variable is predicted from the mediator and the independent variable. Although several comparisons of the variance explained by each of the three equations are possible, the essential comparison involves determining the additional prediction afforded by the independent variable after the mediator has been entered into the equation. If the independent variable does not help in predicting (i.e., does not explain any more of the variance of the dependent variable) or its prediction has been attenuated (i.e., explains less of the variance than when it was entered by itself in the first step), then we can say that a mediator is present.

The study by Evans and Carrere (1991) on traffic congestion and physiological stress among bus drivers provides a good example of the differential effects of mediators, as they have defined the term. Although we have decided to use job control as a moderator, the article by Evans and Carrere presents a clear illustration of its use as a mediator. In their study, levels of epinephrine and norepinephrine for bus drivers after their operating shift for the day, served as the dependent variable. Differential findings for the two outcome measures were obtained. First, when the dependent variable was norepinephrine, the independent variable, traffic congestion, when entered in the prediction equation after the hypothesized mediator variable, job control, did not help in predicting the dependent variable (i.e., did not explain any significant additional variance). When the adrenaline measure was used as the dependent variable, results were similar, but the mediating effect was not as strong (i.e., the independent variable still explained some of the dependent variable's variance but not as much as it did when it was in the equation by itself).

COMMON METHOD VARIANCE

One of the more popular ways to conduct research in social psychology is through the use of a specific data collection method, such as one long instrument that contains the items for the independent variable(s), dependent variable(s), and moderator(s). For example, an investigator who wants to determine the relationship among commuting time, distance, perceived stress, and lateness may distribute, through the mail, a questionnaire to workers who have been chosen in some systematic way. Besides the usual problems of random sampling and representativeness of the respondents, answers provided to the various items and scales may be a function of common method variance.

Keeping the above example in mind, the problem with common method variance can be explained very simply. The individual who is negative about life in general will answer questions on the test that reflect this fact. The common method itself will tend to produce overlap among the scales or measures in the study. Thus, the score on the perceived stress scale as well as commute time, distance, and number of latenesses will be exaggerated in the same direction. The correlations that are calculated will be spuriously high, and techniques, such as correlational or multiple regression analysis, will show links when, in fact, they do not really exist. This threat is far from being a mere theoretical argument. In fact, at least one variable that presents a common method problem–negative affectivity was identified.

NEGATIVE AFFECTIVITY

Considered by some as equivalent to or part of the neuroticism dimension defined in the five-factor general personality model (Digman, 1990; McCrae, Bartone, & Costa, 1987), negative affectivity (NA) has also been seen as equivalent to trait anxiety (Watson & Clark, 1984). It is obvious why this problem is of concern in the stress–strain literature where several researchers view NA as a nuisance variable that may be distorting the relationship between self-reported stressors and strain. This nuisance factor has been described as a generalized cognitive set that is likely to influence a wide range of perceptions about potentially negative phenomena (Clark & Watson, 1991; Burke, Brief, & George, 1993). An individual who is high in NA will have a negative orientation regardless of the specific stimuli to which he or she is exposed.

The more subjective the self-report measure, the greater the likelihood that NA is playing a role. As conceptualized by Burke et al. (1993), the problem exists not only with the independent variable but also with the dependent variable. This implies that observed correlations may be inflated, making it necessary to partial out or remove this factor from self-report stress and strain indicators in the commuting paradigm. The factor has been identified as a legitimate concern by most investigators of the phenomenon, and a reanalysis of some previous data sets have supported this contention (Burke et al., 1993). Nevertheless, others, such as Chen and Spector (1991), contend that NA does not overlap significantly with either stress or strain. Schaubroeck et al. (1992) found that in measuring the relationship between self-report stressors and strain, controlling for NA on the latter significantly attentuated the effects of work stressors (p. 332).

Although this whole issue has not yet been resolved adequately to draw definitive conclusions, some hard and fast rules for the commuting researcher can be stated. First, it seems advisable to use objective measures at all stages of the model including the measures of the potential commuting stressors (time, distance, number of interchanges, number of traffic lights, etc.), physiological indicators (heart rate, blood pressure, etc.), and organizational outcomes (absenteeism, lateness, etc.). When determining attitudinal and emotional strain indicators, the problem is more pronounced. By its very nature, these measures are subjective and may be susceptible to confounding with NA (even Schaubroeck et al., 1992, who did not find stress measures particularly affected, did report the problem with self-report strain).

In such situations, where self-report is inevitable or even desirable, the researcher can still reduce the likelihood of inaccurate inferences from the findings. First, by including an NA measure in the study, it can be partialled (i.e., statistically removed) from all self-report indicators. If that is difficult to accomplish, it may be worthwhile to include several types of indicators of the same construct each measured with a different instrument and, if possible, with a different method. For example, if the job satisfaction of the commuter is being investigated, it can be measured with several distinct scales each constructed somewhat uniquely and measuring a different aspect (job content, employees, etc.) of the construct. Techniques for extracting a latent construct underlying the various measures would increase the likelihood that the common element, job satisfaction, appears in the correlational analysis rather than as a confounded measure. As Burke et al. (1993) so aptly state, "a call for a multimethod approach is a call for increasing not only the quantity but the quality of the data in stress–strain research" (p. 410).

Before leaving this topic, a few points should be emphasized. It is possible that for some individuals the so-called strain reaction will be positive and that the converse of NA, that is, positive affectivity (PA) is the nuisance variable. Thus, an individual who is predisposed to positive emotional states may state that the solo car commute provides an opportunity to be alone, to contemplate, to develop ideas. Investigators have not paid enough attention to the possibility of PA influencing the results, and Burke et al. (1993) argue that it may be just as important in some cases. Moreover, some measures in the field may have both NA and PA components, and since researchers have shown the two affects to be independent of each other, it may be necessary to deal with both nuisance factors within one study (Brief & Robertson, 1989; Burke et al., 1993).

Aware of this last issue, Judge (1993) used a modification of the Weitz (1952) neutral object scale that appears to hold up better over time and is more closely connected to the concept of a "trait" (which is, more or less, permanent) unlike PA or NA measures that are more closely linked to "state" measures and are more liable to be affected by the situation. The word predisposition as used by Judge can be defined as a long-lasting personality characteristic, generally, but not completely invariant from situation to situation. It is interesting to note that Judge's modified Weitz scale, referred to by the originator as a *gripe index,* since it lists several of the common dissatisfactions with life and includes a few commuting-related items. Among these daily commuting hassles cited by the researcher are the following: today's cars, local speed limits, the way people drive, and public transportation.

CAUSE–EFFECT RELATIONSHIPS

One of the major objectives in any scientific discipline is to uncover cause–effect links. Generally, this requires an experimental design that includes control of the independent variables and random assignment of subjects to experimental and control groups. When this is not possible and the researcher is still interested in causal statements, alternative statistical techniques often referred to as "quasiexperimental" need to be employed. Although any such procedure implies that a truly controlled experiment no longer exists and confounding (overlap between variable effects) is likely taking place, many theoretical benefits can still be realized here (Cook & Campbell, 1979). Rodin (1985), although recognizing the limitations inherent in the quasiexperimental approach, still feels that the potential practical or societal benefits are worth the price of a restricted theoretical contribution from the findings.

Neale and Liebert (1986, pp. 10–15) described several types of causal relationships between two or more variables. Each is discussed, in turn, below. In addition, we try to show how each type of causal statement has practical applications to commuting stress. First, a necessary and sufficient relationship is one in which some factor or condition, X, is required to produce an effect and will always do so. The authors state that in social science it is rare to find a causal variable that is a necessary and sufficient condition for an effect variable. In commuting stress, it is also difficult to imagine any predictor that will show this relationship with an outcome variable.

In some cases, the independent variable is viewed as necessary but not sufficient for the occurrence of the dependent variable. For example, if we say that in order to solve a problem in calculus, a student must know basic mathematics, the implication is that the latter is a necessary condition for the former. However, the knowledge of basic principles such as addition or subtraction does not guarantee the ability to understand calculus. Again, it is difficult to cite a good example in the commuting process. Although there is greater uncertainty than would be expected in the natural or physical science, we can view the objective experience as a necessary condition for the subjective experience. The uncertainty enters the picture here because it is possible, albeit highly unlikely, that a person will find the commuting experience as taking a significant amount of time even if there were no commuting experience at all.

Sufficient but not necessary causal relationships are those where the appearance of a specific factor is just one of many possible causes for an outcome. Perspiration as a physiological response to crowding on a hot subway car is such an example. Here, the causal variable may indeed be responsible for the observed change in measured perspiration, but the effect may also be a function of other antecedents. This is a popular research paradigm and most of our conclusions in social science, after controlling for as much of the outside variables as possible, actually refer to this type of cause–effect relationship.

A contributory causal relationship is one in which the predictor is neither necessary nor sufficient for causing the outcome but contributes to it. Neale and Liebert (1986, p. 12) refer to this phenomenon as "chang[ing] the likelihood of an outcome occurring." For example, after a long, tedious commute home, the husband (or wife) may be on edge and any sort of frustration may be enough to set him (or her) off.

Although the authors do not refer to indirect effects in a causal chain, this is really what we are referring to when saying a variable contributes to a relationship.

Causal variables may act as both outcomes and predictors. This is the commonly accepted viewpoint of structural equations where the links are like a chain that can play different roles. It should be emphasized that, strictly speaking, there should be some finite time between the different functions here. Thus, when describing the effects of perceived stress on physiological variables and, in turn, on affective variables, the middle variable should begin after the first one has started and before the third variable has started. Otherwise, the cause and effect factors would not be clear.

It is also common in social research to see one other phenomenon: the feedback loop. If we have two variables X and Y in a causal relationship with each other, i.e., X and Y, then a feedback loop is said to exist if Y, in turn, also is a cause of X, at another point in time. Our model allows for feedback loops among the physiological, affective, and attitudinal variables. Thus, it is possible for a long commute to have physiological and psychological consequences which, in turn, may led to greater absence of lateness behavior. The fact that the individual is absent or late for work may very well trigger all sorts of reactions. A recursive effect could be expected wherein the behavior produces certain physiological responses (higher blood pressure) or psychological responses (greater tension). Finally, as with much of the previous discussion of causal relationships, the time element is critical. Thus, a design that wants to test for such relationships must measure events across time rather than at a specific moment of time. Such longitudinal studies are the preferred technique in true experimental designs, but, many contingencies, including financial, often make it difficult to carry out.

In this chapter, we have tried to point out some of the common methodological issues that confront social researchers, in general, and the investigator of commuting, in particular. Well-designed studies, whether in the laboratory or in the field, can add to our information on the process and relationships involved in the commuting experience. Such an investigation should try to obtain its data from many sources using various methods. Identifying moderators or mediators are especially important for achieving theoretical understandings and verifying the proposed formulation. In the optimal case, data collected from a longitudinal cause–effect study have benefits for both the researcher and practitioner as such data allow for confirmation of hypothesized sequences or linkages and enable the prudent application of intervention techniques.

References

Abbot, B. B., & Baida, P. (1986). Predictable versus unpredictable shock conditions and physiological measures of stress: A reply to Arthur. *Psychological Bulletin, 100*, 384–387.
Abdel-Halim, A. A. (1980). Effects of person–job compatibility on managerial relations to role ambiguity. *Organizational Behavior and Human Performance, 26*, 193–211.
Abdel-Salam, A., Eyres, K. S., & Cleary, J. (1991). Drivers' elbow: A cause of ulnar neuropathy. *Journal of Hand Surgery, 16*(4), 436–437.
Aiello, J. R., Derisi, D. T., Epstein, Y. M. & Karlin, R. A. (1977). Crowding and role of interpersonal distance preference. *Sociometry, 40*, 271–282.
Aizer, A., & Koslowsky, M. (1993). *On the relationship between commuter stress and job performance: A Lisrel approach.* Paper presented at the 24th Israel Psychological Association Conference, Ramat Gan, Israel.
Ajzen, I. (1991). The theory of planned behavior. *Organizational Behavior and Human Decision Processes, 50*, 179–211.
Ajzen, I., & Fishbein, M. (1980). *Understanding attitudes and predicting social behavior.* Englewood Cliffs, NJ: Prentice-Hall.
Altman, I. (1975). *The environment and social behavior.* Monterey, CA: Brooks/Cole.
Altman, I., & Werner, C. (1985). *Home environment.* New York: Plenum Press.
Antonovsky, A. (1979). *Health, stress, and coping.* San Francisco: Jossey-Bass.
Archer, R. P. (1979). Relationships between locus of control, trait anxiety, and state anxiety: An interactionist perspective. *Journal of Personality, 47*, 617–626.
Aronow, W. S., Harris, C. N., Isbell, M., Rokaw, M., & Imperato, B. (1972). Effects of freeway travel on angina pectoris. *Annals of Internal Medicine, 77*, 669–676.
Arsenault, A., & Dolan, S. (1983). The role of personality, occupation, and organization in understanding the relationship between job stress, performance, and absenteeism. *Journal of Occupational Psychology, 56*, 227–240.
Arthur, A. X. (1986). Stress of predictable and unpredictable shock. *Psychological Bulletin, 100*, 379–383.
Averill, J. R. (1973). Personal control over aversive stimuli and its relationship to stress. *Psychological Bulletin, 80*, 286–303.
Baldassare, M., & Katz, C. (1988). *Orange County survey: 1988 final report.* Irvine, CA: Irvine Public Policy Research Organization, University of California.

Bandura, A. (1982). Self-efficacy mechanism in human agency. *American Psychologist, 37,* 122–147.
Baron, R. A. (1976). The reduction of human aggression: A field study of the influence of incompatible reactions. *Journal of Applied Psychology, 6,* 260–274.
Baron, R. A. (1986). *Behavior in organizations.* Boston: Allyn and Bacon.
Bateman, T. S., & Strasser, S. (1984). A longitudinal analysis of the antecedents of organizational commitment. *Academy of Management Journal, 27,* 95–112.
Baum, A., Fisher, J. D., & Singer, J. E. (1985). *Social psychology.* New York: Random House.
Baum, A., & Greenberg, C. (1975). Waiting for a crowd: The behavioral and perceptual effects of anticipated crowding. *Journal of Personality and Social Psychology, 32,* 671–679.
Beck, A. T., Rush, A. J., Shaw, B. F., & Emery G. (1979). *Cognitive therapy of depression.* New York: Guilford Press.
Becker, B. E., & Huselid, M. A. (1992). Direct estimates of SD_y and the implications for utility analysis. *Journal of Applied Psychology, 77,* 227–235.
Beehr, T. A., & Franz, T. (1987). The current debate about the meaning of job stress. In J. M. Ivancevich & D. C. Ganster (Eds.), *Job stress: From theory to suggestion* (pp. 5–18). New York: Haworth Press.
Begley, T. M., & Czajka, J. M. (1993). Panel analysis of the moderating effects of commitment on job satisfaction, intent to quit, and health following organizational change. *Journal of Applied Psychology, 78,* 552–556.
Bell, P. A., & Greene, T. C. (1982). Thermal stress: Physiological comfort, performance, and social effects of hot and cold environments. In G. W. Evans (Ed.), *Environmental stress.* (pp. 75–104) London: Cambridge University Press.
Bentler, P. M. (1989). *EQS: Structural equations program manual.* Los Angeles: BMDP Statistical Software.
Bobko, P. (1990). Multivariate correlational analysis. In M. D. Dunette & L. M. Hough (Eds.), *Handbook of industrial and organizational psychology* (Vol. 1. pp. 637–686). Palo Alto, CA: Consulting Psychologists Press.
Borzo, G. (1992, March 16). Reinventing the commute. *American Medical News,* pp. 29–31.
Boudreau, J. W. (1991). Utility analysis for decisions in human resource management. In M. D. Dunnette & L. M. Hough (Eds.), *Handbook of industrial and organizational psychology* (2nd ed., pp. 621–745). Palo Alto, CA: Consulting Psychologists Press.
Bovenzi, M., & Zadini, A. (1992). Self-reported low back symptoms in urban bus drivers exposed to whole-body vibration. *Spine, 17*(9), 1048–1059.
Brehm, S., & Kassin, S. M. (1990). *Social psychology.* Boston: Houghton Mifflin.
Bretz, R. D., & Thomas, S. L. (1989). Perceived equity, motivation, and final-offer arbitration in major league baseball. *Journal of Applied Psychology, 77,* 280–287.
Brief, A. P., & Robertson, L. (1989). Job attitude organization: An exploratory study. *Journal of Applied Social Psychology, 19,* 719–727.
Broadbent, D. E. (1971). *Decision and stress.* New York: Academic Press.
Bromet, E. J., Dew, M. A., & Parkinson, D. K. (1990). Spillover between work and family: A study of blue-collar working wives. In J. Eckenrode & S. Gore (Eds.), *Stress between work and family* (pp. 133–151). New York: Plenum Press.
Bruning, N. S. & Frew, D. R. (1985). The impact of various stress management training strategies: A longitudinal experiment. Paper presented at the 45th Convention of the Academy of Management, San Diego, CA.
Buckle, P. W., Kember, P. A., Wood, A. D., & Wood, S. (1980). Factors influencing occupational back pain in Bedfordshire. *Spine, 5*(3), 254–258.
Burger, J. M. (1989). Negative reactions to increases in perceived personal control. *Journal of Personality and Social Psychology, 56,* 246–256.

REFERENCES

Burke, M. J., Brief, A. P., & George, J. M. (1993). The role of negative affectivity in understanding relations between self-reports of stressors and strains: A comment on the applied psychology literature. *Journal of Applied Psychology, 78*, 402–412.

Byrne, B. M. (1989). *A primer of LISREL: Basic applications and programming for confirmatory factor analytic models*. New York: Springer-Verlag.

Caldwell, D. F., & O'Reilly, C. A. III (1982). Boundary spanning and individual performance. The impact of self monitoring. *Journal of Applied Psychology, 67*, 124–127.

Campbell, J. P. (1982). Editorial: Some remarks from the outgoing editor. *Journal of Applied Psychology, 67*, 691–700.

Caplice, C., & Mahmassani, H. S. (1992). Aspects of commuting behavior: Preferred arrival time, use of information, and switching propensity. *Transportation Research, 26*, 409–418.

Carayon, P. (1992). A longitudinal study of job design and worker strain: Preliminary results. In J. J. Quick, L. R. Murphy, & J. J. Hurrell, Jr. (Eds.), *Stress and well-being at work* (pp. 19–32). Washington, DC: American Psychological Association.

Catching up on homework. (1993, June). *Home Office Computing*, p. 16.

Cervero, R. (1985). Deregulating urban transportation. *Cato Journal, 5*, 219–238.

Cervero, R. (1986). Unlocking suburban gridlock. *American Planning Association Journal, 52*, 389–406.

Chan, C. C, Spengler, J. D., Ozkaynak, H., & Lefkopoulou, M. T. I. (1991). Commuter exposures to VOCs in Boston, Massachusetts. *Journal of the Air Waste Management Association, 41*, 1594–1600.

Chen, P. Y., & Spector, P. E. (1991). Negative affectivity as the underlying cause of correlations between stressors and strains. *Journal of Applied Psychology, 76*, 398–407.

Clark, L. A., & Watson, D. (1991). General affective dispositions in physical and psychological health. In C. R. Snyder & D. R. Forsyth (Eds.), *Handbook of social and clinical psychology* (pp. 221–245). New York: Pergamon Press.

Cohen, J., & Cohen, P. (1983). *Applied multiple regression/correlation analysis for the behavioral sciences* (2nd ed.) Hillsdale, NJ: Lawrence Erlbaum.

Cohen, S. (1978). Environmental load and the allocation of attention. In A. Baum, J. E. Singer, & S. Valins (Eds.), *Advances in environmental psychology*, Vol. 1 (pp. 1–30). Hillsdale, NJ: Lawrence Erlbaum.

Cohen, S., & Weinstein, N. (1982). Nonauditory effects of noise on behavior and health. In G. W. Evans (Ed.), *Environmental stress* (pp. 47–74). London: Cambridge University Press.

Collins, S. C., & Heywood, S. (1992, November). *Teleworking in rural areas: The elixir of stress*. Poster and paper presented at the second APA/NIOSH conference Stress in the 90's, Washington, DC.

Colquhoun, W. P. (1962). Effects of hyoscine and melcozine on vigilance and short-term memory. *British Journal of Industrial Medicine, 19*, 287–296.

Conte, C. (1985, April 16). The explosive growth of suburbia leads to bumper-to-bumper blues. *Wall Street Journal*, p. 37.

Cook, T. D., & Campbell, D. T. (1979). *Quasi-experimental design and analysis issues for field settings*. Chicago: Rand McNally.

Cooper, C. L., & Payne, R. L. (1992). International perspectives on research into work, well-being, and stress management. In *Stress and well-being at work* (pp. 348–368). Washington, DC: American Psychological Association.

Corey, D. M., & Wolf, G. D. (1992). An integrated approach to reducing stress injuries. In J. C. Quick, L. R. Murphy, & J. J. Hurrell, Jr. (Eds.), *Stress and well-being at work* (pp. 64–78). Washington, DC: American Psychological Association.

Cox, V. C., Paulus, P. B., McCain, G., & Schkade, J. K. (1979). Field research on the effects of crowding in prisons and on off-shore drilling platforms. In J. R. Aiello & A. Baum (Eds.), *Residential crowding and design* (pp. 95–106). New York: Plenum Press.

Cronbach, L. J. (1987). Statistical tests for moderator variables: Flaws in analyses recently proposed. *Psychological Bulletin, 102,* 414–417.

Curry, J. P., Wakefield, D. S., Price, J. L., & Mueller, C. W. (1986). On the causal ordering of job satisfaction and organizational commitment. *Academy of Management Journal, 29,* 847–858.

Damkot, D. K., Frymoyer, J. W., Lord, J., & Pope, M. H. (1982). The relationship between work history, work environment and low-back pain in men. *Spine, 9*(4), 395–399.

Damon, A. (1977). The residential environment, health, and behavior: Simple research opportunities, strategies, and some findings in the Solomon Islands and Boston, Massachussetts. In L. E. Hinkle, Jr., & W. C. Loring (Eds.), *The effect of the man made environment on health behavior* (pp. 241–262). Atlanta: Center for Disease Control, Public Health Service.

Darley, J. M., & Gilbert, D. T. (1985). Social psychological aspects of environmental psychology. In G. Lindzey & E. Aronson (Eds.), *The handbook of social psychology* (pp. 949–991). New York: Newberry Awards Records.

Davis, C. F., & Ridgeway, H. H. (1991). Use of video as an aid in driving. *Transportation Quarterly, 45,* 444–454.

Depue, R. A., & Monroe, S. M. (1986). Conceptualization and measurement of human disorders in life stress research: The problem of chronic disturbance. *Psychological Bulletin, 99,* 36–51.

Digman, J. M. (1990). Personality structure: Emergence of the five-factor mode. *Annual Review of Psychology, 41,* 417–420.

Dohrenwend, B. P., & Shrout, P. E. (1985). "Hassles" in the conceptualization and measurement of life stress variables. *American Psychologist, 40,* 780–785.

Driedger, C. (1987). *Commuting couples.* Kingston, Canada: Industrial Relations Center of Queens University.

Eckenrode, J., & Gore, S. (1990). *Stress between work and family.* New York: Plenum Press.

Eden, D. (1982). Critical job events, acute stress, and strain: A multiple interpreted time series. *Organizational Behavior and Human Performance, 30,* 312–329.

Edwards, J. R. (1988). The determinants and consequences of coping with stress. In C. L. Cooper & R. Payne (Eds.), *Causes, coping and consequences of stress at work* (pp. 53–76). New York: John Wiley & Sons.

Edwards, J. R., Baglioni, A. J., Jr., & Cooper, C. L. (1990). Examining relationships among self-report measures of Type A behavior pattern: The effects of dimensionality, measurement error, and differences in underlying constructs. *Journal of Applied Psychology, 75,* 440–454.

Edwards, J. R., & van Harrison, R. (1993). Job demands and worker health: Three-dimensional reexamination of the relationship between person-environment fit and strain. *Journal of Applied Psychology, 78,* 628–648.

Egan, T. (1994, February 20). Once more with feeling: L.A. tries to do the right thing. *New York Times,* p. B1.

Ellis, A. (1962). *Reason and emotion in psychotherapy.* New York: Stuart.

Ellis, A. (1978). What people can do for themselves to cope with stress. In C. L. Cooper & R. Payne (Eds.), *Stress at work* (pp. 209–222). Chichester: John Wiley & Sons.

Epstein, Y. (1981). Crowding stress and human behavior. *Journal of Social Issues, 37,* 16–144.

Epstein, Y. (1982). Crowding stress and human behavior. In G. W. Evans (Ed.), *Environmental stress* (pp. 133–148). London: Cambridge University Press.

Espindle, M. D. (1992, September). 1992 survey results of readers. *Home Office Computing,* pp. 10–12.
Evans, G. W. (1982). *Environmental stress.* London: Cambridge University Press.
Evans, G. W., & Carrere, S. (1991). Traffic congestion, perceived control, and psychophysiological stress among urban bus drivers. *Journal of Applied Psychology, 76,* 658–663.
Evans, G. W., & Cohen, S. (1987). Environmental stress. In D. Stokols & I. Altman (Eds.), *Handbook of environmental psychology* (pp. 571–610). New York: John Wiley & Sons.
Evans, G. W., & Jacobs, S. V. (1982). Air pollution and human behavior. In G. W. Evans (Ed.), *Environmental stress* (pp. 105–132). London: Cambridge University Press.
Evans, G. W., & Lepore, S. J. (1992). Conceptual and analytic issues in crowding research. *Journal of Environmental Psychology, 12,* 163–173.
Fazio, R. H. (1986). How do attitudes guide behavior? In R. M. Sorrentino & E. T. Higgins (Eds.), *The handbook of motivation and cognition* (pp. 204–243). New York: Guilford Press.
Finder, A. (November 26, 1991a). Yes, subway Nirvana does exist: Just go to Newark. *New York Times,* p. 5.
Finder, A. (December 14, 1991b). At a Queens station: Rush hour at its worst. *New York Times,* p. 1.
Fisher, C., & Locke, E. A. (1992). The new look in job satisfaction theory and research. In J. Cranny, P. Smith, & E. F. Stone (Eds.), *Job satsfaction: How people feel about their jobs and how it affects their performance* (pp. 165–194). Lexington, MA: Lexington Books.
Fisher, S., & Hood, B. M. (1987). The stress of the transition to university: A longitudinal study of psychological disturbance, absent-mindedness and vulnerability to homesickness. *British Journal of Psychology, 78,* 425–441.
Flannelly, K. J., & Mcleod, M. S. (1989). A multivariate analysis of socioeconomic and attitudinal factors predicting commuters' mode of travel. *Bulletin of the Psychonomic Society, 27,* 64–66.
Flannelly, K. J., Mcleod, M. S., Behnke, R. W., & Flannelly, L. (1990). Assessing consumers' interest in using alternative transportation modes of commuting. *Psychological Reports, 67,* 875–878.
Fleming, I., Baum, A., & Weiss, L. (1987). Social Density and perceived control as mediators of crowding stress in high density neighborhoods. *Journal of Personality and Social Psychology, 52,* 899–906.
Fletcher, B. C. (1988). The epidemiology of occupational stress. In C. L. Cooper & R. Payne (Eds.), *Causes, coping, and consequences of stress at work.* Chichester, England: John Wiley & Sons.
Foderara, L. W. (November 15, 1991). Tappan Zee traffic enrages commuters, worries planners. *The New York Times,* p. B5.
Forester, T. (1987). The myth of the electronic cottage. In T. Forester (Ed.), *Computers in the human context: Information technology, productivity, and people.* Cambridge, MA: MIT press.
Fox, M. B. (1983, Spring). Working women and travel: The access of women to work and community facilities. *APS Journal,* 158–170.
Fox, M. L., Dwyer, D. J., & Ganster, D. C. (1991). Stress and control among nurses: Effects on physiological outcomes. In *Proceedings of the National Academy of Management* (pp. 267–271). Miami, FL: National Academy of Management.
Frankenhaueser, M. (1975). Experimental approaches to the study of catecholamines and emotion. In L. Levi (Ed.), *Emotions: Their parameters and measurement* (pp. 209–234). New York: Raven Press.
Frankenhaueser, M., & Jarpe, G. (1963). Psychophysiological changes during infusions of adrenaline in various doses. *Psychophramacologia, 4,* 424–432.

Frankenhaueser, M., Lundberg, V., Fredrikson, M., Melin, B., Tuomisto, M., Myrsten, A., Hedman, M., Bergman-Losman, B. & Wallin, L. (1989). Stress on and off the job as related to sex, and occupational status in white-collar workers. *Journal of Organizational Behavior, 10,* 321–346.

Fremont, J., & Craighead, L. W. (1987). Aerobic exercise and cognitive therapy on the treatment of dysphoric moods. *Cognitive Therapy and Research, 11,* 241–251.

French, J. R. P., Jr., Caplan, R. D., & van Harrison, R. (1982). *The mechanisms of job stress and strain.* New York: John Wiley & Sons.

Frese, M. (1985). Stress at work and psychosomatic complaints: A causal interpretation. *Journal of Applied Psychology, 70,* 314–328.

Frese, M., & Okonek, K. (1984). Reasons to leave shift-work and psychological and psychosomatic complaints of former shift-workers. *Journal of Applied Psychology, 69,* 509–514.

Frese, M., & Zapf, D. (1988). Methodological issues in the study of work stress: Objective vs. subjective measurement of work stress and the question of longitudinal studies. In C. L. Cooper & R. Payne (Eds.), *Causes, coping, and consequences of stress at work.* Chichester: John Wiley & Sons.

Frymoyer, J. W., & Gordon, S. L. (1989). *New perspective on low back pain: American Academy of Orthopaedic Surgeons symposium.* Park Ridge, IL: American Academy of Orthopaedic Surgeons.

Frymoyer, J. W., Pope, M. H., Clements, J. H., Wilder, D. G., MacPherson, B., & Ashikaga, T. (1983). Rish factors in low-back pain. *The Journal of Bone and Joint Surgery, 65a*(2), 213–218.

Frymoyer, J. W., Pope, M. H., Costanza, M. C., Rosen, J. C., Goggin, J. E., & Wilder, D. G. (1980). Epidemiologic studies of low-back pain. *Spine, 5*(5), 419–423.

Gaffuri, E., & Costa, G. (1986). Applied aspects of chronoergohygiene. *Chronobiologia, 13,* 39–51.

Ganster, D. C., Fusilier, M. R., & Mayes, C. (1986). Role of social support in the experience of stress at work. *Journal of Applied Psychology, 71,* 102–110.

GAO. (1989). *Traffic congestion: Federal efforts to improve mobility. Report to the chairman, subcommittee on transportation and related agencies, committee on Appropriations, U.S. Senate.* Washington, DC: United States General Accounting Office.

Gaydos, H. F., & Dusek, E. R. (1958). Effects of localized hand cooling versus total body cooling on manual performance. *Journal of Applied Psychology, 12,* 377–380.

Gellatly, I. R., & Meyer, J. P. (1992). The effects of goal difficulty on physiological arousal, cognition, and task performance. *Journal of Applied Psychology, 77,* 694–704.

Gemmill, G. R., & Heisler, W. J. (1972). Fatalism as a factor in managerial job satisfaction, job strain, and mobility. *Personnel Psychology, 25,* 241–250.

Gerhart, B. (1987). How important are dispositional factors as determinants of job satisfaction? Implications for job design and other personnel programs. *Journal of Applied Psychology, 72,* 366–373.

Gerstel, N., & Gross, H. (1984). *Commuter marriage: A study of work and family.* New York: Guilford Press.

Glass, D. G., & Singer, J. E. (1972). *Urban stress: Experiments on noise and social stressors.* New York: Academic Press.

Goranson, R. E., & King, D. (1970). *Rioting and daily temperature: Analysis of the U.S. riots in 1967.* Unpublished manuscript, York University, Toronto.

Govaerts, K., & Dixon, D. N. (1988). Until careers do us part: Vocational and marital satisfaction in the dual-career commuter marriage. *International Journal for the Advancement of Counselling, 11,* 85–281.

Greenberg, J. (1978). Protestant ethic endorsement and attitudes toward commuting to work among mass transit riders. *Journal of Applied Psychology, 63,* 755–758.

Greller, M., & Parsons, C. K. (1989). Psychosomatic complaints scale of stress: Measure development and psychometric properties. *Educational and Psychological Measurement, 48,* 1051–1065.

Greller, M. M., Parsons, C. K., & Mitchell, D. R. D. (1992). Additive effects and beyond: Occupational stressors and social buffers in a police organization. In J. C. Quick, L. R. Murphy, & J. J. Hurrel (Eds.), *Stress and well-being* (pp. 33–47). Washington, DC: American Psychological Association.

Gubrean, E., Usel, M., Bolay, J., Fioretta, G., & Puissant, J. (1992). Increased risk for lung cancer and for cancer of the gastrointestinal tract among Geneva professional drivers. *British Journal of Industrial Medicine, 49,* 337–344.

Guest, J. (1981). An active employee assistance program. In R. M. Schwartz (Ed.), *New developments in occupational stress, DHHS (NIOSH) Publication No. 81-102.* Washington, DC: U.S. Government Printing Office.

Gulian, E., Matthews, G., Glendon, A. I., Davies, D. R., & Delaney, L. M. (1989). Dimensions of driver stress. *Ergonomics, 32,* 585–602.

Gunn, W. J. (1987). The importance of the measurement of annoyance in prediction of effects of aircraft noise on the health and well-being of noise exposed communities. In H. S. Koelega (Ed.), *Environmental annoyance: Characterization, measurement, and control.* Amsterdam: Elsevier.

Gupta, N., & Jenkings, G. D. (1983). Tardiness as a withdrawal behavior. *Journal of Business Research, 11,* 61–75.

Haaga, D. A., & Davison, G. C. (1993). An appraisal of rational–emotive therapy. *Journal of Consulting and Clinical Psychology, 61,* 215–220.

Hadad, H. (1991, October 27). A specialist makes moves to suburbs easier. *The New York Times,* p. 8.

Hadler, N. M. (1993). *Occupational musculoskeletal disorders.* New York: Raven Press.

Hall, J. K., & Spector, P. E. (1991). Relationships of work stress measures for employees with the same job. *Work and Stress, 5,* 19–25.

Hanisch, K. A., & Hulin, C. L. (1991). General attitudes and organizational withdrawal: An evaluation of a causal model. *Journal of Vocational Behavior, 39,* 110–128.

Hartig, T., Mang, M., & Evans, G. W. (1991). Restorative effects of natural environment experiences. *Environment and Behavior, 23,* 3–26.

Hedberg, G., Jacobson, K. A., Langedeon, S., & Nystrom, L. (1991). Morality in circulatory diseases, especially ischaemic heart disease among Swedish professional drivers: A retrospective study. *Journal of Human Ergology, 20,* 1–5.

Hedge, A., Erickson, W. A., & Rubin, G. (1992). Effects of personal and occupational factors on sick building syndrome reports in air-conditioned offices. In J. C. Quick, L. R. Murphy, & J. J. Hurrell (Eds.), *Stress and well-being* (pp. 286–298). Washington, DC: American Psychological Association.

Henry, J. P., & Meehan, J. P. (1981). Psychosocial stimuli, physiological specificity, and cardiovascular disease. In H. Weiner, M. A. Hofer, & A. J. Stunkard (Eds.), *Brain, behavior, and bodily disease.* New York: Raven Press.

Herzog, T. R., & Bosley, P. J. (1992). Tranquility and preference as affective qualities of natural environments. *Journal of Environmental Psychology, 12,* 115–127.

Hosea, T. M., Simon, S. R., Delatizky, J., Wong, M. A., & Hsieh, C. C. (1989). Myoelectric analysis of the paraspinal musculature in relation to automobile driving. *Spine, 11,* 928–936.

Hunter, J. E., & Schmidt, F. L. (1990). *Methods of meta-analysis.* Newbury Park, CA: Sage.

Ilgen, D. R. (1990). Health issues at work: Opportunities for industrial/organizational psychologists. *American Psychologist, 45,* 273–283.

Ivancevich, J. M. (1986). Life events and hassles as predictors of health symptoms, job performance, and absenteeism. *Journal of Occupational Behavior, 7,* 39–51.

Ivancevich, J. M., & Matteson, M. T. (1988). Promoting the individuals health and well being. In C. L. Cooper & R. Payne (Eds.), *Causes, coping, and consequences of stress at work* (pp. 267–299). Chichester: John Wiley & Sons.

Jackson, S. E. (1989). Does job control control job stress? In S. L. Sauter, J. J. Hurrell, Jr., & C. L. Cooper (Eds.), *Job control and worker health* (pp. 25–53). New York: John Wiley & Sons.

Jansen, G. R. M. (1993). Commuting: Home sprawl, job sprawl, traffic jams. In I. Salomon, P. Bovy, & J. P. Orfeuil (Eds.), *A billion trips a day* (pp. 101–127). Dordrecht, The Netherlands: Kluwer Academic Publishers.

JCPS. (1985). *Demographic change and recent worktrip travel trends. Prepared for the U.S. Department of Transportation, Urban Mass Transportation Administration.* Washington, DC: Joint Center for Political Studies.

Jex, S. M., Beehr, T. A., & Roberts, C. K. (1992). The meaning of occupational stress items to survey respondents. *Journal of Applied Psychology, 77,* 623–628.

Jones, P., Bovy, P., Orfeuil, J. P., & Salomon, I. (1993). Transport policy: The European laboratory. In I. Salomon, P. Bovy, & J. P. Orfeuil (Eds.), *A billion trips a day* (pp. 167–186). Dordrecht, The Netherlands: Kluwer Academic Publishers.

Joreskog, K. G., & Sorbom, D. (1989). *LISREL VII: A guide to the program and applications* (2nd ed.) Chicago: SPSS, Inc.

Judge, T. A. (1993). Disposition, job satisfaction, and turnover. *Journal of Applied Psychology, 78,* 395–401.

Kahn, R. L., & Byosiere, M. (1991). Stress in organizations. In M. Dunnette (Ed.), *Handbook of industrial and organizational psychology.* Palo Alto, CA: Consulting Psychologists Press.

Kahneman, D. (1973). *Attention and effort.* Englewood Cliffs, NJ: Prentice-Hall.

Kain, J. F. (1967). The distribution and movement of jobs and industry. In J. Q. Wilson (Ed.), *The metropolitan enigma: Inquiries into the nature and dimensions of America's urban crisis* (pp. 1–40). Washington, DC: Chamber of Commerce of the United States.

Karasek, R. A. (1979). Job demands, job decision latitude, and mental strain: Implications for job redesign. *Administrative Science Quarterly, 24,* 285–307.

Karasek, R., & Theorell, T. (1990). *Healthy work, stress, productivity, and the reconstruction of working life.* New York: Basic Books.

Karlin, R. A., Rosen, L., Epstein, Y. M., & Woolfolk, R. L. (1979). The use of therapeutic interventions to reduce crowding related arousal: A preliminary investigation. *Environmental Psychology and Nonverbal Behavior, 3,* 219–227.

Kasl, S. V. (1978). Epidemiological contributions to the study of work stress. In C. L. Cooper & R. Payne (Eds.), *Stress at work* (pp. 3–48). Chichester: John Wiley & Sons.

Kasl, S. V. (1987). Methodologies in stress and health: Past difficulties, present dilemmas, future directions. In S. V. Kasl & C. L. Cooper (Eds.), *Stress and health: Issues in research methodology* (pp. 119–146). New York: John Wiley & Sons.

Kassoff, M. J. (1970). *Socioeconomic factors underlying public transit use in the journey to work.* Occasional paper No. 1, Syracuse University, Urban Transportation Institute; U.S. Department of Transportation.

Keating, J. P. (1979). Environmental stressors: Misplaced emphasis. In I. G. Saranson & C. D. Spielberger (Eds.), *Stress and anxiety* (Vol. 6, pp. 55–66). New York: John Wiley & Sons.

Kehoe, J. F. (1979). Choice time and aspects of choice alternatives. In L. C. Perlmuter & R. A. Monty (Eds.), *Choices and perceived control.* Hillsdale, NJ: Lawrence Erlbaum.

REFERENCES

Kelsey, J. L., Githens, P. B., O'Conner, T., Weil, U., Calogero, J. A., Holdford, T. R., White, A. A. III., Walter, S. D., Ostfeld, A. M., & Southwick, W. O. (1984). Acute prolapsed lumbar intervertebral disc: An epidemiologic study with special reference to driving automobiles and cigarette smoking. *Spine, 9,* 608–613.

Kelsey, J. L., Golden, A. L., & Mundt, D. J. (1990). Low back pain/prolapsed lumbar intervertebral disc. *Rheumatic Disease Clinics of North America, 16*(3), 699–716.

Kelsey, J. L., & Hardy, R. J. (1975). Driving of motor vehicles as a risk factor for acute herniated lumbar intervertebral disc. *American Journal of Epidemiology, 102,* 63–73.

Ketcham, B., & Konheim, C. S. (1991, December 7). Don't raise the fare, cut it. *New York Times,* p. 23.

Kluger, A. N. (1992, November). *Commute predictability and strain.* Paper presented at the second APA/NIOSH Stress in the 90's Conference, Washington DC.

Kluger, A. N., Levinsohn, S., & Aiello, J. (1994). The influence of feedback on mood: Linear effects on pleasantness and curvilinear effects on arousal. *Organizational Behavior and Human Decision Processes, 60,* 276–299.

Knox, J. B. (1961). Absenteeism and turnover in an Argentine factory. *American Sociological Review, 26,* 424–428.

Kornhauser, A. (1965). *Mental health of an industrial worker.* New York: John Wiley & Sons.

Koslowsky, M., Kluger, A. N., & Yinon, Y. (1988). Predicting behavior: Combining intention with investment. *Journal of Applied Psychology, 73,* 102–106.

Koslowsky, M., & Krausz, M. (1993). On the relationship between commuting, stress, and attitudinal measures: A LISREL application. *Journal of Applied Behavioral Science, 29,* 485–492.

Krausz, M., & Hermann, E. (1991). Who is afraid of flexitime: Correlates of personal choice of a flexitime schedule. *Applied Psychology: An International Review, 40,* 315–326.

Kutner, D. H. (1973). Overcrowding: Human responses to density and visual exposure. *Human Relations, 26,* 31–50.

Landsberg, H. E. (1969). *Weather and health.* New York: Doubleday.

Landy, F. J. (1985). *Psychology and work behavior.* Homewood, IL: Dorsey Press.

Landy, F. (1992). Work design and stress. In G. P. Keita & S. L. Sauter (Eds.), *Work and well-being* (pp. 115–158). Washington, DC: American Psychological Association.

Landy, F., Rategary, H., Thayer, J., & Colvin, C. (1991).Time urgency: The construct and its measurement. *Journal of Applied Psychology, 76,* 644–657.

LaPiere, R. T. (1934). Attitudes vs. action. *Social Forces, 13,* 230–237.

Lawson, C. (1991, November 7). Distance makes the heart skip for commuter moms. *New York Times,* p. C1.

Lazarus, R. S. (1966). *Psychological stress and the coping process.* New York: McGraw-Hill.

Lazarus, R. S., & Launier, R. (1978). Stress related transactions between person and environment. In L. A. Pervin & M. Lewis (Eds.), *Perspective in interactional psychology* (pp. 287–327). New York: Plenum Press.

Leboyer, C. L., & Naturel, V. (1991). Neighborhood noise annoyance. *Journal of Environmental Psychology, 11,* 75–86.

Leigh, J. P., & Lust, J. (1988). Determinants of employee tardiness. *Work and Occupations, 15,* 78–95.

Lenny, A. (1984). Canyon Corporate Center—From RV's to R&D: Transition to a higher usage. *Urban Land, 43,* 20–24.

Leatherwood, J. D., Dempsey, T. K., & Clevenson, S. A. (1980). A design tool for estimating passenger ride discomfort within complex ride environments. *Human Factors, 22,* 291–312.

Levenson, R. W. (1988). Emotion and autonomic nervous system: A prospectus for research on autonomic specificity. In H. Wagner (Ed.), *Social psychophysiology and emotion: Theory and clinical applications* (pp. 17–42). London: John Wiley & Sons.

Locke, E. A. (1976). The nature and causes of job satisfaction. In M. D. Dunnette (Ed.), *Handbook of industrial and organizational psychology* (pp. 1297–1349). Chicago: Rand McNally.

Long, R. J. (1987). *New office information technology: Human and managerial implications.* London: Croom Helm.

Lundberg, U. (1976). Urban commuting: Crowdedness and catecholamine excretion. *Journal of Human Stress, 2,* 26–32.

MacLennan, B. W. (1992). Stressor reduction: An organizational alternative to individual stress management. In J. C. Quick, L. R. Murphy, & J. J. Hurrell (Eds.), *Stress and well-being* (pp. 79–95). Washington, DC: American Psychological Association.

Mahmassani, H. S., & Chang, G. L. (1986). Experiments with departure time choice dynamics of urban commuters. *Transportation Research, 20,* 297–320.

Martin, J. (1971). Some aspects of absence in a light engineering factory. *Occupational Psychology, 45,* 77–89.

Maslach, C., & Jackson, S. E. (1981). The measurement of experienced burnout. *Journal of Occupational Behavior, 2,* 99–113.

McClaney, M. A., & Hurrell, J. J. (1988). Control, stress, and job satisfaction. *Work and Stress, 2,* 217–224.

McCrae, R. R., Bartone, P. T., & Costa, P. T. (1987). Validation of the five factor model of personality across instruments and observers. *Journal of Personality and Social Psychology, 49,* 710–721.

McFarlane-Shore, L., Newton, L. A., & Thronton, G. C. (1990). Job and organizational attitudes in relation to employee behavioral intentions. *Journal of Organizational Behavior, 11,* 57–67.

McGrath, J. E. (1976). Stress and behavior in organizations. In M. D. Dunnette (Ed.), *Handbook of industrial and organizational psychology* (pp. 1351–1395). Chicago: Rand McNally.

Mckee, G. H., Markham, S. E., & Scott, K. D. (1992). Job stress and employee withdrawal from work. In J. C. Quick, L. R. Murphy, & J. J. Hurrell, Jr. (Eds.), *Stress and well- being at work* (pp. 153–164). Washington, DC: American Psychological Association.

McLean, A. A. (1973). Occupational mental health: Review of an emerging art. In R. L. Noland (Ed.), *Industrial mental health and employee counseling* (pp. 107–137). New York: Behavioral Publications.

Meichenbaum, D., & Cameron, R. (1983). Stress inoculation training: Toward a general paradigm for training skills. In D. Meichenbaum & M. E. Jaremko (Eds.), *Stress reduction and prevention* (pp. 115–154). New York: Plenum Press.

Meichenbaum, D. (1985). *Stress innoculation training.* New York: Pergamon Press.

Mento, A. J., Steel, R. P., & Karren, R. J. (1987). A meta-analytic study of the effects of goal setting on task performance: 1966–1984. *Organizational Behavior and Human Decision Processes, 39,* 52–83.

Miller, S. (1987). Monitoring and blunting: Validation of a questionnaire to assess styles of information seeking under threat. *Journal of Personality and Social Psychology, 52,* 343–353.

Mitra, A., Jenkins, G. D., & Gupta, N. (1992). A meta-analytic review of the relationship between absence and turnover. *Journal of Applied Psychology, 27,* 879–889.

Mobley, W. H. (1982). *Employee turnover: Causes, consequences, and control.* Reading, MA: Addison-Wesley.

Monahan, J., & Loftus, E. F. (1982). Psychology of law. *Annual Review of Psychology, 33,* 441–476.

Montag, I., & Comrey, A. L. (1987). Internality and externality as correlates of involvement in fatal driving accidents. *Journal of Applied Psychology, 72,* 339–343.

More companies are using flexible work arrangements. (1993, October). *Personnel Journal*, p. 22.
Motowidlo, S. J., Packard, J. S., & Manning, M. R. (1986). Occupational stress: Its causes and consequences for job performance. *Journal of Applied Psychology, 71*, 618–629.
Mowday, R. T., Porter, L. W., & Steers, R. M. (1982). *Employee–organizational linkages: The psychology of commitment, absenteeism, and turnover.* New York: Academic Press.
Muchinsky, P. M. (1977). Employee absenteeism: A review of the literature. *Journal of Vocational Behavior, 10*, 316–340.
Murphy, L. R. (1988) Workplace interventions for stress reduction and prevention. In C. L. Cooper & R. Payne (Eds.), *Causes, coping and consequences of stress at work* (pp. 301–342). Chichester: John Wiley & Sons.
Narayanan, V. K., & Nath, R. (1982). A field test of some attitudinal and behavioral consequences of flexitime. *Journal of Applied Psychology, 67*, 214–218.
National Center for Health Statistics. (1989). *Vital and Health statistics: Health characteristics by occupation and industry, United States, 1983–85* (PHS No. 90-1598). Washington, DC: Author.
National Safety Council (1988). *Accident survey, 1987.* New York: Author.
Neale, J. M., & Liebert, R. M. (1986). *Science and behavior: An introduction to methods of research.* New York: Prentice-Hall.
Netermeyer, R. G., Johnston, M. W., & Burton, S. (1990). Analysis of role conflict and role ambiguity in a structural equation framework. *Journal of Applied Psychology, 75*, 148–157.
Nicholson, N., & Goodge, P. M. (1976). The influence of social, organizational, and biographical factors on female absence. *Journal of Management Studies, 13*, 234–254.
Nicosia, G., Hyman, D., Karlin, R. A., Epstein, Y. M., & Aiello, J. R. (1979). Effects of bodily contact on reactions to crowding. *Journal of Applied Social Psychology, 9*, 508–523.
Novaco, R. W., Kliewer, W., & Broquet, A. (1991). Home environmental consequences of commute travel impedance. *American Journal of Community Psychology, 19*, 881–909.
Novaco, R. W., & Sandeen, B. A. (1992, November). *Mitigating the stress of commuting to work: Ridesharing and the interactional effects of gender.* Paper presented at the APA/NIOSH Conference on Stress in the 90's: A changing workforce in a changing workplace. Washington, DC.
Novaco, R. W., Stokols, D., Campbell, J., & Stokols, J. (1979). Transportation, stress, and community psychology. *American Journal of Community Psychology, 7*, 361–380.
Novaco, R. W., Stokols, D., & Milanesi, L. (1990). Objective and subjective dimensions of travel impedance as determinants of commuting stress. *American Journal of Community Psychology, 18*, 231–257.
One week later, Los Angeles still in big trouble (1994, January 25). *Associated Press as reported in Jerusalem Post*, p. 4.
Orfeuil, J. P., & Bovy, P. (1993). European mobility is different: A global perspective. In I. Salomon, P. Bovy, & J. P. Orfeuil (Eds.), *A billion trips a day* (pp. 13–19). Dordrecht, The Netherlands Kluwer Academic Publishers.
Orpen, C. (1981). Effect of flexible working hours on employee satisfaction and performance. *Journal of Applied Psychology, 66*, 113–115.
Orski, C. K. (1985). Suburban mobility: The coming transportation crisis? *Transportation Quarterly, 39*, 283–296.
Osborn, D. R., & McCarthy, M. (1987). The economical and ecological advantages of mass-transit subsidies. *Personnel Journal, 66*, 140–147.
Page, R. A. (1977). Noise and helping behavior. *Environment and Behavior, 9*, 311–334.
Passell, P. (1991, October 30). Economic scene: Transit green, gridlock blues. *New York Times* p. D2.

Passell, P. (1992, November 24). Cheapest protection of nature may lie in taxes, not laws. *The New York Times* pp. C1,C8.
Paterson, R. J., & Neufeld, R. W. J. (1989). The stress response and parameters of stressful situations and issues concerning control and its implementation. In R. W. J. Neufeld (Ed.), *Advances in the investigation of psychological stress* (pp. 7–67). New York: John Wiley & Sons.
Payne, R. (1988). Individual differences in the study of occupational stress. In C. L. Cooper & R. Payne (Eds.), *Causes, coping and consequences of stress at work* (pp. 209–232). Chichester: John Wiley & Sons.
Pearson, R. (1989). Move the work or move the people? *Nature, 338,* 98.
Perlmuter, L. C., & Monty, R. A. (1977). The importance of perceived control: Facts or fantasy? *American Scientist, 65,* 759–765.
Perrewe, P. L., & Ganster, D. C. (1989). The impact of job demands and behavioral control on experienced job stress. *Journal of Organizational Behavior, 10,* 213–229.
Piazzi, A., Bollino, G., & Mattioli, S. (1991). [Spinal pathology in self-employed truck drivers]. *Med Lav, 82*(2), 122–130.
Pierce, J. L., & Newstrom, J. W. (1983). The design of flexible work schedules and employee responses: Relationships and processes. *Journal of Organizational Behavior, 4,* 247–262.
Pietri, F., Leclerc, A., Boitel, L., Chastang, J. F., Morcet, J. F., & Blondet, M. (1992). Low- back pain in commercial travelers. *Scandinavia–Journal of Work Environment and Health, 18,*(1), 52–58.
Pines, A. M., Aronson, A., & Kafry, D. (1981). *Burn-out from tedium to personal growth.* New York: Free Press.
Pisarski, A. E. (1987). *Commuting in America: National report on commuting patterns and trends.* Westport, CT: ENO Foundation for Transportation.
Pisarski, A. E. (1992). *Travel behavior issues in the 90's.* Washington, DC: Office of Highway Information Management, U.S. Department of Transportation.
Popp, P. O., & Belohlav, J. A. (1982). Absenteeism in a low status environment. *Academy of Management Journal, 25,* 677–683.
Porter, L. W., & Lawler, E. E. (1968). *Managerial attitudes and performance.* Homewood, IL: Irwin.
Poulton, E. C. (1978). A new look at the effects of noise: A rejoinder. *Psychological Bulletin, 85,* 1068–1079.
Poulton, E. C. (1979). Composite model for human performance in continuous noise. *Psychological Review, 86,* 361–375.
Powell, T. J., & Enright, S. J. (1990). *Anxiety and stress management.* London: Routledge.
Proshansky, H. M., Ittelson, W. H., & Rivlin, L. G. (1970). *Environmental psychology: People and their physical settings.* New York: Holt, Rinehart and Winston.
Quick, J. C., Murphy, J. J., & Hurrell, J. J. (1992). *Stress and well-being at work.* Washington, DC: American Psychological Association.
Regular Common Carrier Conference. (1990). *Motor carrier safety survey, 1989.* Alexandria, VA: Author.
Rhodes, S. R., & Steers, R. M. (1990). *Managing employee absenteeism.* Reading, MA: Addison-Wesley.
Robinson, A. A. (1989). Lung cancer, the motor vehicle and its subtle influence on body functions. *Medical Hypotheses, 28,* 39–43.
Robinson, A. A. (1991). Cancer death due to all causes, its relationship with vehicle travel in Australia, Japan, and European countries. *Medical Hypotheses, 36,* 166–171.
Rodin, J. (1985). The application of social psychology. In G. Lindzey & E. Aronson (Eds.), *The handbook of social psychology* (3rd ed., pp. 805–882) New York: Random House.

REFERENCES

Ronen, S. (1981). Arrival and departure patterns of public sector employees before and after implementation of flexitime. *Personnel Psychology, 34,* 817–822.

Roskies, E. (1987). *Stress management for the healthy Type A: Theory and practice.* New York: Guilford Press.

Rosse, J. G. (1991). Understanding employee withdrawal from work. In J. Jones, B. D. Steffy, & D. W. Bray (Eds.), *Applying psychology in business* (pp. 668–682). New York: Lexington Books.

Rosse, J. G., & Hulin, C. L. (1985). Adaptation to work: An analysis of employee health, withdrawal, and change. *Organizational Behavior and Human Decision Processes, 36,* 324–347.

Rusbult, C. E., & Farrell, D. (1983). A longitudinal test of the investment model: The impact on job satisfaction, job commitment, and turnover of variations in rewards, costs, alternatives, and investments. *Journal of Applied Psychology, 68,* 429–438.

Russell, C. J., & Bobko, P. (1992). Moderated regression analysis and Likert scales: Too coarse for comfort. *Journal of Applied Psychology, 77,* 336–342.

Russell, D. W., Altmaier, E., & van Velzen, D. (1987). Job related stress, social support, and burnout among classroom teachers. *Journal of Applied Psychology, 72,* 269–274.

Sagie, A., & Koslowsky, M. (1993). Organizational attitudes and behaviors as a function of participation in strategic and tactical change decisions: An application of path–goal theory. *Journal of Organizational Behavior, 15,* 37–47.

Sarbin, T. R. (1969) Schizophrenic thinking: A role-theoretical analysis. *Journal of Personality, 37,* 190–206.

Sauter, S. L., Hurrell, J. J., & Cooper, C. L. (1989). *Job control and worker health.* New York: John Wiley & Sons.

Schaefer, M. H., Street, S. W., Singer, J. E., & Baum, A. (1988). Effects of control on the stress reactions of commuters. *Journal of Applied Social Psychology, 18,* 944–957.

Schaubroeck, J., & Ganster, D. C. (1993). Chronic demands and response to challenge. *Journal of Applied Psychology, 78,* 73–85.

Schaubroeck, J., Ganster, D. C., & Fox, M. L. (1992). Dipositional affect and work-related stress. *Journal of Applied Psychology, 77,* 322–335.

Schmidt, F. L., Hunter, J. E., Outerbridge, A. N., & Trattner, M. H. (1986). The economic impact of job selection methods on size, productivity, and payroll costs of the federal work force: An empirically based demonstration. *Personnel Psychology, 39,* 1–29.

Schriber, J. B., & Gutek, B. A. (1987). Some time dimensions of work: Measurement of an underlying aspect of organizational culture. *Journal of Applied Psychology, 72,* 642–650.

Schuler, R. S., & Jackson, S. E. (1986). Managing stress through PHRM practices: An uncertainty interpretation. *Research in Persononnel and Human Resources Management, 4,* 183–224.

Seligman, M. E. P. (1975). *Helplessness: On depression, development, and death.* San Francisco: Freeman.

Seligman, M. E. P., & Miller, S. M. (1979). The psychology of power: Concluding comments. In L. C. Perlmuter & R. A. Monty (Eds.), *Choices and perceived control.* Hillsdale, NJ: Lawrence Erlbaum.

Sells, S. B., & Will, D. P. (1971). *Accidents, police incidents, and weather: A further study of the city of Fort Worth, Texas, 1968.* Fort Worth: Group Psychology Branch, Office of Naval Research and Institute of Behavioral Research, Texas Christian University.

Selye, H. (1976). *The stress of life* (2nd ed.). New York: McGraw-Hill.

Seyfarth, J. T., & Bost, W. A. (1986). Teacher turnover and the quality of worklife in schools: An empirical study. *Journal of Research and Development in Education, 20,* 1–6.

Shamir, B. (1992). Home: The perfect workplace. In S. Zedeck (Ed.), *Work, families, and organizations* (pp. 272–311). San Francisco: Jossey-Bass.

Sherrrod, D. R., & Downs, R. (1974). Environmental determinants of altruism: The effects of stimulus overload and perceived control on helping. *Journal of Experimental Social Psychology, 10,* 468–479.

Simonson, E., Baker, C., Burns, N., Keiper, C., Schmitt, O. H., & Stackhouse, S. (1968). Cardiovascular stress (electrocardiographic changes) produced by driving an automobile. *American Heart Journal, 75,* 125–135.

Sims, C. (1991, November 4). Motorists are still shunning car pools: They want to be alone. *The New York Times,* p. B1.

Singer, J. A., Lundberg, U., & Frankenhauser, M. (1978). Stress on the train: A study of urban commuting. In A. Baum, J. A. Singer, & S. Valins (Eds.), *Advances in environmental psychology* (pp. 41–56). Hillsdale, NJ: Lawrence Erlbaum.

Singer, J. A., Neale, M. S., & Schwartz, G. E. (1987). The nuts and bolts of assessing occupational stress: A collaborative effort with labor. In L. R. Murphy & T. F. Schoenborn (Eds.), *Stress management in work settings.* Cincinnati: Public Health Service.

Skov, T., Cordtz, T., Jensen, L. K., Saugman, P., Schmidt, K., & Theilade, P. (1991). Modification of health behaviour in response to air pollution notification in Copenhagen. *Soc Sci Med, 33,* 621–626.

Smith, B. H. (1991). Anxiety as a cost of commuting to work. *Journal of Urban Economics, 29,* 260–266.

Smith, O. L. (1991). Computer-assisted flexible routing of mass transit bus systems. *Transportation Quarterly, 45,* 581–597.

Smith, P. C., Kendall, L. M., & Hulin, C. L. (1969). *The measurement of satisafction in work and retirement: A strategy for the study of attitudes.* Chicago: Rand McNally.

Spector, P. E., Dwyer, D. J., & Jex, S. M. (1988). Relation of job stressors to affective, health, and performance outcomes: A comparison of multiple data sources. *Journal of Applied Psychology, 73,* 11–19.

Spector, P. E., & Jex, S. M. (1991). Relations of job characteristics from multiple data sources with employee affect, absence, turnover intentions, and health. *Journal of Applied Psychology, 76,* 46–53.

Spence, J. T., Helmreich, R. L., & Pred, R. S. (1987). Impatience versus achievement strivings in the Type A pattern: Differential effects on students' health and academic achievement. *Journal of Applied Psychology, 72,* 522–528.

Spielberger, C. D., Jacobs, G. A. Crane, R. G., Russell, S. F., Westbury, S. L., Barker, L., Johnson, E. H., Knight, J., & Marks, E. (1979). *Preliminary manual for the State–Trait Personality Inventory.* Tampa, FL: University of South Florida Human Resources Institute.

Spyridakis, J., Barfield, W., Conquest, L., Haselkorn, M., & Isakson, C. (1991). Surveying commuting behavior: Designing motorist information systems. *Transportation Research, 25,* 17–30.

Steers, R. M., & Rhodes, S. R. (1978). Major influences on employee attendance: A process model. *Journal of Applied Psychology, 63(4),* 391–407.

Steffy, B. D., & Jones, J. W. (1988). Workplace stress and indicators of coronary disease risk. *Academy of Management Journal, 31,* 686–698.

Steffy, B. D., & Maurer, S. D. (1988). The dollar-productivity impact of the human resource function: Conceptualization and measurement. *Academy of Management Review, 13,* 271–286.

Stern, E., & Tretvik, T. (1993). Public transport in Europe: Requiem or revival. In I. Salomon, P. Bovy, & J. P. Orfeuil (Eds.), *A billion trips a day* (pp. 129–147). Dordrecht, The Netherlands: Kluwer Academic Publishers.

REFERENCES

Stockford, L. O. (1944). Chronic absenteeism and good attendance. *Personnel Journal, 23,* 202–207.
Stokols, D. (1992). Establishing and maintaining healthy environments: Toward a social ecology of health promotion. *American Psychologist, 47,* 6–22.
Stokols, D., Novaco, R. W., Stokols, J., & Campbell, J. (1978). Traffic congestion, Type A behavior, and stress. *Journal of Applied Psychology, 63,* 467–480.
Strahilevitz, M., Strahilevitz, A., & Miller, J. (1979). Air pollutants and the admission rate of psychiatric patients. *American Journal of Psychiatry, 136,* 205–207.
Stuart, P. (1993, January). Employees buy awards with rideshare points. *Personnel Journal, 72,* 65–69.
Sumi, T., Matsumoto, Y., & Miyaki, Y. (1990). Departure time and route choice of commuters on mass transit systems. *Transportation Research, 24,* 247–262.
Svenson, H. O., & Anderson, G. B. J. (1983). Low back pain in 40 to 47 year old men. *Spine, 8,* 272–276.
Tainsh, J. (1973). An investigation of the effects of traveling on later decision making. *Public Transport, 16,* 306.
Taylor, A. S., & Lounsbury, J. W. (1988). Dual-career couples and geographic transfer: Executives' reactions to commuter marriage and attitudes toward the move. *Human Relations, 41,* 407–424.
Taylor, P., & Pocock, C. (1972). Commuter travel and sickness: Absence of London office workers. *British Journal of Preventive and Social Medicine, 26,* 165–172.
Thompson, S. C. (1981). Will it hurt less if I can control it? A complex answer to a simple question. *Psychological Bulletin, 90,* 89–101.
Tien, J., O'Donnell, V. F., Barnett, A., & Mirchandani, P. B. (1979). *Street lighting projects.* Washington, DC: U.S. Department of Justice.
Turnage, J. J. (1990). The challenge of new workplace technology for psychology. *American Psychologist, 45,* 171–178.
Ulrich, R. S., Simons, R. F., Losito, B. D., Fiorito, E., Miles, M. A., & Zelson, M. (1991). Stress recovery during exposure to natural and urban environments. *Journal of Environmental Psychology, 11,* 201–230.
Vroom, V. H. (1964). *Work and motivation.* New York: John Wiley & Sons.
Watson, D., & Clark, L. A. (1984). Negative affectivity: The disposition to experience aversive emotional states. *Psychological Bulletin, 96,* 465–490.
Weinman, J. D. (1982). The office environment as a source of stress. In G. W. Evans (Ed.), *Environmental stress* (pp. 256–285). London: Cambridge University Press.
Weinstein, N. D. (1978). Individual differences in reactions to noise: A longitudinal study in a college dormitory. *Journal of Applied Psychology, 63,* 458–466.
Weisman, S. R. (1991, October 3). Seoul's traffic prompts emergency measures. *New York Times,* p. 11.
Weitz, J. (1952). A neglected concept in the study of job satisfaction. *Personnel Psychology, 5,* 201–205.
Wells, J. A. (1982). Objective job conditions, social support, and perceived stress among blue-collar workers. *Journal of Occupational Behavior, 3,* 70–94.
Wilder, D. G., Woodworth, B. B., Frymoyer, J. W., & Pope, M. H. (1982). Vibration and the human spine. *Spine, 7,* 243–254.
Williams, A., Livy, B., Silverstone, R., & Adams, P. (1979). Factors associated with labor turnover among ancillary staff in two London hospitals. *Journal of Occupational Psychology, 52,* 1–16.
Williams, C. E., Stevens, K., & Klatt, D. (1969). Judgements of the acceptability of aircraft noise in the presence of speech. *Journal of Sound and Vibration, 9,* 263–275.

Williams, L. J., & Hazer, J. T. (1986). Antecedents and consequences of satisfaction and commitment in turnover models: A reanalysis using latent variable structural equation methods. *Journal of Applied Psychology, 71,* 219–231.

Wilson, R. J., Anderson, S. A., & Fleming, W. M. (1987). Commuter and resident students' personal and family adjustment. *Journal of college Student Personnel, 28,* 229–233.

Winfield, F. (1985). *Commuter marriage: Living together, apart.* New York: Columbia University Press.

Wren, C. (1991, December 31). Soweto journal: Gangs of random killers stalk commuter trains. *The New York Times,* p. 4.

Zerega, A. (1981). Transportation energy conservation policy: Implications for social science research. *Journal of Social Issues, 37,* 31–50.

Zimring, C. (1982). The built environment as a source of psychological stress: Impacts of buildings and cities on satisfaction and behavior. In G. W. Evans (Ed.), *Environmental stress* (pp. 151–178). London: Cambridge University Press.

Zuckerman, M. (1979). *Sensation seeking: Beyond the optimal level of arousal.* Hillsdale, NJ: Lawrence Erlbaum.

Index

Absenteeism, as commuting stress outcome, 3, 5, 14–15, 16, 79, 80, 81–82, 126
  costs of, 15
  flex-time and, 184
Accidents
  motor vehicle, 4
    commuters' fear of, 155
    economic costs of, 176
    fatal, U.S./European comparison, 36
    helicopter use for management of, 176–177
    relationship to driver's locus of control, 117–118
    substance abuse-related, 73
    by truck drivers, 73, 76
  in the workplace, 124, 126
    burnout-related, 54
Adolescents
  average commuting time of, 21
  mass transportation use by, 31
  as "transportation disadvantaged," 26
Aerobic exercise, as commuting stress coping strategy, 137
African-Americans, mass transportation use by, 26–27
Age factors
  in commuting-related attrition, 83
  See also Adolescents; Older adults
Aggression, thermal stress-related, 50
Air pollution, motor vehicle-related, 4, 37, 38, 53
  economic costs of, 173–174

Air pollution, motor vehicle-related (*cont.*)
  as effect variable, 52–53
  in Europe, 36
  health effects of, 66–67, 74–75
    cancer, 69–70, 71
    cardiovascular symptoms, 66–67
  taxation as reduction strategy for, 174, 175–176
Air pollution legislation, 75, 175–176
  as car-pooling incentive, 169–170
Alcohol abuse, as motor vehicle accident cause, 73
American Journal of Community Psychology, 3
AMTRAK, 73–74
Angell, Dee, 167
Angina pectoris, commuting stress-related, 62
Anticipation, of crowding-related stress, 47–48
Anxiety
  attitudinal effects of, 123
  of automobile commuters, 87
  crowding-related, 46
  environmental stress-related, 39
  of railroad engineers, 74
Arousal
  effect on urinary epinephrine excretion, 76
  noise-related, 40–41, 55
  predictors of, 3–4
  task-related factors in, 12–13, 55, 56
  temperature-related, 50
Arousal–performance U curve, 56

Arrival times
    flex-time and, 183–185
    predictability of, 170–171
    preferred, 113–114
Asocial behavior, noise-related, 43
Assertiveness skills, use in crowded situations, 149–150
Attention diversion, 130
Attitude–behavior links, 118, 124, 125
Attitude changes, strain-related, 5
Attitudinal effects, 80
    on car-pool drivers and passengers, 90
    commuting stress model of, 122
    measures of, 84–87
    relationship to behavior, 85, 123, 125, 171–172
    relationship to environmental stress, 39–40
    relationship to negative affectivity, 195
    relationship to physiological strain, 127
Attributions, 111
Audiotapes, use by commuters, 143
    as commuting stress coping strategy, 151
    headphone safety with, 152
    implications for car pooling, 166
Automobile accidents: *see* Motor vehicle accidents
Automobile commuters
    attitudes toward mass transportation, 171–172
    blood chemistry of, 67
    control/loss of control experienced by, 90, 98–99, 144
    driving stress of, 95
    female, 33
        alternative route use by, 35
        dissatisfaction with commuting experience, 92
        job involvement of, 92
        horn-honking behavior of, 153
        locus of control of, 117–118
        taxation of, 174–176
Automobile commuting/driving
    as air pollution cause: *see* Air pollution, motor vehicle-related
    alternative route use in, 34, 35
    challenge situations during, 55–56
    comparison with car pooling, 165–166
    comparison with mass transportation, 21, 22, 30, 48–49, 52, 53, 89–90, 91, 142
    cost of, 87, 167
    crowding-related stress in, 148

Automobile commuting/driving (*cont.*)
    fears associated with, 51, 155
    following California earthquake, 89, 172
    gender differences in: *see* Women, automobile commuting by
    health effects of, 61–62
        back problems, 61, 63–66, 71, 76–77
        cancer, 61, 69–70, 71
        cardiovascular problems, 61, 62, 66–67, 71
        colds and flu, 63
        solutions to, 74–76
    information costs associated with, 96–97
    noise stress during, 4, 40, 41–42
        coping strategies for, 150–151, 152
        drivers' emotional responses to, 44–45
        effect on passengers' comfort, 66
        effect on task-related arousal, 55
        model of, 43–45
        physical impact of, 41–42
        relationship to antisocial behavior, 43
        U.S./European comparison of, 36
    non-mass transportation alternatives to, 20–21
    safety and security precautions in, 51, 156
    Seattle, Washington, case study of, 33–35
    speed of, 7, 32, 84
    violation of spatial norms during, 46
    winter driving conditions of, 153
    as work time, 143
    See also Freeway driving
Automobile exhaust: *see* Air pollution, motor vehicle-related
Automobile ownership
    by African-Americans, 26–27
    by Hispanics, 28
    relationship to mass transportation use, 20–21, 25–26, 31
    U.S./European comparison of, 35–36
Automobiles
    audiocassette use in, 143, 151
        implications for car pooling, 166
    auditory environment of, 151
    automated travel guidance systems in, 179
        mapping programs, 144, 179
    climate control in, 153, 155
    energy use by, 52
    federal occupancy guidelines for, 4
    increasing number of, 1
    noncommuting use of, 24

Automobiles (cont.)
  operating costs of, 20
  purchase costs of, U.S./European comparison, 36
  seating positions in, as back problem risk factor, 65, 74
  types of, relationship to herniated disk occurrence, 64–65
  weight-distance tax on, 174

Back pain/problems, motor vehicle driving-related, 61, 63–64, 71
  psychological factors in, 76–77
  solutions to, 74
Beacon, New York, train commuting from, 162–163
Behavioral anchored rating scale (BARS), 115, 116
Behavioral effects, of commuting, 79–84
  commuting distance variable in, 79
  commuting stress model of, 124
  commuting time variable in, 79
  relationship to attitudinal effects, 85, 123, 125, 171–172
  See also Absenteeism; Job turnover; Lateness; Performance; Performance decrements; Performance enhancement; Satisfaction
Behavior change, self-efficacy model of, 132
Belgium, mass transportation use in, 36
Benefit assessment districts, 161
Benzene, commuters' exposure to, 67
Bicycling, as commuting method, 20–21, 138–139, 161
Birch, Richard, 162
Blood chemistry, of automobile drivers, 67
Blood pressure levels
  of commuters, 62–63
    car-pool passenger/single-automobile commuter comparison, 165
    female commuters, 92
  of transportation workers, 72
Boating, as commuting method, 20–21
Body, stress adaptation by, 11–12
Body contact, in crowds, 149–150
Boeing Corporation, back-injury claims filed against, 71
Branch offices, 126
Breast cancer, automobile driving as risk factor for, 70

Burnout
  as commuting stress model variable, 122–123
  as environmental stress reaction, 53–56
Bus drivers
  epinephrine levels in, 63
  herniated disks in, 72
  perceived job control by, 98–99
  traffic-related physiological stress in, 193–194
Buses
  average commuting time on, 21–22
  commuters' use patterns of, 23, 24
  computer-controlled flexible routing of, 178
  crowding on, 148
  information costs of, 96–97
  as most frequently used mass transit form, 22, 23
  scheduling
    flexible routing, 178
    relationship to commuting density, 163
  special lanes for, 52
  vibrational frequency of, 66
Bus riders, attitudes toward automobile commuting, 49
Bus service, for corporate parks, 160
Bus stops, effect on commuters' stress reactions, 162

California Clean Air Act of 1989, 169–170
California earthquake, commuting patterns after, 89, 172
Cancer, automobile driving as risk factor for, 61, 69–70, 71
Carbon burning, as transportation taxation basis, 175–176
Cardiovascular symptoms
  of automobile drivers, 61, 62, 66–67, 68–69, 71
  of transportation workers, 72
Car heaters, health risks of, 67
Car-jacking, 155
Car-pool drivers
  attitudes toward automobile commuting, 49
  commuting strain experienced by, 90
  control experienced by, 100
  female, 92
  hostility and anxiety levels of, 87

Car pooling, 164–170
    automobile commuters' attitudes toward, 165–166, 167
    as automobile commuting alternative, 20–21
    comparison with automobile commuting/driving, 165–166
    crowding-related stress in, 147–148
    decrease in, 165
    economic advantages of, 167
    federal funding for, 52
    "high-occupancy vehicle" lanes for, 179
    incentives for, 166–170
        employers' programs, 53, 75, 164–165
        governmental programs, 52, 164–166
        joint government–corporation programs, 168–170
        punishment as, 168–169
        tax-related, 176
        trip reduction schemes, 161
    stresses associated with, 166
    unpopularity of, 52
Car-pool passengers, 90
    female, 92
Car telephones: see Mobile telephones
Catalyst (organizational survey company), 183
Catecholamine levels
    commuting-related increase, 62
    crowding-related increase, 77
    stress-related increase, 76
Cause–effect relationships, 190, 196–198
    contributory, 197–198
    direct and indirect, 127–128
Cellular telephones: see Mobile telephones
Cerebrovascular disease (stroke), automobile driving as risk factor for, 68–69
Challenge situations, 54–56
Chest pain, commuting stress-related, 63
Chicago, Illinois, railroad commuting in, 22
Choice, commuting stress reduction effects of, 170–171
Clean Air Act of 1990, 175
    Amendments, Section 182 (d), 75
Clinical psychologists, involvement in commuting stress management, 3
Clinicians, involvement in commuting stress management, 2–3
Clothing, for thermal stress management, 50, 149, 152, 153–154
Cognitive-behavioral techniques, as commuting stress coping strategy, 13

Cognitive relabeling, as commuting stress coping strategy, 130
Cognitive restructuring, as commuting stress coping strategy, 139–142, 150
Cognitive style, relationship to commuting stress, 140
Colds/flu, commuting as risk factor for, 63
Cold stress, 49–50, 152, 153–154, 155
College students, commuting by, 96
Combat stress, 12
Commitment, as stress moderator, 133–134
Common method variance, 194
Communication, during commuting, 146–147
Communication skills training, as commuting stress coping strategy, 129–130
Community, responsibility for mass transportation, 161
Community planners, use of commuting pattern data by, 17
Community psychologists, involvement in commuting stress management, 2–3
Commuters
    choice of travel mode by, 48–49
    Protestant work ethic of, 142–143
    See also Automobile commuters
Commuter satisfaction: see Satisfaction
Commuter Transportation Service, 165
Commuting, 1–16
    commuters' perception of, 8–10
    direct effects of, 4–5
    increase in, 1
    indirect effects of, 5–6
    mediator variables in: see Mediators, of commuting stress
    mobile telephone use during, 143, 146–147, 166, 177
    moderating variables in: see Moderators, of commuting stress
    organizational consequences of, 14–16
    physiological stressors in, 14
    as positive experience, 58, 143
    preparation for, 134–136, 145
    psychological stressors in, 14
    as response phenomenon, 37–38
    taking advantage of, 142–147
    time/distance variables in, 6–7; see also Impedance
    variability in responses to, 5
    variability of, 39
    as "window" of time, 146
    as work time, 142–144, 146

INDEX

Commuting (*cont.*)
  work-to-home, 8–9
    commuters' attitudes toward, 114
    exercise during, 138
    family responsibilities associated with, 34, 92, 93
Commuting couples, 93–95; *see also* Dual-career couples
Commuting distance
  of female commuters, 34, 94, 95
  relationship to job absenteeism, 81
  relationship to job decisions, 93
  relationship to commuting time, 6–7; *see also* Impedance
  relationship to job turnover, 83
  relationship to lateness, 82
  relationship to physical symptoms, 63
  U.S./European comparison of, 36
  See also Impedance
Commuting measures, 88–89
Commuting patterns, 17–36
  after California earthquake, 89, 172
  in Europe, 35–37
  General Accounting Office data on, 18–20
  importance of, 17–18
  Joint Center for Political Studies data on, 18, 20–31
    commuter flows, 23–24
    commuting time, 21–22
    gender differences, 29–30, 31
    household demographics, 20, 21, 24–26
    job location, 23–24
    older workers' commuting patterns, 29
    residential factors, 23–24
    "transportation disadvantaged" commuting patterns, 26–28
  Nationwide Personal Transportation Survey data on, 18, 31–33
  Seattle, Washington, case study of, 18, 33–35
  stage process of, 73
Commuting research
  inconsistency of findings in, 107
  methodology, 189–198
    cause-effect relationship, 127–128, 190, 196–198
    common method variance, 194
    comparison of laboratory and field studies, 189–190

Commuting research (*cont.*)
  methodology (*cont.*)
    confirmatory factor analysis, 120–121
    for control variables assessment, 102–103
    correlational analysis, 194
    covariance structure analysis, 191
    demographic factors, 20–21, 24–26, 33, 191
    detection of moderators and mediators, 192–194
    field studies, 190–191
    inadequacy of, 80–81, 107
    latent factors, 120–121, 122–123, 191–192
    meta-analysis, 81, 107–108
    multiple regression analysis, 80, 109, 192, 193–194
    negative affectivity, 194–196
    path analysis, 191
    "quasiexperimental" statistical techniques, 196–198
    structural equation modeling, 80, 109, 191–192, 198
  professionals' involvement in, 2–4
  publication of, 158–159
  theory development in, 108
Commuting speed: *see* Driving speed
Commuting stages, relationship to job absenteeism, 81–82
Commuting stress
  gender differences in: *see* Women, as commuters
  individual variables in, 38–39, 108
  interdomain transfer effects in, 39, 86
  "properties of the person" concept of, 38–39
Commuting stress disorders, 3
Commuting stress model, 118–128
  attitude–behavior link, 118, 124, 125
  confirmatory factor analysis, 120–121
  direct and indirect links, 127–128
  feedback loops, 127
  latent factors, 120–121, 122–123
  mediators, 111–112
  moderators, 112–118, 121
    locus of control, 117–118
    negative affectivity, 117–118
    time urgency, 113–117
  multiple regression analysis, 109
  organizational implications, 124
  outcome variables, 125–127

Commuting stress model (*cont.*)
  predictability/outcome variables relationship, 119–120
  quantitative variables, 120
  stages, 118–124
    stage I (potential stressors), 120
    stage II (perceived stress), 118, 121
    stage III (physiological reactions), 118, 121–122
    stage IV (emotional/attitudinal strain responses), 118, 122–123
    stage V (job avoidance), 118, 123–124
    stage VI (behavioral/performance indicators), 118
  structural equation modeling, 109, 120–121, 124
  subjective and objective predictors, 121
  theoretical framework, 108, 109–111
    expectancies theory, 110–111
    person–environment fit, 109–110, 121
  time urgency moderators, 120
Commuting time
  of African-Americans, 27
  average, 21–22, 32
  increase of, 32
  Joint Center for Political Studies data on, 21–23
  gender differences in, 30
  relationship to herniated disk occurrence, 65–66
  relationship to job absenteeism, 81–82
  relationship to job satisfaction, 91
  relationship to performance, 84
  relationship to physical symptoms, 63
  in rush-hour Manhattan, 9
  in Seattle, Washington, 33, 34
  unpredictability of, 9
  work-to-home, 34
  See also Impedance
Companies
  as air pollution cause, 53
  car-pooling incentives of, 164–165
  commuting stress coping stategies of: *See* Coping strategies, organizational
Companions, during commuting, 151
Computers
  in automobiles, 35, 144
  in buses, 178
  laptop, 143
  notebook, 143

Concentration
  noise-related decrease in, 45
  relationship to task demand, 13
Confirmatory factor analysis, 120–121
Confounding, definition of, 196–197
Control, 97–106
  actual and perceived, 99–103
  causal linkages in, 128
  of environment, 98–99
  experienced by automobile drivers, 89–90, 144
  relationship to flex-time, 183–185
  relationship to mass transportation use, 170–171
  relationship to mode of transportation, 89
  use of mapping and video systems for, 144
  See also Locus of control; Predictability, of commuting experience
Control groups, 196
Convection, as heat loss mechanism, 153–154
Conversation
  as commuting stress coping strategy, 151
  effect of noise on, 43
  as noise stress source, 152
Coping
  causal variables in, 128
  commuting stress model of, 128
  definition, 131
  effect on stress determinants, 131
Coping strategies, 14
  for commuting-related fears, 156
  general, 129–133
  governmental, 157–158, 159–179
    car-pooling incentives, 164–165, 168–170
    corporate compliance-focused strategies, 160–161
    individual compliance-focused strategies, 161–163
    ordinances, 161
    taxation, 174–176
    technological strategies, 177–179
  individual, 118, 129–156
    cognitive restructuring, 139–142, 150
    commitment, 133–134
    commute as work time, 142–144, 146
    for crime prevention, 155–156
    for crowding, 147–150
    for environmental stressors, 147–155

Coping strategies (*cont.*)
  individual (*cont.*)
    exercise, 136–139
    failure to implement, 132–133
    job turnover, 84
    meditation, 139
    mobile telephones, 143, 146–147
    for noise, 150–152
    optimizing commuting departure times, 147
    organization and self-discipline, 134–136, 145–146
    practice of, 132
    of Seattle commuters, 34–35
    selection of, 131–132
    sequential implementation of, 132
    taking advantage of the commute, 142–147
  instrumental, 129–130
  organizational, 118, 126, 157–158, 180–187
    assessment of stressors, 181–182
    corporate relocation, 126, 127, 181
    flex-time, 2, 48, 183–185
    job sharing, 183
    part-time work, 183
    selection of, 182–183
    telecommuting, 180, 181, 183, 185–187
    worker control, 99
  palliative, 13–14, 129, 130
  for physical symptoms, 74–76
  societal, 118
  for stress management, 13–14
  withdrawal as, 15
Core body temperature, maintenance of, 152, 153, 155
Coronary artery disease patients, automobile driving by, 67
Corporate parks, 160
Corporations, relocation by, 126, 127, 181
Correlational analysis, 194
Cortisol levels, of female commuters, 92
Courtesy, of mass transportation riders, 148–149
Covariance analysis, of commuting–outcome relationship, 80
Crime
  on mass transportation, 51, 127, 155–156
  in poorly lit environments, 51

Crowding, as commuting stressor, 37, 38, 45–49
  anticipation of, 47–48
  coping strategies for, 147–150
  definition of, 147
  effect on catecholamine levels, 77
  as fight-or-flight response cause, 44
  long-term effects of, 47
  model of, 45–46, 147–148
  relationship to spacing of train stations, 162
  standing during, 137
  thermal stress and, 50, 154

Deadline control, relationship to time urgency, 115, 116
Deafness, in transportation workers, 72
Deep breathing, as noise stress coping technique, 151
Demographic factors
  in mass transportation use, 20–21, 24–26, 33
  path analysis of, 191
Departure times
  flex-time and, 183–185
  in mass transportation, 147
  optimization of, as coping strategy, 147
  patterns of, 32
  work-to-home, 34
Dependent variables, multiple regression analysis of, 192–193
Depression
  burnout-related, 54
  cognitive style-related, 140
  environmental stress-related, 39
Direct action, as stress response, 13
Discomfort, as commuting-related stressor, 37
Distance: *see* Commuting distance
Driving behavior inventory (DBI), 37–38
Driving speed
  as commuting impedance measure, 7
  patterns of, 32
  relationship to performance, 84
Driving stress measure, 95
"Dropping out," 54
Drug abuse, as motor vehicle accident cause, 73
Dual-career couples, 93–95
  job transfer decisions by, 94
  mass transportation use by, 25–26, 29, 30
Dutchess County Planning Department, 162

Eating behavior, relationship to time urgency, 114, 115
EEG (electroencephalogram), of automobile drivers, 67
Efficiency, commuting-related decrease, 5
Electroencephalogram (EEG), of automobile drivers, 67
Elevated trains, 21–22, 23, 24
Ellis, Albert, 13
Emotional effects, of commuting, 11, 12, 79, 80
  on commuting couples, 94
  commuting stress model of, 122
  measures of, 86–87
  relationship to burnout, 54
  relationship to environmental stress, 39–40
  relationship to negative affectivity, 195
  relationship to noise, 42–43
Employees
  commitment of, 134
  residential requirements for, 157–158
Employers
  car-pooling programs of, 75, 164–165, 168–170
  employee residential requirements of, 157–158
  use of commuting pattern data by, 17
  See also Companies; Coping strategies, organizational; Corporations
Energy conservation, 51–52
Entrapment, burnout-related, 54
Environmental ecological psychology, 3
Environmental psychology
  applied to commuting stress management, 2–3
  of time urgency, 116–117
Environmental stressors, 37–59
  combined effects of, 56–57
  coping strategies for, 131
  effect on emotional and attitudinal states, 39–40
  effect on physical health, 39
  energy conservation as, 51–52
  individual responses to, 58–59
  interface with individual reactions, 108–109
  lighting as, 51
  relationship to behavioral alternatives, 44
  tranquility of environment and, 50–51
  See also Air pollution, motor vehicle-related; Crowding; Noise

Epinephrine levels
  crowding-related increase of, 77
  effect of traffic congestion on, 193–194
  stress-related increase of, 76
  of train commuters, 162
EQS software, 109
Esophageal cancer, automobile driving as risk factor for, 69, 70
Ethylbenzene, commuters' exposure to, 67
Europe, commuting behavior in, 35–36
European Economic Community, automobile ownership rate in, 35–36
Evaporation, as heat loss cause, 154
Evening commute, 8–9
  commuters' attitudes toward, 114
  exercise during, 138
  family responsibilities associated with, 34, 92, 93
Exercise, as commuting stress coping strategy, 136–139
  during evening commute, 138
  integration into the commuting experience, 138–139
  during morning commute, 137–138
  in the workplace, 138
Expectations, unrealistic, 13
Expectation theory, 110–111
Eye contact
  in crowded situations, 149
  with strangers, 156

Family relationships, effect of commuting on, 5, 39, 84, 86
Family responsibilities, relationship to commuting stress
  as evening commute component, 34, 92, 93
  in female commuters, 92–93, 94–95
  flex-time and, 184
Farmer's Insurance company, 169
Fatigue
  environmental stress-related, 39
  as motor vehicle accident cause, 73, 76
Fears, commuting-related, 51, 127, 155–156
Federal Aid Highway Program, 19
Federal Highway Administration, 18–19
Feedback loops, 127, 198
Field studies, methodological issues in, 190–191
Fight-or-flight reaction, 12, 44
Fitness, physical effects of, 137
Fitness centers, in the workplace, 138

INDEX

Flex-time, 2, 48, 183–185
Fluids, average daily intake of, 154
Formaldehyde, commuters' exposure to, 67
France
    commuting distances in, 36
    mass transportation use in, 36
Freeway driving
    commuters' dissatisfaction with, 85
    relationship to absence-sick days, 82
Freud, Sigmund, 145
Frustration tolerance
    effect of noise on, 41–42
    relationship to personality type, 87

Gasoline
    price of, 20
    volatile organic compounds content of, 66–67
Gasoline usage, calculation of, 175
Gastric disorders, in transportation workers, 72
Gastrointestinal tract
    effect of stress on, 12
    effect of vibration on, 68
General Accounting Office, traffic congestion report of, 18–20
General adaptation syndrome, 11–12
Goal achievement, motivation theory of, 111
Goals
    crowding-related threat to, 148, 150
    as performance motivators, 168
Gorgon, Peter, 163, 164
Government, commuting-related programs and strategies of, 157–158, 159–179
    car-pooling incentives, 164–165, 168–170
    corporate compliance-focused strategies, 160–161
    individual compliance-focused strategies, 161–163
    ordinances, 161
    taxation, 174–176
    technological strategies, 177–179
Government experts, involvement in commuting stress management, 2–3, 4
Government subsidies
    for highway construction and management, 163–164
    for mass transportation, 163
    for train stations, 162
Grand Central Station, express-train commuting to, 162–163

Great Britain, back pain prevalence in, 71
Greece, mass transportation use in, 36
Greyhound bus company, 97
Gripe index, 196
Growth moratoriums, traffic-induced, 161

Handicapped persons, mass transportation use by, 148–149
"Hassles," commuting-related, 7
    gripe scale of, 196
Headphones, safe use of, 152
Health effects, of commuting: *see* Physical symptoms, commuting-related
Health measures, of subjective impedance, 87
Heart disease
    commuting as risk factor for, 66–67, 68–69, 71
    in transportation workers, 72
Heart rate, effect of commuting on, 62, 67–68
Heat stress, 49–50, 152, 154–155
Helicopter riding, effect on musculoskeletal system, 72
Helicopters
    use in traffic congestion management, 176–177
    use in traffic information gathering, 177
Help-giving behavior, effect of noise on, 43
Helplessness, relationship to depression, 140
Hemorrhoids, in transportation workers, 72
Herniated lumbar intervertebral disks, motor vehicle driving-related, 61, 64–65, 71
    prevention of, 74
High-occupancy vehicle lanes, 179
Highway construction, federal funding of, 19
Highways
    driving speed, 7
    electronic toll collection, 179
    high-tech traffic control mechanisms, 179
    maintenance cost, 163–164
    technologically "smart," 177
Hispanics, mass transportation use by, 28
Homelife: *see* Family relationships
Home Office Computing, 185, 187
Honolulu, automobile commuters' attitude survey in, 171

Hopelessness
  burnout-related, 54
  depression-related, 140
Hospital patients, self-administration of pain medications, 10
Hostility, of automobile commuters, 87
Household demographics, relationship to mass transportation use, 20, 21, 24–26
Houston, Texas, commuting patterns in, 159
Humidity, 50, 152, 153–154, 155
Hydration, for thermal stress prevention, 154–155
Hyoscine, effect on short-term memory, 57

Imagery, as environmental stressor coping strategy, 131
Impedance, 7
  cardiovascular effects of, 62–63, 68
  as commuting stress mediator, 112
  as commuting stress moderator, 120
  definition of, 68, 85–86
  direct and indirect linkages in, 128
  experienced by female commuters, 84
  health measures of, 82, 87
  high, definition, 86
  low, definition, 86
  measurement of, 8
    variations in, 88
  objective, implications for organizational coping strategies, 181–182
  physical impedance index of, 88
  relationship to absenteeism, 82
  relationship to control, 99–100
  relationship to locus of control, 117, 190
  relationship to performance, 84
  subjective, 8–9
    comparison of morning/evening commutes, 114
    direct and indirect linkages in, 128
    examples of, 191
    implications for organizational coping strategies, 181–182
    interaction with time urgency, 115, 116
    as stressor–strain relationship moderator, 162
Income levels, relationship to mass transportation use, 28, 30

Independent variables
  objective, 112
  as perceived demand/perceived stress alternatives, 9–10
  subjective, 112
Industrial psychologists, involvement in commuting stress management, 3
Information costs, of different modes of transportation, 96–97
Information gathering, as commuting stress coping strategy, 129–130
Information highway, 186, 187
Input/output (I/O) context, of job stress, 7–8
Interdomain effect, in commuting stress effects, 39, 86
Interstate highways
  federal toll prohibition for, 164
  traffic congestion on, 18–19
Intervening variables, 192
  driving stress as, 95
Ischemic heart disease
  in automobile drivers, 68–69
  in transportation workers, 72
Israel, employee residency requirements in, 158

Japan
  automobile ownership rate in, 35–36
  employee commitment in, 134
Job avoidance, 118, 123–124
  relationship to withdrawal behavior, 124, 125
  See also Absenteeism; Lateness
Job changes, implications for car pools, 167
Job control: *see* Control
Job Description Index (JDI), 116, 122–123
Job dissatisfaction
  relationship to job avoidance, 124, 126
  See also Job satisfaction
Job involvement, of female commuters, 92
Job satisfaction, 84
  attitudinal factors in, 86
  as commuting stress model factor, 122–123
  environmental stress-related, 40
  measurement of, 122–123
  relationship to commuting time, 91
  relationship to workers' use of time, 115
  relationship to working at home, 186–187
  work conditions associated with, 136

INDEX

Job sharing, 183
Job strain model, 99
Job stress
  input/output (I/O) context of, 7-8
  relationship to lack of control, 9
Job transfers, of dual-career couples, 94
Job turnover
  as commuting stress outcome, 14, 15
  as coping strategy, 84
  precedent behavior of, 85
  relationship to job satisfaction, 85
Joint Center for Political Studies, commuting pattern data on, 18, 20-31
  commuter flows, 23-24
  commuting patterns of older workers, 29
  commuting patterns of "transportation disadvantaged," 26-28
  commuting time, 21-22
  gender differences in commuting patterns, 29-30, 31
  household demographics data, 24-26
  residential factors, 232-4
Journal of Applied Psychology, 126
Journal of Environmental Psychology, 37
Journal of Human Stress, 37

Kain, John, 164
Knowledge, cumulation of, 107
Korean War, combat-related stress research during, 12

Laboratory studies, comparison with field studies, 189-190
Lack of control, over commuting experience, 9-10, 140
  by automobile commuters, 90, 98-99
  crowding-related, 47, 48
  noise-related, 40-42, 43, 44, 45
Langeloh, Eric B., 167
Laptop computers, 143
Lateness, 3, 5, 14, 15, 16, 79, 80, 82
  negative effects of, 140
  organizations' responses to, 115
  tolerance of, 115
  workplace tolerance of, 114
Latent factors, 120-121, 122-123, 191-192
Learned helplessness, 10, 41, 132, 140
Leisure time, relationship to commuting stress, 136
Leukemia, motor vehicle driving-related, 70
Life satisfaction, 84

Lifestyle, effect of commuting on, 1-2, 96
Lighting, as crime deterrent, 51
LISREL, 80, 106, 109, 120
List making, 115
Liver cirrhosis, automobile driving as risk factor for, 69
Lockheed corporation, worker absenteeism in, 82
Locus of control, as commuting stress moderator, 117-118
  relationship to automobile accidents, 117-118
  relationship to impedance, 117, 190
  relationship to neuroticism, 118
  relationship to stressor perception, 3
London, mass transportation users' lack of safety, 127
Long Island Expressway, "high-occupancy vehicle" lanes, 179
Longitudinal studies, 198
Los Angeles
  automobile commuting time in, 1
  proposed alternative commuting methods for, 172
Lung cancer, automobile driving as risk factor for, 69, 70

Macrostressors, 38
Manhattan
  rush-hour commuting time in, 9
  See also New York City
"Margin of safety" effect, in stress response, 56-57
Maslach Burnout Inventory, 122
Mass transportation
  age of riders, 29
  arrival time predictability of, 170-171
  automobile commuters' attitudes toward, 171-172
  average commuting time, 21-22
  characteristics of users of, 20-21
  community's responsibility for, 161
  comparison with automobile commuting, 21, 22, 30, 48-49, 52, 53, 89-90, 91, 142
  for corporate park employees, 160
  cost to taxpayers, 163
  crime associated with, 51, 127, 155-156
  crowding on, 45-49, 46, 148-150
  demand-driven systems, 164
  departure times, 147
  in Europe, 36

Mass transportation (*cont.*)
  fares, 20, 171
    decrease of, 174–175
    increase of, 173–174, 175
  government subsidies for, 75, 173
  information costs associated with, 96–97
  planning approaches to, 2
  predictability of service, 170–171
  prevalence of use, 20, 22, 30, 33
    relationship to automobile ownership, 20–21, 25–26, 31
    relationship to household demographics, 20, 21, 24–26
  riders' courtesy on, 148–149
  speed of, 32
  tax-based subsidies for, 174–176
  trip reduction schemes for, 161
  working on, 142–144
Meclozine, effect on short-term memory, 57
Mediators, of commuting stress, 8–10, 111–112
  differential effects of, 193–194
Meditation, as commuting stress coping strategy, 139
Mental exhaustion, burnout-related, 54
Meta-analysis, 81, 107–108
Metropool, Inc., 167
Miami, Florida, heavy-rail system of, 163
Microstressors, 38
Mister Spock (television character), 151
Mobile telephones, 143, 146–147, 166
  traffic advisory services of, 177
Model, of commuting stress: *see* Commuting stress model
Mode of transportation, as commuting stress moderator, 89–91; *see also* specific modes of transportation
Moderated regression analysis, 192–193
Moderators, of commuting stress, 10, 80, 88–97
  commuting measures of, 88–89
  control as, 98–106
  detection of, 192–193
  gender as, 91–93
  increasing strength of effect of, 193
  information costs as, 96–97
  lifestyle as, 96
  Likert-type, 193
  locus of control as, 117–118
  mode of transportation as, 89–91
  moderated regression analysis of, 192–193
  multiple regression analysis of, 192

Moderators, of commuting stress (*cont.*)
  negative affectivity as, 117–118
  problems of commuting couples, 93–95
  time urgency as, 113–117
Mood
  effect of air pollution on, 52
  relationship to subjective impedance, 87
Morning, exercise during, 137–138
Morning commute, 8–9
  exercise during, 137–138
  preparation for, 135–136, 145
Mothers, commuting-related stress experienced by, 93, 94–95
Motivation theory, 111
Motor vehicle accidents, 4
  commuters' fear of, 155
  economic costs of, 176
  fatal, U.S./European comparison, 36
  relationship to drivers' locus of control, 117–118
  substance abuse-related, 73
  by truck drivers, 73, 76
Multiple regression analysis, 80, 109, 192, 193–194
Muscle strain, commuting-related, 137
Music, as commuting stress coping strategy, 143, 151, 152

Nationwide Personal Transportation Survey, 18, 31–33
Negative affectivity
  as commuting stress moderator, 117–118
  as nuisance variable, 194–196
Neighborhood noise, 44
Nervous energy, relationship to time urgency, 115
Neuroticism
  negative affectivity as, 194
  relationship to locus of control, 118
Neutral object scale, 196
Newark, New Jersey, subway system, 172–173
New Jersey, mass transportation use in, 21
New Jersey Transit, 173
New York City
  Battery Park, 161
  mass transit system, 21
    impact of proposed fare increase on, 173–174
    riders' lack of safety on, 127
  railroad commuters in, 22
  subway system, 40
    crowding on, 46–47

INDEX

New York State Thruway Authority, 179
New York Times, 159
Night, noise disturbances during, 43
Noise, as commuting stress factor, 4, 40–45
  combined with thermal stress, 57
  coping strategies for, 150–152
  effect on automobile passengers' comfort, 66
  effect on task-related arousal, 55
  emotional impact of, 42–43
  model of, 43–45
  physical impact of, 41–42
  U.S./European comparison, 36
Noise filters, 152
Norepinephrine excretion levels
  effect of traffic congestion on, 193–194
  of female commuters, 92
Notebook computers, 143
Nurses
  commuting-related stress reactions of, 90–91
  subjective–objective stress measures for, 121

Older persons
  mass transportation use by, 29, 31, 148–149
  as "transportation disadvantaged," 26
Ordinances, for traffic reduction, 161
Organization, as commuting stress coping strategy, 134–136, 145–146
Organizational antecedents, of stress, 38
Organizational behavior
  as dependent variable, 14–16
  as independent variable, 16
Organizational behavior studies, of commuting, 2–3
Organizational commitment, 122
Organizational effectiveness, 180
Organizations
  commuting stress coping strategies of:
    see Coping strategies, organizational
  employee commitment to, 134
  See also Companies; Corporations

Palliative coping strategies, 13–14, 129, 130
Parking, employer-provided, tax-based subsidies for, 164
Parking areas
  in corporate parks, 160
  crime risk in, 156
Parking reduction ordinances, 161

Participative decision making (PDM) process, 169
Part-time work, as commuting stress coping strategy, 183
Path analysis, 191
Pena, Frederico, 89
Pennsylvania
  mass transportation use in, 21
  railroad commuters in, 22
Perceived control, 13
Perception
  of commuting-related stress, 37–38
  of noise, 43
  relationship to stressor response, 10
Perception variables, 8–10
Performance
  flex-time and, 184
  "margin of safety" in, 56–57
  relationship to arousal, 56
  relationship to satisfaction, 127
Performance decrements
  of automobile commuters, 90, 165
  burnout-related, 54
  of car-pool passengers, 165
  as commuting stress model variable, 124
  noise-related, 40
  strain-related, 5
Performance enhancement
  noise-related, 40
  stress-related, 12
Personality traits, as commuting stress moderators, 10
  locus of control, 117–118
  negative affectivity, 117–118
  time urgency, 113–117
Person–environment fit, 109–110, 121
Personnel Journal, 159
Personnel managers, involvement in commuting stress management, 2
Personnel Psychology, 126
Petroleum products, as automobile fuel, 52
  economic costs of, 51
Physical impedance index, 88
Physical symptoms, commuting-related, 61–77
  back problems, 61, 63–66, 76–77
  burnout and, 54
  cancer, 61, 69–70, 71
  cardiovascular symptoms, 62–63, 66–69, 71
  chronic, 124
  cohort studies of, 61–62

Physical symptoms, commuting-related (*cont.*)
  colds/flu, 63
  commuting stress model of, 122
  coping strategies for, 74–76
  environmental stress responsivity effects, 39
  herniated lumbar intervertebral disks, 61, 64–65, 71
  liver cirrhosis, 69
  physiological indicators of, 62–63
  stressor–emotional reaction–physiological effect relationship of, 76–77
  subjective impedance relationship of, 123
Physicians, commuting by, 96
Physiological factors
  in strain response, 12
  in stress response, 12, 13, 14
Planned behavior theory, 125
Portland, Oregon, trolley system, 163
Positive affectivity, as nuisance variable, 195
Positive thinking, as commuting stress coping strategy, 130, 142, 149
Predictability, of commuting experience, 102–106
  measurement of, 122
  operationalization of, 103–106
  relationship to mass transportation use, 170–171
  relationship to perceived control, 100–101
  state, 102
  trait, 102
Preferred time of arrival (PAT), 113–114
Pregnant women, mass transportation use by, 149
Privacy, automobile commuters' desire for, 91
Problem-solving, organizational, 129–130
Problem-solving skills, as stress inoculation, 142
Productivity
  commuting-related decrease in, 1, 5
  relationship to workers' use of time, 115
"Properties of the person" concept, of commuting stress, 38–39
Protestant work ethic, 142–143
Psychiatric admissions, relationship to air pollution, 52
Psychiatrists, involvement in commuting stress management, 3

Psychological effects/stressors, in commuting, 14, 86–87
Psychologists, involvement in commuting stress management, 2–3
Psychosocial factors, in stress, 12–13

Quantitative overload, 34
Quasiexperimental statistical techniques, 196–198

Railroad engineers, of high-speed trains, 73–74, 76
Rational emotive therapy, 13, 140, 141–142
Reasoned action theory, 125
Rectal cancer, automobile driving as risk factor for, 69, 70
Reframing, as commuting stress coping strategy, 130, 131, 142
Regional Plan Association, 166, 167
Relaxation techniques, as commuting stress coping strategy, 130, 131, 142, 151
Relocation, by corporations, 126, 127, 181
Remote work, 186
Repetition, of stressful events, 46
Residential/office complexes, 160–161
Residential offices, 126
Residential satisfaction, 84, 86
Road capacity, urban, 1
Road districts, 161
Rush hour, environmental stressors associated with, 183

Safety issues, of mass transportation, 51, 127, 155–156
Salary, effect on commuting-related attrition, 83
Santa Monica Freeway, 172
Satisfaction, 84–86
  as commuting stress model factor, 122, 123
  measures of, 123
  relationship to job turnover, 83
Scheduling
  of buses, 178
  flex-time, 2, 48, 183–185
  relationship to time urgency, 115, 116
Search for meaning, as commuting stress coping strategy, 130
Seattle, Washington, commuting behavior study of, 33–35
Self-discipline, as commuting stress coping strategy, 134–136, 145–146

INDEX

Self-efficacy model, of behavior change, 132
Self-employment, as commuting alternative, 93
Self-image, relationship to stressor perception, 3
Self-instructional training, 142
Self-report measures, effect of negative affectivity on, 195–196
Self-speech/self-talk, as commuting stress coping strategy, 140–141, 149, 151
Selye, stress theory of, 11–12
Senior citizens: *see* Older persons
Seoul, South Korea, traffic congestion in, 176–177
Separation, experienced by commuting couples, 93–94
Service industries, working hours in, 32
Sex factors
  in commuting time-related stress, 192–193
  in preferred time of arrival, 114
  in stressor–strain relationships, 109
  in stress response, 5
  See also Women, as commuters
Sexual contact, in crowds, 149–150
Shoewear, of commuters, 149
Sick days, 82
Social psychology, privacy model of, 91
Social support, as stress moderator, additive effect of, 57
Social workers, involvement in commuting stress management, 3
Society, effect of commuting stress on, 86
Software, for structural equation modeling, 109
  EQS, 109
  LISREL, 80, 106, 109, 120
Somatic control, over environmental stressors, 131
South Africa, train commuters' lack of safety in, 127
South Korea, helicopter use for traffic management in, 176–177
Spatial norms, violation of, 45–46; *see also* Crowding
Speech patterns, relationship to time urgency, 114, 115
Spouses, of commuters, 123
Stage fright, 12
Standing, during commute, 137, 149

Stomach cancer, automobile driving as risk factor for, 69, 70
Strain
  air pollution-related, 52
  causes of, 52, 148
  definition of, 8
  distinguished from stress, 7–8
  measurement of, 8
  organizational consequences of, 5
  physiological responses to, 12
Streetcars, 21–22, 23, 24
Stress
  acute versus chronic, 10
  definition of, 8, 11, 131
  distinguished from strain, 7–8
  general adaptation syndrome of, 11–12
  intervention models of, 6
  measurement of, 8
  organizational antecedents of, 38
  performance-enhancing effects of, 12
  physiological responses to, 12, 13, 14
  psychosocial factors in, 12–13
  Selye's theory of, 11–12
  transactional view of, 37–38
"Stressed out," 11
Stressful events
  as macrostressors, 38
  as microstressors, 38
  repetition of, 46
Stress inoculation training, 13, 132, 142
Stress management
  cognitive-behavioral techniques, 13
  in organizations, 6
  social workers' involvement in, 3
  for Type A personalities, 130
  See also Coping strategies
Stressors
  definition of, 11
  individual responses to, 58
  interactive effects of, 134–135
  objective versus subjective, 10
  physiological, 12, 13, 14
  positive relationship with effect indicators, 58
  relationship to coping strategy, 131
  superadditive effects of, 56–57
  thresholds for, 131
Stressor–strain relationship
  assessment of stressor stimuli in, 182
  direct and indirect links in, 127–128
  inconsistency of, 57–58
  sex factors in, 109

Stress response
  individual factors in, 3–4
  sex factors in, 5
Structural equation modeling, 80, 109, 191–192
  causal variables in, 198
  software programs for
    EQS, 109
    LISREL, 80, 106, 109, 120
Substance abuse, as motor vehicle accident cause, 73
Suburban commuters, mothers as, 94–95
Suburbs
  corporate relocations to, 126, 127, 181
  population growth of, 30–31
  mass transportation use in, 31
    preferred modes of, 23, 24
  redesign of, 2
  traffic congestion in, 1
Subsidies: see Government subsidies
Subways
  average commuting time on, 21–22
  commuters' use patterns of, 23, 24
  crime associated with, 155–156
  crowding on, 46, 46–47, 48, 50
  fares
    average commuters' expenditure on, 174
    relationship to ridership, 173, 174–175
  lighting problems in, 51
  noise stress in, 40–41, 151–152
  platforms, unaesthetic appearance of, 51
  profit-making, 172–173
  suburban, 173
  thermal stress in, 50
  volatile organic compound exposure in, 67
Superadditive effects, of stressors, 56–57
Sweden, back pain prevalence in, 71

Tappan Zee Bridge, New York State
  commuting time across, 101
  traffic congestion management on, 179
Task demand, relationship to arousal, 12–13
Taxation, as mass transportation subsidy source, 174–176
Taxi cabs, 21–22, 23
Teachers, commuting-related attrition of, 83

Technology
  application to transportation problem management, 177–179
  implications for telecommuting, 186, 187
Telecommuting, 2, 180, 181, 183, 185–187
Temperature-humidity index (THI), 153
Thermal stress, 49–50
  combined with noise, 57
  coping strategies for, 152–155
Thermoregulation, 50
Time, relationship to distance, 6–7; see also Impedance
Time awareness, 115, 116
Time factors, in causal relationships, 198
Time management, 129–130
Time period, of commute: see Commuting time
Time-saving behavior, relationship to time urgency, 115, 116
Time urgency, 145–146
  behavioral anchored rating scale (BARS) of, 115, 116
  as commuting stress moderator, 115–117, 120
  components of, 114–117
Tolls
  electronic collection of, 179
  for single-passenger versus car-pool vehicles, 168–169
Toluene, commuters' exposure to, 67
Traffic accidents: see Accidents, motor vehicle-related
Traffic congestion
  control measures for, 4
  General Accounting Office report on, 18
  helicopters for management of, 176–177
  as major contemporary problem, 175
  technological management of, 177–179
  in urban areas, governmental/organizational solutions to, 159–161
Traffic delays, average hours per employed person, 1
Traffic impact fees, 161
Traffic information, sources of, 35
Trains
  average commuting time on, 21–22
  commuters' lack of safety on, 127

INDEX

Trains (*cont.*)
  commuters' use patterns of, 23, 24
  decreased service to suburban areas, 23
  elevated, 21–22, 23, 24
  high-speed, 36, 73–74
  increasing use of, 22–23
  information costs of, 96
  noise exposure on, 42
  vibrational frequency of, 66
  See also Subways
Train stations, effect on commuters' stress reactions, 162
Trait anxiety, negative affectivity as, 194
Tranquility, environmental, 50–51
Transactional view, of stress, 37–38
Transit vouchers, 164
Transportation, regional problems in, 159–160
Transportation workers, health problems of, 63, 71–74
  prevention and management of, 75–76
Trip planning, information costs of, 96–97
Trip reduction schemes, 161
Truck drivers
  herniated disks in, 72
  motor vehicle accidents by, 73, 76
Trucks, weight-distance tax for, 174
Truck usage, U.S./European comparison of, 36
Turkey, mass transportation use in, 36
Type A behavior pattern scale (TABP), 116
Type A personality
  coping strategy program for, 130
  relationship to frustration tolerance, 87
  relationship to stressor perception, 3
Type B personality, relationship to frustration tolerance, 87

Ulnar nerve compression, 66
Uncertainty
  crowding-related, 47
  as organizational stress component, 101–102
  reduction of, 35
  relationship to mass transportation use, 171
  relationship to perceived stress, 101
Urban areas
  commuting methods in, 22, 23
  interstate highway traffic congestion in, 18–19

Urban areas (*cont.*)
  mass transportation use in, 21, 33
    decline of, 20, 22
    most commonly used transportation modes, 22–23, 24
    by "transportation disadvantaged," 26–27
  See also names of specific cities

Van pooling, 166
Variables
  causal relationships among, 196–198
  definition of, 6–8
  direct and indirect links in, 127–128
Vibration, motor vehicle-related
  as back pain risk factor, 74
  cardiovascular effects of, 68
  effect on passengers' comfort, 66
  as herniated disk risk factor, 64–65, 72
Video systems, for automobiles, 144
Visual impairment, in transportation workers, 72
Volatile organic compounds, 66–67
Vouchers, transit, 164

Walking, as commuting method, 20–21, 161
  as commuting-related stress coping strategy, 138, 139
  speed of, 32
"Walkman," as commuting stress coping strategy, 143, 152
Washington, D.C., subway system, 40, 163
Weather, as commuting-related stressor, 38, 152; *see also* Cold stress; Thermal stress
Weight-distance tax, 174
Weighting, empirical, 120–121
Weitz neutral object scale, 196
Wind chill, 153
Winter, commuting during, 153
Withdrawal behaviors
  as commuting stress response, 14–16
  as coping strategy, 15
  indicators of, 126
  relationship to job avoidance, 124, 125
  relationship to strain, 5
  relationship to workers' use of time, 115
Wolf, Stewart, 12
Wolff, Harold, 12

Women, as commuters
  automobile commuting by, 33
    alternative route use, 35
    dissatisfaction with commuting experience, 92
    job involvement of, 92
  as car-pooling passengers, 165
  commuting distance of, 34, 94, 95
    relationship to job absenteeism, 81
    relationship to job decisions, 93
  commuting stress experienced by, 34, 35, 91–93
  commuting time of, 30
  lateness of, 82
  mass transportation use by, 25, 29–30, 31, 33
  physiological stress reactions of, 63
  as "transportation disadvantaged," 26
Work and Stress, 37

Workers' compensation, for herniated lumbar disks, 71
Working
  during the commute, 142–144
  at home, 186–187
Workplace
  effect of commuting stress on, 86
  exercise in, 138
  preferred arrival time at, 113–114
Workplace tolerance, 113–114
Work schedules, flex-time, 2, 48, 183–185
World Resource Institute, 175
World War II, combat-related stress research during, 12

Xylene, commuters' exposure to, 67

Zupan, Jeffrey M., 166